This book is about celebrating
the arrival
of a Jewish baby

This book was read by

_____

Name of parents, grandparents, relatives, friend

To prepare for the arrival of

_____

Child's Name

_____

Birth Date

_____

Celebration Date(s)

_____

This book was a gift from

_____

Also by Anita Diamant

The New Jewish Wedding
Living a Jewish Life

The *NEW* Jewish Baby Book

NAMES
CEREMONIES
CUSTOMS

A Guide For Today's Families

ANITA DIAMANT

JEWISH LIGHTS Publishing
Woodstock, Vermont

The New Jewish Baby Book: Names Ceremonies, Customs, A Guide for Today's Families
Copyright © 1994 and © 1993 by Anita Diamant

Library of Congress Cataloging-in-Publication Data
The new Jewish baby book: names, ceremonies, customs, a guide for today's families/ by Anita Diamant
    p.   cm.
    Includes bibliographical references and index
    ISBN 1-879045-28-1: $15.95
    1. Jewish children—Religious life.   2. Baby books.   3. Names, Personal—Jewish.
    4. Brit milah.   5. Brit bat.   6. Judaism—Customs and Practices.
    I. Title.
    BM727. D53 1993
    296.4'4—dc20   93-25870
                                                    CIP

First paperback edition

10 9 8 7 6 5 4

Cover design by Nancy Malerba

Manufactured in the United States of America

Published by JEWISH LIGHTS Publishing
A Division of LongHill Partners, Inc.
P.O. Box 237
Sunset Farm Offices, Route 4
Woodstock, Vermont 05091

Tel: (802) 457-4000 *Fax:* (802) 457-4004

# *The New Jewish Baby Book* is written for:

- People who are about to have a baby or who have just become parents.
- People who are looking for a Jewish name for their baby.
- New parents who wish to fully understand what it means to circumcise a baby boy with Jewish rituals and ceremonies.
- New parents who wish to celebrate the arrival of a baby girl in a meaningful Jewish way.
- New adoptive parents who are looking to express their joy in Jewish terms.
- Professionals and lay-leaders in the Jewish community—rabbis, cantors, *mohels,* educators, and synagogue leaders—who have contact with new parents.
- Jewish family members and friends who may not be familiar with the ceremony being planned by the new parents.
- Non-Jewish family members and friends who will be attending a Jewish ceremony for the new baby and want to understand the history and meaning of the customs and rituals.

This book is different from the other baby books on your night stand. It has nothing to say about Kegel exercises or breathing through labor pains. In these pages you will find no advice about nursing, cradle cap, or sibling rivalry. *The New Jewish Baby Book* is designed to help you make your first decisions as the parents of a Jewish child—decisions that include the choice of a name and the ways to publicly welcome your baby into the covenant and community of Judaism.

The New Jewish Baby Book describes contemporary, liberal★ Jewish practice among expectant or new parents who want to celebrate their child's and family's connection to Judaism and the Jewish people. In America today, parents are choreographing a wonderful new dance that combines ancient traditions with modern insights and practices: Words borrowed from the 4,000-year-old practice of *brit milah* (the covenant of circumcision) resound with new meanings in ceremonies for daughters and for adopted children. And Hebrew letters and Jewish symbols add a special dimension to the modern American custom of sending birth announcements.

This is not an etiquette book full of "do's" and "don'ts." Nor is it a book of religious prescriptions. You will find very few "shoulds" in these pages. *The New Jewish Baby Book* is a guide to choices drawn from the wealth of Jewish mythic, historic, religious, culinary, and literary traditions that surround the arrival of a new baby.

Our great-grandparents would have been mystified by a book like this. In the close-knit Jewish communities of the past, most people participated in life-cycle rituals as a matter of course. Long before anyone became a parent, she or he knew the hows, whens, wheres, and whys of the Jewish celebrations that followed the birth of a baby. For most American Jews today, however, "community" is more goal than reality. As we move from one milestone, one rite of passage, to the next, many of us find ourselves rediscovering and reconstructing Jewish practice.

New parents who want to make meaningful decisions about Jewish names and celebrations for their babies often find themselves at sea. Most people join synagogues when their children reach school age, so many parents-to-be and new moms and dads aren't in touch with the "experts"—rabbis and cantors—who could help provide resources and guide choices.

★ *"Liberal" Judaism is used throughout this book as a synonym for non-Orthodox Judaism and refers to Conservative, Reconstructionist, and Reform Judaism as well as the practice of most non-affiliated Jews.*

Besides, few expectant parents worry about Jewish rites of passage until their baby arrives. If this is your first child, you are probably devouring pregnancy and childbirth books in preparation for the Big Day. If you have other children, you've probably marshaled all your strength to get through this pregnancy without selling off one of the older ones.

Another reason that Jewish parents avoid preparing for the ritual welcoming of a new baby is the evil eye. Even in 20th-century America, many expectant Jewish parents are reluctant to bring a crib into the house until the baby is born, because of superstitions rooted in eastern European folklore.

As a result, parents often find themselves trying to pull together a meaningful, thoughtful rite of passage when they have the least energy to prepare for one. *The New Jewish Baby Book* is the resource for this time.

The first section, *Chai—Life,* is about the mystery and awe of pregnancy and birth. From private moments alone with your spouse to baby showers, this chapter helps you acknowledge and celebrate in distinctively Jewish ways.

The second section, *A Jewish Name,* provides some guidelines for your first Jewish decision as a parent—what to call your baby. The lists of names for boys and girls contain suggestions from around the world, some as old as the Bible, some as new as the land of Israel.

The next portion of *The New Jewish Baby Book* is entitled *Brit,* which means covenant. We Jews are sometimes described as the choosing people—a people who choose to enter into a covenant with God, a relationship that involves mutual obligations. From the beginning of Jewish history, that relationship has been sealed by *brit milah,* the covenant of circumcision. Today, there are also new covenant ceremonies to celebrate the birth of a girl, *brit bat.* Different as they are, *brit milah* and *brit bat* both initiate children into the covenant and both announce that they belong to the people of Israel.

The *Brit* section is divided into three parts, the first of which concerns circumcision and includes everything parents need to know about its laws, rituals and customs, including the historical, biblical, and theological underpinnings of *brit milah,* a frank discussion of the fears and emotions surrounding circumcision, advice on how to find and talk to a *mohel* (a person trained in the practice of ritual circumcision), and information about circumcision for adopted sons.

The chapter on *brit bat* is a guide to Jewish ceremonies that celebrate the birth of a daughter. This section contains several sample ceremonies as well as a description of the elements, prayers and rituals most commonly included in *brit bat* ceremonies.

The final chapter in this section, "*Hiddur Mitzvah*—Beautiful Touches," includes suggestions for ways to enhance the celebration of any covenant celebration with written guides, ritual objects, music, and words.

Whatever your circumstances—whether you know the sex of your unborn child, whether your baby is already here, or whether you are adopting—the entire *Brit* section is a resource for you. This part of the book provides a historical context for your family's celebration, and each section includes readings and translations that can be used in a variety of settings.

Simcha means joy, and this section is all about celebrating that feeling. Because Jewish law commands that there be a celebratory meal—called a *s'udat mitzvah*—after a *brit,* you will find information here about food, photography, gifts, and ways of making your celebration a delight for all concerned. "Celebrations and Customs" describes the full round of parties and practices that surround the arrival of a baby, including the ancient practice of *pidyon haben*—redemption of the first-born. The chapter on announcements talks about spreading news in distinctively Jewish ways.

The section entitled *Modern Life* presents a Jewish perspective on issues that are, for the most part, unique to our times. Acknowledging the fact that an increasing number of Jews are fulfilling the commandment to "be fruitful and multiply" by means of adoption, this section includes information about Jewish law, resources for Jewish adoptive families, and adoption ceremonies.

Another fact of modern life is that the extended Jewish family now includes many Jews by choice, non-Jews committed to raising Jewish children, and non-Jewish grandparents, cousins, aunts, uncles—even stepbrothers and stepsisters. *The Changing Jewish*

Family outlines some of the issues and emotions that may arise in families that include non-Jews and offers suggestions for ways non-Jewish family members can participate in the celebrations for a new Jewish baby. Additionally, the appendices for non-Jews attending *brit* ceremonies are designed so they may be copied and given to people at or before the celebration.

Finally, *The First Year* describes some of the ways that parents celebrate the seasons of their first twelve months with a new baby, from the first *Shabbat* at home together to parties that celebrate a child's weaning.

In the Bible, "Be fruitful and multiply" is the first *mitzvah*—the first commandment. In the Jewish tradition, having children is not only a primary religious obligation; it is considered the crown of human experience and the source of the greatest possible happiness. The arrival of a new Jewish baby has always been greeted with happiness, ceremony, and a wealth of customs. *The New Jewish Baby Book* was written to help you find meaning and joy in this long and varied tradition.

The Midrash says, "With each child, the world begins anew." Mazel tov!

Contents

Contents

for my parents
Maurice and Hélène Diamant

Acknowledgments

Y̶ou may not see them, but Rabbi Lawrence Kushner's spiritual fingerprints are all over this book. I first met Larry in 1981, while researching an article for the *Boston Phoenix.* He became what journalists call "a source." And although the years have made us into friends as well, he remains for me, always, a source.

A great many other people provided insight, information, and wonderful creative ideas. In updating and revising *The New Jewish Baby Book,* I want especially to thank Dr. Robert Levenson, who provided medical and spiritual insights about circumcision; Jane Redmont for her sensitive input about non-Jewish readers; and Rabbi Barbara Penzner for her files, her careful listening, and her loving support.

Thanks also to Rabbi Susan Abramson, Elaine Adler, Dr. Joseph Adolph, Rabbi Al Axelrad, Fern Amper and Eli Schaap, Toni Bader, Naomi Bar-Yam, Judith Baskin, Janet Buchwald, Debra Cash, Betsy Cohen, Howard Cooper, Ora Gladstone, Dr. Victor Himber, Carol Katzman and Michael Katzman, Marga Kamm, Gail Libowsky Kazin and Jerry Kazin, Rabbi Neil Kominsky, Jonathan Kremer, Karen Kushner, Gila Langner, Amy Mencow and Billy Mencow, Phyllis Nissen, Rabbi Jeffrey Perry-Marx, Cantor Sam Pesserof, Betsy Platkin Teutsch, Joel Rosenberg, Stephanie Ritari, Arthur Samuelson, Rabbi Dennis Sasso, Cantor Robert Scherr, Rabbi Daniel Shevitz, and Danny Siegel. Thanks also to Hanna Tiferet Siegel and Rabbi Daniel Siegel, Alvin Schultzberg, Rabbi Rifat Soncino, Rabbi Edward S. Treister and Rochelle Treister, Ella Taylor, Moshe Waldoks, Shoshana Zonderman, and Saul E. Perlmutter.

I am also grateful to the Jewish Women's Resource Center of the National Council of Jewish Women, New York Section, and the National Tay-Sachs and Allied Diseases Foundation.

Acknowledgments

Special thanks to all the artists and poets whose words and images grace these pages, and to Louisa Williams, for making sure that my language was concise and as graceful as possible.

Stuart Matlins, the publisher of Jewish Lights Publishing, is the reason there is a *New Jewish Baby Book,* and the reason it's a better, more useful, more beautiful book.

My husband, Jim Ball, provided invaluable technical assistance as well as cheerful support, especially in the final pangs of production. And, of course, I would never have written this book were it not for my daughter. Emilia's birth showed me the gap on the bookshelf where this book needed to be. She is a joy and a wonder.

Foreword

Eve had witnessed several of the animals in the Garden of Eden giving birth to their young. She once watched intently as a hippo gave birth, heard the noises which the mother made and saw how she immediately tried to clean her newborn of its afterbirth by licking it from head to toe. She thought of that scene as she began to feel the child in her womb pushing downward as it reached towards life. And after what seemed like an eternity of pain because of the contractions, when she finally saw her baby emerge, she exclaimed: *kaniti ish et Adonai,* "I have gained a male [child] with God['s help]" (Genesis 4:1).

Although her words are somewhat amorphous, anyone who has been blessed with the birth of a child can understand something of what this first mother felt. The verb *kanah* in Hebrew can mean to purchase or to gain, but has the clear connotation of "in perpetuity." In bringing Cain into the world, Eve sensed that birthing a child had as much to do with the future as with the present. It was through this little child that both she and Adam were guaranteed a future beyond themselves.

But there was more. As they acted upon the spark of divinity in both of them, having been created in God's image, they solidified their relationship with the Divine. It was as if Eve might have actually said: *Kaniti et Adonai,* "[through the birthing of their child] I gained a greater sense of God." *Kanah* also has the connotation of "create," and in their creative act, Adam and Eve experienced the presence of God as never before. In the Garden of Eden, everything was provided for them; nothing demanded their responsibility. Outside the paradisal Garden in the struggle in the real world, Adam and Eve came to know the exaltation of the creating of life as well as the responsibility that it entails.

The world outside the Garden of Eden into which Cain was thrust was much more complex and difficult than that in which his parents grew. If Adam and Eve had only to choose between eating or not eating the fruit of the Tree of Knowledge, Cain surely had choices to make at every turn.

All the more so our own children, who are born into a world in which the complexities of life and relationships can be overwhelming. We know this all too well even as Jews. The high rate of intermarriage, the increasing incidence of single parent families, the equality of men and women; all have had an impact on the way we must view the rites and rituals surrounding the birth, naming and entry of children into the covenantal relationship between God and the Jewish people. New Jewish parents or prospective parents are confronted with a host of difficult questions, ranging from possible welcoming and naming ceremonies for a baby girl to how to include non-Jewish family members in an appropriate way in the *brit milah* of their newborn son. Jewish professionals, rabbis, cantors, educators and *mohalim* also are forced to help single or gay parents who have adopted a child create meaningful ceremonies as well as assist non-Jewish relatives in understanding the significance of bringing a child to the Jewish people.

Anita Diamant's *The New Jewish Baby Book* is an invaluable resource and guide for Jewish parents and their families as they deal with the birth of their child. It will help educate them as to the origin, meaning and importance of all the rituals and customs associated with the birth of a new child, while presenting them with any number of possible alternative ceremonies for *brit milah* and *brit bat,* an extensive list of male and female Hebrew names, and guideposts for how to handle these events.

For liberal Jews today, the issues and choices surrounding the birth of a child are manifold, and most Jewish adults need much help in educating themselves so as to know how to respond in personally meaningful ways. Anita Diamant will assist new Jewish parents in making intelligent choices which can enhance the spiritual significance of this most important moment in their lives and in the lives of their families.

In dealing sensitively with the oftentimes painful realities of Jewish family life today, especially as they surface when a child is born and in raising and responding to the myriad of questions new parents always have, Anita Diamant has presented them with perhaps their first baby gift. *The New Jewish Baby Book* will enable them not only to experience the authentically Jewish way, while being respectful of the traditions of other family members, but also to grow in knowledge and commitment themselves as Jews.

Rabbi Norman J. Cohen,
Dean, New York School,
Hebrew Union College –
Jewish Institute of Religion

Preface

The Rabbis taught that mother, father, and the Blessed Holy One are partners in the creation of new life. Yet, for too long, the spirituality of childbirth has been a well-kept secret in the contemporary American Jewish community. Ask any mother (and often, fathers, too) the story of her child's birth, and you invite a flood of sacred stories, intense feelings, indescribable joy, and a sense of closeness to God. Everyone knows that the time of childbirth is a time when parents come very close to God, but the secret is closely guarded because so few Jews are able to speak of this truth out loud. Here is a book that is willing to do just that.

As a young rabbi serving a large, traditional congregation some years ago, I often wove stories about my young daughter into my sermons. I talked about her as my own first fruit, as a teacher who brought me the most valuable lessons about living—about gratitude, about wonder, about patience, about laughter, about God's presence in the everyday miracles of life. And yes, I told stories about her birth—an occasion so sacred to me that it compares in my own experience to my people's experience of Sinai—the day the gateway to God opened wide before my eyes. I consistently received the most heartfelt responses to these sermons, from both women and men. People were moved and grateful to hear their own experience of the extraordinary holiness of childbirth affirmed.

Anita Diamant's work is a beautiful expression of the profound spirituality of the experience of pregnancy and childbirth. This book is an invaluable contribution to any Jewish bookshelf, as it nourishes and gives voice to parents' sense of overpowering wonder at the process of preparing for and responding to the birth of a child. The book pulsates with the awe and joy and fear that are the real stuff of this time of life for parents. It eloquently voices what goes on in the heart and spirit of new parents, and gives parents easy access to the many ways in which Jewish tradition expresses those very same sentiments in its ancient rituals.

Preface

As in *The New Jewish Wedding Book,* Anita uses her clear and delightful journalist's style to open the door to the many meanings and practices of Jewish traditions around the birth of a baby. The book brims over with usable suggestions on how to celebrate and sanctify the experience of childbirth, giving even newcomers to Jewish tradition an enticing invitation to enter into the dynamics of Jewish teachings, allowing their own hearts to speak through time-honored Jewish idiom.

In doing this, Anita not only gives parents ways to express the inexpressible, but invites all kinds of Jews to enter into a partnership with Jewish tradition. In Anita's account, Judaism becomes a friend, a partner, as parents are empowered to link their own needs and longings with the tradition's teachings to create ceremonies and spiritual responses that are both personally powerful and Jewishly meaningful.

Laced with Anita's characteristic lightness and good humor, the book offers a menu of possibilities, a plethora of opportunities for responding to childbirth with creativity, spiritual awareness, and Jewish authenticity. The book brims over with tantalizing tidbits—interpretations, suggestions, reminders, exquisite touches to sanctify and beautify childbirth rituals. This is all done with deep respect for the diversity of our Jewish community as well as the needs of individuals, and particular awareness of the changing character of the Jewish family in our community (hence valuable sections on adoption, infertility, and the interfaith family).

This book is not a *halachic* encyclopedia. In fact, it contains an occasional item that may be problematic for traditional Jews, and so they may wish to discuss the key elements of their own ceremonies with a rabbi. But the book is of enormous value even to the most traditional of Jews, for its comprehensiveness, its liturgical creativity, its good humor, and its spiritual depth.

To new and expectant parents using this book, may it help nourish your joy and wonder as you bring a child into your life, and may it invite you to fully claim your partnership with God, as you create your new family. Mazal Tov!

Rabbi Amy Eilberg
Director, Kol Haneshama
San Francisco

Introduction

Like so many of my middle-class American baby-boom peers, I postponed child-bearing until I was just about as grown-up and in control of my life as I was likely to get. So when I was thirty-four and pregnant for the first time, I was excited, afraid, ambivalent. I was riveted by the sight of small babies swaddled in Snugglis, strapped to their mothers and fathers. How wonderful, I thought. My husband and I were going to join this ancient sorority and fraternity of parents. On the other hand, I worried. About everything.

I asked my friends who already had children hundreds of questions—about car seats, about diaper services, about breast-feeding, about labor, about changes in relationships with spouses, about coping with sleeplessness, about patience. I read the books my friends recommended, and even more important, I watched them cope and their children thrive.

Although the ultrasound suggested that my baby would be a girl, my husband and I had a boy's as well as a girl's name ready. The baby would be Emilia or Eliot, in memory of my maternal grandmother, Esther Leah. But apart from her name, my husband and I didn't think about the Jewish dimensions of our child's impending birth. Nor did we have any inkling of the over-powering, inarticulate awe we felt at the miracle of her birth—feelings we felt required the blessings of our tradition and our community.

After we became the proud and exhausted parents of Emilia, we scrambled to put together some sort of welcoming ritual that would coincide with my parents' visit from out of town. But it's not easy to write a ceremony that expresses the inexpressible, especially when you're sleep-deprived.

What sources we could find were few and scattered. On the night before Emilia's *brit bat* (covenant for a daughter) ceremony, we found ourselves shuffling through a sheaf of ceremonies borrowed from our rabbi's files, trying to cobble together a ritual that would feel right to us.

The ceremony was held after *Shabbat* morning services at Congregation Beth El of the Sudbury River Valley. It was beautiful and moving, and apparently no one knew how breathless we were about the whole thing.

When we talked with friends who had had baby boys at about the same time, they expressed even more bewilderment. Although most did not hesitate to have their sons circumcised, their lack of understanding about the religious significance of the rite—and about how they might participate in it—left them feeling dazed, out of control, and something less than joyful at their sons' circumcisions.

I wrote *The New Jewish Baby Book* in response to these feelings of awe and bewilderment, and in hopes that parents would feel inspired and empowered to use Jewish tradition as a means for expressing their own great joy.

Every Jewish baby is a link in a chain that extends back to Sinai, when according to Midrash (the Jewish literature of biblical interpretation) the souls of all the Jews—even those yet unborn—were present for the giving of the Torah, the first five books of the Hebrew Bible.

Every Jewish baby is a triumph of life over death, especially in a century that has witnessed the annihilation of so many Jewish children.

And every Jewish baby embodies the ancient longing for redemption; for a world as innocent and peaceful as a newborn's face.

A story is told: God commands us to perform countless acts of love. How can we begin to obey such a difficult commandment? The answer lies (or soon will lie) in your arms. In every smile, every diaper change, every sleepless night, every lullaby, every wordless prayer of thanks, in the unending ways we care for and teach and protect our children, we perform countless acts of love. And the world is made holier. And so are we.

Introduction

Dear reader, if you are looking at these words while preparing for the arrival of a child, I wish you an easy wait, a short labor, and a healthy baby—who sleeps.

Anita Diamant
West Newton, Mass.
June 1993—Tammuz 5753

PART
1

Chai — Life

Conception

Judaism, which sanctifies so many of life's passages with *brachot* (blessings), and *mitzvot* (sacred obligations), is comparatively silent about the awe-inspiring experiences of conception, pregnancy, and birth. Until recently, the expectation of conception began with every Jewish wedding. Thus, the bridal *mikvah* (ritual immersion) not only marked the beginning of a woman's sexual activity but her decision to become a mother as well as a wife.[1]

Mikvah, however, is foreign to most American Jews. Today many married couples wait years before having a child. Still, the decision to begin a family or add to it is such an important one that some people have created simple, private rituals to mark their decision in distinctly Jewish ways.

Deciding to have a child alters a couple's sexual relationship. Physical intimacy becomes a means to what Judaism considers a sacred end. A choice so momentous suggests a self-conscious separation—in Hebrew *havdalah*—between one stage of life and another.

Jewish tradition encourages love-making on *Shabbat,* and particularly on Friday night. According to *Midrash* (Judaism's imaginative literature of biblical interpretation), the Sabbath reunites God's male and female aspects. The joy, peace, and relaxation associated with Friday evening was thought to make for a particularly auspicious time for conception.[2]

In the rhythms of modern life, Friday night also happens to be a perfect time to make a separation between one way of doing things and another. The workweek is over. It's time to concentrate on each other.

There are no rules. There is barely any precedent for these private moments. You choose what you feel comfortable with: A special, leisurely meal, lit by *Shabbat* candles, perhaps a bubble bath. You could read your *ketubah* (marriage contract), or recite the *shehecheyanu*—the prayer of thanksgiving that marks all manner of beginnings. And love.

When the Baal Shem Tov, the great Jewish mystic and founder of Hasidism, was asked why people love children so much, he answered that a child is still very close to his or her conception. And because there was so much ecstasy at the conception, it still shows in the child.

Some couples choose to acknowledge their decision to become Jewish parents with *mikvah*. Although the ritual bath is most commonly associated with *tohorat hamishpachah* (the laws regulating women's sexual availability vis-à-vis menstruation), that is by no means its only use. *Mikvah* is a way of preparing for various kinds of encounters with the Holy—the source of life and death. Some traditional Jews—men and women—visit the *mikvah* before every *Shabbat* and in preparation for the holiday of *Yom Kippur.* According to Jewish folklore, *mikvah* is an antidote for infertility.

The traditional blessing recited during *mikvah* is:

בָּרוּךְ אַתָּה יְיָ, אֱלֹהֵינוּ מֶלֶךְ הָעוֹלָם,
אֲשֶׁר קִדְּשָׁנוּ בְּמִצְוֹתָיו, וְצִוָּנוּ עַל הַטְּבִילָה.

*Ba-ruch a-ta Adonai, Eh-lo-hei-nu meh-lech
ha-o-lam, a-sher ki-d'sha-nu b'mitz-vo-tav,
v'tzi-va-nu al ha-t'vi-lah.*

Holy One of Blessing Your Presence Fills
Creation, You sanctify us with Your
commandments and command us
concerning immersion.

Here is a more personal prayer (in Hebrew, a *kavannah*) for *mikvah*:

> Now as I immerse myself, I begin a new cycle, a cycle of rebirth and renewal in your world and Your people Israel. I prepare in hopes of creating new life according to the *mitzvah* of *p'ru urvu* (be fruitful and multiply), and for the sanctification of that life in *chupah* (the marriage canopy), Torah (Jewish learning) and *ma-asim tovim* (acts of loving kindness).[3]

Pregnancy

Pregnant women have always evoked respect, affection, and excitement in the Jewish community. In the life of the *shtetl* (the Jewish villages of eastern Europe), pregnant women were pampered and protected in the belief that unpleasantness might hurt the baby. In many communities, pains were taken not to let the evil spirits—especially Lilith, Adam's first wife—know that a baby was due at all.[1]

Shabbat can provide couples with a way of privately marking the milestones of pregnancy. After the bustle of the week (and after the older children are asleep), Friday night can be the perfect time to recall the "events" of the week; the end of morning sickness, the first kick, the first meeting of your childbirth class.

And whether or not you think of yourselves as religious, pregnancy makes everyone a supplicant. Mostly, the prayers of expectant parents are simple: Dear God, please make it a healthy baby. (Also, please make these hemorrhoids go away.) While such fervid requests of God will not be found in the synagogue prayerbook, prayers like these are as old as memory and some were published as *t'chinoht,* Yiddish petitionary prayers of eastern European women. Our great-grandmothers doubtless shared many prayers for their baby's health and for an easy birth, but that oral tradition is largely lost to us.

There is a formal set of prayers said during pregnancy by traditional Jews during the daily prayer service.[2] However, many liberal Jews are uncomfortable with the language of these prayers, and with the fact that most are the sole responsibility of the father. Pregnancy has inspired Jewish parents to write new prayers and poems that express the anticipation and excitement of this time. The following prayer, written during her pregnancy by Rabbi Judy Shanks, revives the tradition of *t'chinoht* in modern terms.

With all my heart, with all my soul, with all
my might,
I pray for the health of this child.
I pray for it to be perfect in mind and body,
To issue safely and easily from me
At the proper time,
To grow steadily and sturdily
In a home filled with joy at its presence,
To be nurtured into a person who greets the
world
with passion, enthusiasm, dance, love, humility,
faith.

With all my heart, with all my soul, with all
my might,
I pray for the health of this world.
I beg its leaders to temper their insanity
with reason,
So that my child may be born into a world that
seeks longevity,
not annihilation.
Let the world join in the thrill of creation,
And turn its back on the lust for destruction.
Let my child never know the pain and absurdity
of warfare
Let it take part in the dances of peace.

With all my heart, with all my soul, with all
my might,
I pray for God to watch over me and my family,
I pray for strength and courage when I labor to
bring forth this child,
I pray for the capacity to return my husband's
love for me,
I pray for the ability to love and nurture this
child,
I pray to feel God's presence now and always.[3]

Celebrating Pregnancy

Although pregnancy and childbirth have become more of a joint adventure for expectant fathers and mothers than ever before, the physical changes and challenges of having a baby makes sisters of all mothers. Jewish women have taken advantage of two customs to celebrate this part of life—*Rosh Chodesh* and the baby shower.

Rosh Chodesh, the celebration of the new moon, is a semi-holiday that falls on the first day of every lunar month. According to tradition, women were exempt from all work on *Rosh Chodesh.* Since the 1960s, groups of American and Israeli women have formed groups that meet to celebrate the "head of the month," with study, prayer, liturgy, and rituals that celebrate the unique qualities of Jewish women's spirituality. *Rosh Chodesh* groups have created beautiful ceremonies of preparation for their pregnant members and rituals of passage for women who are newly delivered.[4]

The baby shower, an American tradition, is usually sanctified only by Hallmark. But with the addition of a few distinctive Jewish touches, a shower can become a memorable event and a milestone on the road to becoming a Jewish parent.

Here are some ideas for ways to make a baby shower unique:

- Ask the guests who are mothers to contribute photographs of themselves when they were pregnant, and photographs of their babies, to be collected into a friendship album for the new mother. Put a picture of the mother-to-be on the cover and leave room for her own baby pictures on the last few pages of the book.

- Ask each guest to bring a fruit that symbolizes her wish for the mother-to-be: an apple for wisdom, a pineapple for generosity, figs for strength, and so forth.[5]

- After everyone is assembled, ask every woman to recite her Hebrew name and her matrilineage—the name of her mother, grandmothers, great-grandmothers, and other female relatives as far back as she can.

- Ask guests to bring presents that are specifically Jewish, such as gift certificates for home-cooked *Shabbat* meals, Jewish children's books, a *tzedakah* (charity) box for the baby's room, a colorful *mezuzah* to hang on the nursery door post, a Chanukah *draydl* (spinning top).

- Invite the father and his friends to the baby shower, and ask the men who are fathers to share their stories about becoming parents.

Birth

Agony, joy, wonder, terror, laughter, anger, tears, remember to breathe, crying out, despair, courage, profanity, prayer, the wonderful nurses, awe, a miracle.

The struggle, pain, power, and triumph of giving birth is the most intense encounter with the Holy that most of us will ever know. After the baby is born—held, kissed, studied, cradled, nursed, admired—language seems utterly inadequate. At this moment when there are no words, Jewish tradition provides two timeless prayers.

בָּרוּךְ אַתָּה יְיָ, אֱלֹהֵינוּ מֶלֶךְ הָעוֹלָם,
הַטוֹב וְהַמֵּטִיב.

*Ba-ruch a-ta Adonai, Eh-lo-hei-nu meh-lech
ha-o-lam,
ha-tov v'ha-mei-tiv.*

Blessed are You Adonai Ruler of Creation,
Who is good and does good.

and

בָּרוּךְ אַתָּה יְיָ, אֱלֹהֵינוּ מֶלֶךְ הָעוֹלָם,
שֶׁהֶחֱיָנוּ וְקִיְּמָנוּ וְהִגִּיעָנוּ לַזְּמַן הַזֶּה.

*Ba-ruch a-ta Adonai, Eh-lo-hei-nu meh-lech
ha-o-lam,
sheh-heh-cheh-ya-nu v'ki-y'ma-nu v'hi-gi-a-nu
la-z'man ha-zeh.*

Blessed are You Adonai Ruler of Creation, Who
has kept us alive, and sustained us and enabled us
to reach this moment.

The other traditional words that seem appropriate at the birth
of a child are the opening lines of *brit milah* and *brit bat,* the
covenant ceremonies, respectively, for boys and girls:

בָּרוּךְ הַבָּא.

Ba-ruch ha-bah.

Blessed is he who comes.

or

בְּרוּכָה הַבָּאָה.

B'ru-chah ha-ba-ah.

Blessed is she who comes.

This new blessing was written by Seth Riemer, Betsy Platkin-
Teutsch, and David Teutsch expressly for the moment when
parents hold their child for the first time.

בָּרוּךְ אַתָּה יְיָ, אֱלֹהֵינוּ מֶלֶךְ הָעוֹלָם,
מְשַׂמֵּחַ הָאֵם בִּפְרִי בִטְנָה
וּמֵגִיל הָאָב בְּיוֹצֵא חֲלָצָיו.

*Ba-ruch a-ta Adonai, Eh-lo-hei-nu meh-lech
ha-o-lam,
m'sa-mei-ach ha-eim bif-ri vit-nah
u-mei-gil ha-av b'yo-tzei cha-la-tzav.*

Blessed are You, the Incomparable our God, the
Sovereign of All Worlds, Who lets the mother
rejoice in the fruit of her womb, and the father
with his offspring.[1]

PART

2

A Jewish Name

Naming

Parents are passionate about the choice of their child's name, but everyone handles the decision-making process differently. Some people select names before they conceive, and others spend the pregnancy poring over lists, asking friends and relatives for reactions to the top contenders. Others wait until after the baby is born before settling on what to call him or her. Some couples keep the names they select a secret, while others refer to the mother's belly by its soon-to-be name.

Whatever your style, this section provides some history, practical advice, and a list of contemporary Jewish names to help you make your decision.

What's in a Name?

Choosing your baby's name is a second conception that begins the task of shaping the human being—the *mensch*—your child will become. By placing this important choice within a Jewish context, you have already begun to give your child an identity, a community, and a way of being in the world.

For Jews, a name is a complicated gift. A baby named Daniel or Rebecca may recall a loved relative who has died, but it is also a link to every Daniel or Rebecca back to biblical times. Your child's name places him or her squarely in the unfolding story of your family and the Jewish people.

Names have always had powerful associations in Jewish tradition. *Hashem*, "the Name," is one of many indirect ways of referring to God. The dozens of alternatives—*Adonai* (Lord) and *Eloheinu* (Our God) being the best-known—express a belief that God's real name is unpronounceable and unknowable, because that

"Name" somehow contains the essence, power, and unity that *is* God.

The great founder of Hasidism, Israel ben Eliezer, was called the Baal Shem Tov, master of the good name, not simply because he enjoyed a reputation for goodness. His name suggests that he possessed great insight into the power and wisdom of God's name.

The Bible portrays naming as the first independent human act. Adam's job in Eden was to name the beasts of the field, the birds of the air, and every living thing. This was no make-work project. The Hebrew for "word," *davar* is also the Hebrew for "thing," suggesting a close connection between names and natures. There is something about human names that seems to confirm this insight. Naming a baby feels like a self-fulfilling prophecy; a beautiful name will predict a beautiful soul, a strong name suggests endurance. Like Adam's task in the Garden of Eden, giving the "right" name to your baby is a wonder-filled exercise of creative power.

The Torah highlights dramatic name changes in two famous stories that defined the Jewish people. Abram and Sarai become Abraham and Sarah after they accept the covenant and become the parents of the Jewish people. Even more striking is the name change of Jacob, a word that means "supplanter" and refers to Jacob's victorious struggle with his brother, Esau. But after Jacob wrestles with the angel, he gets a completely new name—Israel, "wrestler with God," and becomes the patriarch of the twelve tribes.

Proverbs 22 says, "A good name is rather to be chosen than good oil," oil being a measure of wealth. "A good name" probably refers to reputation, but the tradition stresses the idea that names have an inherent value and power. There is a story that the Jews enslaved in Egypt had become lax in their faith but were saved from total assimilation by maintaining two signs that set them apart: They retained the custom of circumcision, and they held onto their Hebrew names.

Acknowledging the importance of naming, the Midrash advises, "One should examine names carefully in order to give his son a name that is worthy so that the son may become a righteous person, for sometimes the name is a contributing factor for good as for evil." Still, the power attributed to a "good" name is only as strong as the person who bears it. The tradition also stresses that a good name is earned. The Mishnah, the first part of the Talmud, says, "The crown of a good name excels all other crowns, including the crown of learning, of priesthood and even of royalty."[1]

Names in the Bible

During biblical times, people had only one name, and every child was given a name that was entirely his or her own. Over the thousand years described in the Bible, there is only one Abraham, one Sarah, one Miriam, one Solomon. None of the twenty-one kings of Judah was named after David, the founder of the dynasty.

There are 2,800 personal names in the Bible, of which less than five percent are used today.[2] The relatively few biblical names still in use have a wide range of origins. Many are theophoric, which means they exalt God. Names with the prefixes or suffixes *el, eli, ya, yahu* all refer to the Holy One: Elisha—God is my salvation; Raphael—God has healed; Netanyahu—gift of God.

Other biblical names describe the circumstances of birth or a person's historical role. Moses comes from Pharaoh's daughter's explanation, "I drew him out of the water." Chava, Eve's Hebrew name, comes from the root word for life, *chai.*

The Bible is full of names taken from nature, and to North American ears they resonate with Native American associations: Deborah—bee; Jonah—dove; Tamar—palm tree. This tradition has been revived with a passion in modern Israel with modern names such as Tal and Tali—dew; Elon and Elana—oak; Oren—fir tree; Namir—leopard.

Sacred and Secular

Despite their importance and durability, biblical Hebrew names have always competed with names from other languages and cultures. Even during the Talmudic period, Aramaic, Greek, and Roman names outnumbered biblical names among Jews. During the Middle Ages in eastern Europe, Jewish males were usually given both a secular name, called a *kinnui,* and a religious name, a *shem kadosh.* Eventually, the secular name became so dominant that some parents didn't bother giving a Hebrew name, a development that so alarmed the rabbis of the time that they decreed it mandatory to give a Hebrew name.[3]

Still, it remained common for men to have two names; one for use in the secular world, the other for religious purposes. The process for selecting secular names varied. The most straightforward method was to seek a direct translation of a Hebrew name; thus, in France, men called Chayim in synagogue were often known as Vive on the street. In Germany, the use of the first name Wolf was probably based on the biblical Benjamin, whose tribe was associated with that animal. However, equally often, people chose a secular name because it sounded like or shared a letter with a Hebrew name, or simply because it was popular in the surrounding culture.

Girls rarely had two names. The one that sufficed was sometimes Hebrew, as in Rachel or Hannah. But through constant use, Yiddish names took on the venerable status of biblical ones. Feigel, for example, a very popular name among Polish Jews in the 19th century, has an obscure etymology and may be based on words meaning violet, bird, or even fig.[4] Yiddish names often pose a problem for modern parents who go looking for Grandma Bayla's Hebrew name when she never had one.

Customs differed somewhat in the Sephardic world. Although girls were commonly given only one name, Syrian boys were never called by an Arabic name only. Equivalents in Hebrew and Arabic were hyphenated, as in Shelomo-Shelem (peace) or Yehuda-Aslan (lion).[5]

The disparity between boys' and girls' names is based on traditional gender roles in Jewish religious and communal life. A man's Hebrew name appears on legal documents, such as a *ketubah* (marriage contract), and is called when he reads from the Torah. Since women were not called to the Torah, and since the *ketubah* outlined only the groom's responsibilities, a Hebrew name was not considered necessary for women. As the status of Jewish women has changed, so has their need for Hebrew names.

With the opening of the ghettos in Europe, names taken from society at large become increasingly common. Although this was intended to blur the differences between Jews and gentiles, by end of the 19th century in northern Europe and in early 20th century America, a new category of Jewish-gentile names had emerged. Jews seemed drawn to certain names; in pre-World War I Germany, for example, Ludwig, Morritz, and Sigfried were so identified with Jews that non-Jews began to avoid them. Isadore (which actually means "gift of Isis") was a very popular secular name for Isaac and Israel and became so identified with the Jews that it became a Nazi epithet. In America, Hymie, a nickname for Hyman, which was a popular Americanization of Chaim, became an anti-Semitic slur as well.[6]

Jewish immigrants to America often selected new names when they arrived in the *goldene medina,* the golden land. Although some traditional names never completely disappeared, many Yiddish and Hebrew names seemed too foreign for the new country. So the Yiddish Blume (flower) blossomed into Rose, Lily, and Iris. The old country Tzvi (deer) who was known in Yiddish as Hersch (deer) became Harry. Also in America, Jews embraced the custom of giving a "middle" name.

American Jews have continued the custom of giving children a secular name and a Hebrew name, which often share only an initial consonant. A boy named for Uncle Moshe may be called to the Torah as Moshe, but his birth certificate will read Mark. A baby girl named for her grandmother Shayna may get the Hebrew name Shoshana and be called Susan by her friends. Although some people find this custom silly or worse, "phonetic assimilation" actually has ancient precedents. Under Greek rule, for example, men with the Hebrew name of Menachem commonly answered to Menaleus.

Naming after Relatives

Although the custom of naming children after parents or grand-parents is not found in the Bible, it is a very ancient practice. It was common among the Egyptian Jews of the 6th century B.C.E.,* who most likely borrowed the idea from their non-Jewish neighbors.

It is a never-ending source of amazement to Jews of Ashkenazic, or eastern European descent, who name their children only after relatives who have passed away, that Sephardim name their children after living relations. In some Sephardic communities, the practice follows a precise pattern; the first son is named after the father's father, the first daughter is named after the father's mother; the second son is named after the mother's father, the second daughter after the mother's mother. Beyond that, names may be selected to honor any family member or friend.[7]

Because the vast majority of American Jews are of Ashkenazic descent, the custom of naming after a deceased relative is most common here. In many cases, parents give the baby the same Hebrew name as the person honored, and then select a secular name on the basis of the initial letter or sound of the Hebrew. Which is how it came to pass that Baruch ("blessed") becomes Barry, Bradley, Bruce, and Brian, which is a Celtic or Gaelic name that means strength. One Grandma Naomi of blessed memory was even honored with a namesake called Natalie, which means Christmas child.

Superstition

Names have been associated with witchcraft since the beginning of human speech, probably due to the global suspicion that the soul is identical to and identified by a person's name. Thus, in some

---

* B.C.E. stands for Before the Common Era, which Jews prefer to B.C., or Before Christ.

cultures, a secret name—one that expresses a person's true self—is given at birth and guarded against enemies and evil forces.

Superstitions about the power of names abound in Jewish culture and are even acknowledged in the Talmud, which states, "Four things can abrogate the fate of man, and they are charity, supplication, change of name, and change of action." Name changes were often used to "fool" the angel of death.

Considering the high infant mortality rate of earlier times, we can easily understand why death and demons were thought to be particularly drawn to babies. In Poland, newborn boys who were ill or somehow at risk were given names like *Alte* or *Alter* (which mean, respectively, "another," and "old one") or *Zaida* (grandpa) to confuse the evil spirits. Not only would such a name confuse Death, who would come looking for a baby and instead find an old man. It implied that the child would live long enough to grow old and become a grandfather. Similarly, a name like Chayim (life) was given as a talisman.

Ashkenazic Jews superstitiously shunned the practice of naming children after living relatives to prevent the grim reaper from making a mistake and taking a child in place of a grandparent. Sephardic Jews had a different attitude toward the angel of death, assuming he might err in favor of longevity for both generations if fathers and sons bore the same name.

Modern American Jews who otherwise mock all forms of superstition tend to follow the advice of the medieval rabbi Judah Hechasid, who wrote, "Although one should not believe in superstitions, it is better to be careful." Thus many parents would no sooner consider naming their child after a living grandparent than they would think of leaving the baby out in a snowstorm.

Fashion

Throughout history, rabbis and scholars have railed against the demise of authentic Jewish names and warned against the assimilation that comes from choosing secular names for children. But the mishmash of Jewish naming customs is at least as old as the Babylonian exile (586 B.C.E.).

Throughout history, names have been as vulnerable to fashion as hemlines. The Talmudic period saw a burst of new Hebrew names (Meir, Nahman, Ahavah) as well as a revival of obscure ones (Hillel and Gamliel). But even then, many Jews were giving their babies distinctly non-Jewish names from the vernacular, which for many generations was Aramaic.

Jewish names were not handed down from Sinai; they have been hammered out of history. Take, for example, that extremely Jewish name, Esther, which is Persian in origin and shares its root with Ishtar, the great fertility goddess of the ancient Middle East. Although the Hebrew name for Esther is Hadassah, no one argues the Jewish pedigree of Esther. Likewise Mordecai, the other hero of the Purim story, has a Persian name, and an idolatrous one at that, because it means "devotee of the god Marduk."

Despite history's lessons, Jewish use of non-Jewish names has been a constant source of irritation to those who consider themselves conservators of tradition. The Hellenization of Jewish names (Jason for Joshua) dismayed the rabbis of late antiquity. Alexander, a name with no Jewish lineage, has enjoyed a loyal following since biblical times and continues to be extremely popular.

Every generation adopts a new set of names that reflect the local customs and the changing fashions of the times. In America, Sam and Rose and Molly and Jake gave birth to Sylvia and Charles and Rosalyn and Leonard. They, in turn, named their children Ellen and Alan, Gail and Barry, Karen and Ken, who then raised the generation of Kim and Bradley, Jennifer and Josh, Stacey and Jesse.

A recent trend in Jewish American naming demonstrates a return to roots. Biblical names like Sarah and Benjamin and Rebecca and Aaron are enormously popular. And there has been a run on selected "ethnic" immigrant names—witness the rash of announcements proclaiming a new generation of Rose and Max. Another new fashion, especially among American Jews who have spent time in Israel, is to give children modern Hebrew names.

Some people advocate the selection of unambiguously Jewish names for several reasons. For one thing, names like Jacob and Aviva may help children develop a Jewish identity. Ruth and David also make life simpler because such names work well in the three settings American Jews are likely to inhabit: in thoroughly American situations like public school; in religious life, as when one is called to the Torah; and as a visitor to—or resident of—the state of Israel.

Modern Hebrew Names

With the founding of the state of Israel in 1948, Hebrew was revived and reconstructed as a modern language. In the process, the lexicon of Jewish names exploded. Many who went to Palestine after the Holocaust were eager to cast off all reminders of the Diaspora, including their names. Some chose to translate Yiddish names to Hebrew. Shayna (pretty one) became Yaffa, Gittel (good one) became Tovah. Others simply chose a Hebrew name, and, reversing the old custom, picked one on the basis of the initial letter. Thus, Mendel and Morritz became Menachem and Meir.

The first generation of *sabras,* children born in Israel, inspired a host of new names. There were translations; a baby girl named for her aunt Raizel (rose) would be called Varda. And there was a resurrection of ancient biblical names that had not been heard for generations, such as Amnon, Yoram, Avital, Tamar. Even names of evil bibical characters surfaced, such as Aviram, who was swallowed by the Earth in retribution for his instigation of the rebellion against Moses.

As the people gave life to the land, the land inspired names such as Kinereth (a sea), Arnon (a stream bed), Barak (lightning) and Ora (light). Boys' names inspired a generation of new girls' names; Ariella from Ariel, Gabriella from Gabriel. And some names serve boys and girls: Yona (dove), Ayala and Ayal (deer), Leor and Leora (light), Liron and Lirona (song).

The knowledge that Jewish history was being made led to the coining of names like Aliyah (wave of immigration), Or-Tzion (light of Zion), and even Balfour (for the British Foreign Secretary who in 1917 issued a declaration announcing England's favorable attitude toward the establishment of a Jewish state in Palestine).

Israeli names have a music and life all their own, with diminutives and abbreviations applied to even the most ancient Hebrew names. One American who moved to Israel wrote, "It is of course the traditional names that give rise to all those icky diminutives: Yosef (Yossi), Avraham (Avi), Yaakov (Kobi), Yitzchak (Itzik and Tzachi). David inevitably becomes . . . Dudu, which to me always evokes a disposable diaper.

"Rachel meanwhile yields Racheli and Rochi, Shoshana is truncated to Shoshi, Ruth Ruti, Channah Channi, and my own Esther becomes Esti."[8]

A recent trend has been the addition of a final "t" sound to the end of girls' names, adding an extra feminine emphasis to even the most ancient; thus Leah has become Le'at.

Your Family, Your Names

Setting off in search of the perfect name for your Jewish baby may lead to interesting genealogical territory, as you mine for the Hebrew names of parents, grandparents, uncles, and aunts after whom you wish to name your child. This process may also send you to your *bar* or *bat mitzvah* certificate to find your own.

Traditionally, a child's full Hebrew name includes his or her parents' names as well. No one is simply David or Leora. David is *David ben Mosheh v'Rivkah*, David the son of Moses and Rebecca. Leora is *Leora bat Refa-el u-Malkah*, Leora the daugher of Raphael and Malkah. If you're not sure of your own Hebrew name, ask your parents. And if you don't have one, now might be a good time to select one.

In many families, the choice of a baby's name gives rise to intergenerational and/or inter-*machatunim* (in-law) conflict. However, there is at least one way to make a child's name a way of knitting families together: give the baby lots of middle names. A child named Sharon Esther-Leah Rivkah can honor three relatives. And think how impressive it will sound when she is called to the Torah!

And remember: How and why you chose a particular name will be of great interest to your child. Children love to hear stories about themselves, and the origin of a name can make a fascinating tale. Someday, you can tell your Ruth or Saul about their biblical namesakes, about Bubbe Ruth or Zayde Saul, about the names you considered and rejected, about the day you found their name in this very book. The richer and more numerous your stories, the better. You will be asked to tell them again and again and again.

Naming an Adopted Child

In general, adoptive parents and birth parents select names using the same criteria. The same customs, superstitions, and arguments apply no matter how your baby finds his or her way into your arms. Thus, among American Jews, most adoptive children are named in memory of family members who have died. And typically, a child's full Hebrew name includes his or her adoptive parents' names as well, as in *Doron bat Eliezer v'Elisheva*, Doron, the daughter of Eli and Elizabeth.

However, it is also possible to give an adopted baby the traditional "generic" convert's name, which is still used by most adult Jews by choice. Thus, Doron would be *Doron bat Avraham Avinu v'Sarah Immeinu*, Doron the daughter of Abraham our patriarch and Sarah our matriarch.[9]

What Makes This List Different from All Other Lists

No list of names is complete. The compilation that follows is not a scholarly work or a definitive dictionary, but a guide for naming a Jewish child in an English-speaking world at this point in history.

For example, you will not find all the 2,800 names that appear in the Bible in this book. The long-suffering Job is not mentioned here. Nor can there be any comprehensive catalog of modern Hebrew names since Israeli society propagates new ones so quickly, any list would be incomplete before the ink was dry. The names below reflect the author's best effort to catalog names that conform to current American tastes and trends.

Although you may find all the help you need on the following pages, there are other places to turn. A sympathetic rabbi, cantor, or *mohel* can be a great help. And if you want advice in selecting a modern Hebrew name, talk to an Israeli.

The best published resource on names is *The Complete Dictionary of English and Hebrew Names* by Alfred J. Kolatch (Jonathan David Publishers, 1984). A volume of nearly 500 pages, Kolatch's book includes a remarkable Hebrew vocabulary index. So if you wish your baby's name to reflect a quality, such as compassion, you will find suggestions under that heading.

All the names on the lists below have a Jewish pedigree of some sort. (With a little effort, you can find a Jewish precedent for the use of almost any name. Legend has it that some Danish Jews were named Christian after King Christian X, who wore a yellow badge when the Nazis ordered the Danish Jews to wear them.)[10]

What you will find here, in addition to biblical names, are many traditional and modern Hebrew names, some Yiddish, and a few Sephardic names. Also included are ethnic English-language names that are associated with American Yiddishkeit (Jewishness) and have experienced a renaissance in the last few years.

Many of the names that appear below are beautiful in sound and meaning; Eliora (God is my light), Gila (joy), Rimona (pomegranate). Then again, some are simply melodic. For example, Aderet, which sounds lovely, means cloak. On the other hand, the timeless biblical name Leah means weariness. Unlike Americans, Israelis don't rule out names just because they have an unhappy literal meaning or biblical source. Hence the popularity of the ill-fated Dina and the little-known Naftali.

For many generations, children born on Jewish holidays were given names appropriate to the dates of their birth; thus, babies were named Shabbatai, Pesach, and Yom Tov. It was a safe bet that anyone called Mordecai or Esther arrived during Purim. Those names have fallen out of fashion with a majority of American Jews, but because they still have currency in Israel, some appear below.

Finally, fashion, by definition, changes with each generation, if not every season. Names considered unthinkably old-fashioned only a decade ago have been reclaimed with a vengeance—just go count the Sarahs and Aarons in the synagogue nursery school.

Speaking of Sarah, sources for girls' names reflect Judaism's undeniably patriarchal past. Thus there are fewer female prophets, warriors, and priests in the Bible after whom to name girls. The paucity of historical records about female Jewish scholars, leaders, and public figures compounds the problem.

However, there is a form of *yichus* (hereditary status) attached to many women's names that date from more recent history. Emma recalls modern Jewish heroines like political activist Emma Goldman and poet Emma Lazarus. And there may well be heroines in your own family saga. Great-grandma Pearl, who put her children through college by working in a sweatshop where she was a union organizer is no less lofty a namesake than Avital, wife of King David. Your Pearl of blessed memory can be honored with a daughter named Penina or Margalit.

When Using This List Remember

- The first version of each name is given in English, followed by alternative English spellings, followed by a transliteration of the Hebrew pronunciation if it differs significantly from the English. Unless otherwise noted, translations are from Hebrew. Not all the translations given are literal. In some cases, a more poetic rendering is provided.

- All English versions of Hebrew names are transliterations, which means there is no exact correlate; Dina, Deena, Dena, and Dinah are all correct. Choose the spelling you prefer, or make up your own. The final "h" on names ending with a vowel are sometimes dropped, so you can choose Malkah or Malka.

- In most—though not all—Hebrew names, the accent falls on the second syllable. Thus, A*dam*. There are always exceptions; for example, Yeho*shua*. If you are unsure, ask your rabbi or anyone who is more familiar with the Hebrew language.

- A number of names are given with variations that change the meaning somewhat. Most common are the suffixes *-i, -li,* and *-iel.* For example, Ron, which means joy or song, can become Roni (my joy), Ronli (joy is mine), or Roniel (joy of God).
- There is no "J" sound in Hebrew. Wherever a "J" appears, the Hebrew sound is "Y." Thus, Jonina is Yonina. In most cases, and especially where there is no common English J-sound version, such names are listed under "Y." However, where an English version is possible (Jasmine or Yasmin), both are given under the listing for "J."

A Son!

A

AARON, ARON, AHARON אהרן

Teaching, singing, shining, or mountain. The Aramaic root means messenger. Aaron was the older brother of Moses and Miriam, the first Israelite high priest and progenitor of all priests. Rabbinic tradition stresses his love of peace.

ABBA אבא

Father. It might seem odd to name your son "Daddy," but then, Israeli statesman Abba Eban has worn it well.

ABEL הבל

Breath. The son of Adam and Eve, and the ill-fated brother of Cain.

ABIR אביר

Strong.

ABNER, AVNER אבנר

Literally, father of light. Avner ben Ner was King Saul's uncle and the commander of his army.

ABRAHAM, AVRAHAM אברהם

Father of a mighty nation. Abraham, the first Hebrew, began life as Abram, but when he accepted the covenant, by circumcising himself and establishing the practice among his people, the Hebrew letter Hay, which appears twice in the unpronounceable name of God (Yud Hay Vav Hay) was added to his name. The Arabic equivalent is Ali Baba.

ABRAM, AVRAM אברם
Exalted father. Abraham's original name.

ABSALOM, AVSHALOM אבשלום
Father of peace. King David's third son. A later Absalom played a prominent part in the defense of Jerusalem against the Emperor Pompey.

ACHIYA אחיה
God is my brother. One of King David's warriors. Achi means brother.

ADAM אדם
Earth. In Phoenician and Babylonian, it means mankind. The first man. Not a popular name among Jews until modern times.

ADIN עדין
Beautiful, pleasant, gentle. A biblical name, its variations include Adi, Adina, Adino, Adiv.

ADLAI עדלי
Refuge of God, from the Aramaic. The biblical Adlai was a shepherd.

ADMON אדמון
The name of a red peony that grows in the upper Galilee.

AKIBA, AKIVA עקיבא
Akiva is derived from the same root as Jacob, Ya'akov, which means supplanter, or "held by the heel." Rabbi Akiva was a 1st-century scholar and teacher, the founder of a famous academy. Common nicknames include Koby and Kivi.

ALEXANDER אלכסנדר
Protector of men. Ever since the 3rd century B.C.E., when
Alexander the Great spared Jerusalem from harm, Jewish boys
have been named in his honor. As the story goes, the high
priest of Jerusalem was so grateful for Alexander's largesse that
he proclaimed that all Jewish males born in the city for a year
would bear the conquerer's name, and it has remained popular
ever since, in many forms, including Sander (Yiddish), and
Sasha (a Russian diminutive). Nicknames include Alex and
Sandy.

ALON אלון
Oak tree. One of the sons of Shimeon. A very popular name in
Israel.

ALYAN עלין
Heights. One of the sons of Seir in the Bible.

⁄ AMAL עמל
Work. A member of the tribe of Asher.

AMATZ, AMAZIAH אמץ, אמציה
Strong, courageous.

AMI עמי
My people. A popular Israeli name, the root is found in many
other names, a few of which follow.

AMICHAI עמיחי
My people is alive.

AMIEL עמיאל
God of my people.

AMIKAM עמיקם
Nation arisen.

AMIN אמין
Trustworthy.

AMIR אמיר
Mighty, strong.

AMIRAM עמירם
My people is lofty.

AMITAI אמיתי
True, faithful. Amitai was the father of Jonah.

AMNON אמנון
Faithful. Amnon was the oldest son of David.

AMOS עמוס
Burdened. A prophet who preached social morality in the
Northern Kingdom of Israel during the 8th century B.C.E.
A popular Israeli name.

AMRAM עמרם
A mighty nation. Amram was the father of Moses, Miriam, and
Aaron.

ANSHEL אנשעל
Yiddish for Asher.

ARI ארי
A shortened form of Aryeh, but a popular name in its own
right.

ARIEL אריאל
Lion of God. Also a poetic name for the city of Jerusalem.
Ari and Arik are diminutives.

ARNON ארנון
Roaring stream. In the Bible, the Arnon was a stream in the
frontier of the Moab, a kingdom east of the Dead Sea.

ARYEH אריה
Lion. The biblical Aryeh was an army officer.

ASA אסא
Healer. A king of Judea.

ASHER אשר
Blessed, fortunate. Asher was the son of Jacob and Zilpah and the leader of one of the twelve tribes of Israel.

AVI אבי
Father. A diminutive of Avraham, but also used as a name on its own, this is the prefix/root for many names, some of which follow.

AVICHAI אביחי
My father lives.

AVIDAN אבידן
Father of justice, or God is just.

AVIEL אביאל
God is my father.

AVIEZER אביעזר
Father helper.

AVIGDOR אביגדור
Father protector. Popular in Israel.

AVIMELECH אבימלך
Father king.

AVINOAM אבינעם
Father of delight.

AVISHAI אבישי
In Aramaic, "gift of God." A grandson of the biblical Jesse.

AVISHALOM אבישלום
Father of peace.

AVIV אביב
Spring.

AVROM אברם
Yiddish for Abraham.

AZI עזי
Strong.

AZRIEL עזריאל
God is my help.

B

BARAK ברק
Lightning. A biblical soldier, during the reign of Deborah.

BARAM ברעם
Son of the nation.

BARUCH ברוך
Blessed. Baruch was a friend to the prophet Jeremiah. The Yiddish version, Bendit, is probably based on the name Benedict.

BEN-AMI בן־עמי
Son of my people. The prefix/root *ben,* or son, gives rise to many names.

BENJAMIN, BINYAMIN בנימין
Son of my right hand. Benjamin was the younger of Rachel's sons and Jacob's favorite. As the only one of the twelve brothers who did not participate in Joseph's sale into slavery, Benjamin was honored by having the Holy Temple built on territory allotted to his tribe.

BEN-ZION בֶּן־צִיּוֹן
Son of Zion. Benzi is a popular nickname.

BERYL בעריל
A Yiddish diminutive for bear, which is sometimes further shortened to Ber. The Hebrew equivalent is Dov.

BOAZ בֹּעַז
Strength and swiftness. The great-grandfather of King David, Boaz was a wealthy, land-owning Bethlehemite who married Ruth.

C

CALEB, CALEV כָּלֵב
Of the twelve spies sent by Moses to Canaan, only Caleb and Joshua brought back a favorable report, for which they were allowed to enter the promised land.

CHAIM, HAYYIM חַיִּים
Life.

D

DAN דָּן
Judge. Dan was the fifth son of Jacob, and first-born of Bilha, Rachel's maidservant. Dani is a variant.

DANIEL דָּנִיֵּאל
God is my judge. The hero of the book of Daniel was an interpreter of visions who predicted the future triumph of a messianic kingdom.

DAVID דָּוִד
Beloved. David, the shepherd who killed Goliath became king first of Judah and later of Israel. According to legend, the Messiah will be a descendant of David. The name has been a favorite since Talmudic times.

DEROR, DERORI, DROR דרור, דרורי
Freedom. Also, a bird. A popular Israeli name.

DEVIR דביר
Holy place. In the Bible, Devir was a king of Eglon.

DOR דור
A generation.

DORAN, DORON דורן, דורון
Gift.

DOTAN דותן
Law. In the Bible, Dotan was a place in Palestine, north of Samaria.

DOV דב
Bear.

E

EFRAYIM, EPHREM, EPHRAIM אפרים
Fruitful. Efrayim was one of Joseph's sons—Jacob's grandsons. His name is mentioned in the traditional Friday night blessing for sons.

EFRON עפרון
A bird.

ELAZAR אלעזר
God has helped. Aaron's third son, Elazar became the high priest after him. There have been many famous Elazars throughout history, including Elazar ben Jair, a commander at Masada, whose eloquence persuaded the city's defenders that suicide was preferable to surrender or defeat.

ELI, ELY עלי
Ascend. In the Bible, Eli was a high priest and the last of the
Judges in the days of Samuel.

ELIAKIM אליקים
God established.

ELIEZER אליזער
My God has helped. Eliezer was the name of Abraham's
steward, Moses' son, and a prophet in the time of Jehosaphat.
Three great Talmudic scholars and many great German rabbis
were called Eliezer.

ELIHU אליהוא
He is my God. Elihu appears in the Bible as a young friend of
Job.

ELIJAH, ELIAHU אליהו
The Lord is my God. Elijah the prophet lived during the 9th
century B.C.E., and led the fight against the cult of Baal.
According to tradition, he ascended to heaven in a chariot of
fire but did not die. Elijah became a figure in Jewish folklore,
appearing to common folk disguised as a beggar. Elijah is
viewed as a herald of the Messiah, and his presence is invoked
during Passover and at circumcisions. The name is translated
into Elie in French, Elia in Italian. English versions include
Eliot, Ellis, and Elias. Elya is a common Israeli nickname.

ELISHA אלישע
God is my salvation. Elisha the prophet succeeded Elijah. In
Second Kings, there are miraculous stories about his long life.

ELKANAH אלקנה
God created.

EMANUEL, EMMANUEL עמנואל
God is with us.

ENOCH חנוך
Dedicated. Enoch was Cain's son, born after Abel died.

ESHKOL אשכול
A cluster of grapes. In Hebrew letters, Eshkol signifies a gathering of scholars. Levi Eshkol (1895–1969) was Israeli prime minister from 1963 to 1969.

ETAN, EYTAN איתן
Strong.

EVEN אבן
Stone. Eben and Eban are common English versions.

EYAL איל
A stag.

EZEKIEL יחזקאל
God will strengthen. Ezekiel was a prophet who lived during the 6th century B.C.E., during the last days of the first Temple. Ezekiel's description of the divine throne was the major text for Jewish mysticism (*Maaseh Merkavah*).

EZRA, EZRI עזרא, עזרי
Help. A priest and scribe of the 5th century B.C.E., Ezra led the return from Babylon to Jerusalem, where he became a key figure in the reconstruction of the Temple. He is credited with introducing the square Hebrew alphabet.

G

GABRIEL, GAVRIEL גבריאל
God is my strength. Gabriel the angel visited Daniel in the biblical tale. In Israel, the diminutive Gabi is also used as a full name. Gavirol is a Sephardic variation, with Gavri as a nickname.

GAD גד
Happy. Gad was one of Jacob's sons.

GAL, GALI גל, גלי
A wave or a mountain. Also, Galya.

GAMALIEL, GAMLIEL גמליאל
God is my reward. The name of many Talmudic scholars.

GAN גן
Garden.

GARON גרון
A threshing floor.

GEDALIA, GEDALIAH, GEDALIAHU גדליה, גדליהו
God is great. Gedaliah was a governor of Judea.

GERSHOM, GERSHON, GERSON גרשום, גרשון
I was a stranger there. Moses named his older son Gershom, referring to the Egyptian captivity. The name has served many teachers, including Gershom Scholem, the great 20th-century scholar of Jewish mysticism.

GIBOR גבור
Strong, hero.

GIDEON גדעון
A mighty warrior. A biblical warrior, reputed to have fathered seventy sons. Gidi is a popular nickname.

GIL, GILL, GILI, GILLI גיל, גילי
Joy. Gili means "my joy."

GILAD, GILEAD, GILADI גלעד, גלעדי
A place name that refers to a mountain range east of the Jordan River.

GUR, GURI, GURIEL גור, גורי, גוריאל
Respectively, young lion, my young lion, and God is my lion.
Guryon is another variation.

H

HADAR הדר
Adornment. A biblical king of Edom.

HANAN חנן
Grace or gracious. A shortened form of Yohanan.

HAREL הראל
Mountain of God. A biblical place name.

HASKEL, HASKELL השכל
Wise.

HASKEL, HASKELL חזקעל
Yiddish form of Ezekiel.

HERSCH, HERSH הערש
In Yiddish, a deer. The diminutives and variations of Hersch are
numerous: Herschel, Hesh, Heshel, Herzl, Hirsh, Hirsch. Tzvi
is the Hebrew equivalent.

HILLEL הלל
Praised. The name was often given in honor of the great scholar
Hillel, who was born in Babylon in 75 B.C.E.

HIRAM חירם
Noble-born. Hiram was king of Tyre, circa 969–936 B.C.E. He
helped plan, build, and equip the Temple in Jerusalem.

HOD הוד
Splendor, vigor. Hod was a member of the tribe of Asher.
Popular in Israel.

I

ILAN אילן
Tree. An alternative transliteration for Alon.

IRA עירא
From the Arabic, swiftness.

ISAAC, ITZAK, YITZHAK יצחק
Laughter. Isaac was the son of Abraham and Sarah, and the first Jew to be circumcised on the eighth day of life. The name has remained popular throughout Jewish history. Isaac Luria, the Safed mystic, established the Lurianic Kabbalah. Nicknames include Ike, Issa, and Yitz.

ISAIAH, YISHAYAHU ישעיה, ישעיהו
God is salvation. Isaiah was a prophet in Jerusalem in the 700s B.C.E. Isa is a popular nickname.

ISRAEL, YISRAEL, YISROEL ישראל
Wrestler with God. The name given to Jacob after he wrestled with the angel. Israel is a synonym for the Jewish people.

ISSACHAR יששכר
There is a reward. Issachar was the son of Jacob and Leah, one of the leaders of the twelve tribes of Israel.

ITAI, ITTAI אתי
Friendly. Itai was one of David's warriors.

ITIEL איתיאל
God is with me. Itiel was a member of the tribe of Benjamin.

ITTAMAR איתמר
Island of palm. Ittamar, whose name signifies gracefulness, was one of Aaron's sons. Ismar is an Ashkenazic transliteration of the name.

J

JACOB, YACOV, YA'ACOV יעקב
Held by the heel, supplanter. The third of the patriarchs, Jacob fathered the twelve tribes. His name was changed to Israel after his wresting match with an angel. There are many nicknames and derivatives of Jacob, from James to Jack to Jake to Yankele.

JARED, YARED ירד
To descend.

JEDEDIAH, YEDADIAH ידידיה
The name of priestly ancestral houses, mentioned in the book of Nehemiah.

JEREMIAH, JEREMY, YIR'MIAHU ירמיה, ירמיהו
God will uplift. Jeremiah the prophet lived around 625 B.C.E. His gloomy forecasts aroused resentment and he spent many years in jail.

JESSE, YISHAI ישי
Wealthy. Ruth's grandson, Jesse was the father of King David.

JETHRO, YITRO יתרו
Abundance, riches. Father of Zipporah and Moses' father-in-law, Jethro was a Midianite priest.

JOEL, YOEL יואל
God is willing. Joel was one of the twelve minor prophets who preached in Judea.

JONAH, YONAH יונה
Dove. Jonah was the prophet of whale fame.

JONATHAN, YONATAN יונתן
God has given. Jonathan, the son of Saul, is remembered for his friendship with David. Yoni is a popular Israeli nickname.

JORDAN, YARDEN ירדן
Descend. Jori is a popular Israeli nickname.

JOSEPH, YOSEF יוסף
God will increase. Almost twenty-five percent of Genesis is devoted to Joseph's story. A dreamer as well as a shrewd politician, his name has been a favorite throughout Jewish history. Jose, the Aramaic form of the name, was popular in Talmudic times.

JOSHUA, YEHOSHUA יהושע
The Lord is my salvation. Joshua succeeded Moses and led the Hebrews into the land of Israel. Moses changed his successor's name from Hoshea by adding a yud, one of the letters of God's name; thus, Yehoshua.

JOSIAH, YOSHIAHU יאשיהו
God has protected. Son of Amnon, Josiah became a king of Judah when he was eight years old.

JUDAH, YEHUDA יהודה
Praise. Judah was the fourth son of Jacob and Leah and received special blessings from his father. Yehuda is the source of the words Judaism, Jewish and Jew. There have been many famous Judahs, including Judah Halevi, a great Hebrew poet.

K

KADMIEL קדמיאל
God is the ancient one.

KALIL כליל
Crown or wreath.

KANIEL קניאל
A reed or stalk. In Aramaic, Kaniel means spear.

KATRIEL כתריאל
God is my Crown.

KENAN קינן
To acquire. A nephew of Abraham in the Bible.

KOBY קובי
A nickname for Jacob.

KOCHAV כוכב
Star.

KORE, KOREI קורא
Quail, or to call.

L

LABAN לבן
White. Laban was Rebecca's brother, father of matriarchs Rachel and Leah, and grandfather of the twelve tribes of Israel. An unsavory character.

LAVI לביא
Lion.

LAZAR לאזאר
A Greek form of Eliezer and a popular Yiddish name.

LEOR ליאור
I have light.

LEV לב, לייב
Heart in Hebrew. In Yiddish, Leib means lion. Label is a Yiddish nickname.

Levi לוי
Attendant. The name signifies devotion. In the Bible, Levi was the third of Jacob's sons born to Leah. His descendants became the Levites, the priests of the Temple.

Liron לירון
Song is mine.

Lotan לוטן
To envelope, or protect. Popular in Israel.

M

Maimon מימון
Aramaic for luck or good fortune. The philosopher, Moses ben Maimon, known as Maimonides, is the most illustrious bearer of the name.

Malachi מלאכי
Messenger or angel. The last of the prophets.

Malkam מלכם
God is their king.

Mattathias, Mattityahu מתתיהו
Gift from God. Mattathias, a name linked with Hanukkah, was the father of Judah Maccabee, the patriarch of the Hasmonean dynasty. Common nicknames include Matt, Matti, Matia.

Max
Once common among Jewish immigrants to America, Max has recently become popular. A contraction of Maxmilian, Latin for great or famous, this is not a Hebrew name.

Meged מגד
Goodness, sweetness.

MEIR, MEYER מאיר
One who shines.

MENACHEM מנחם
Comforter. Menachem, a biblical king known for his cruelty. This was the name given to boys born on the 9th of Av, the day of mourning for the destruction of the Temple. Yiddish derivatives include Mendel and Mannes.

MENASSEH, MANASSEH, MENASHE מנשה
Causing to forget. The older of Joseph's sons, Menasseh and his brother Ephraim are mentioned in the *Shabbat* blessing for sons.

MERON מרון
Troops. Also a town in Israel. A popular Israeli name.

MICAH מיכה
Who is like God. Micah was a prophet in Judah during the 8th century B.C.E., who denounced oppression by the ruling classes.

MICHAEL מיכאל
Who is like God. Michael was the angel closest to God, and God's messenger who carried out divine judgments. Variations on Michael include: Mike, Mickey, Mitchell, and the Russian, Misha.

MIRON מירן
A holy place.

MORDECHAI מרדכי
Persian for warrior or warlike. Mordechai, Queen Esther's cousin, helped save the Jews of Shushan. A name commonly given to boys born during Purim, its Yiddish nicknames include Mottel, Motke, and Mordke. Motti is the Israeli diminutive.

MORI מורי
My teacher.

MOSES, MOSE, MOSHE משה
Saved from the water. Also Egyptian for son or child. The leader and teacher who brought the Israelites out of bondage in Egypt. Variations on the name include Moss, Moise (French), and Moishe (Yiddish). Jewish immigrants to America named their Moishes Milton, Melvin, and Morris.

N

NAAMAN נעמן
Sweet, beautiful. A general in the army of Aram.

NACHMAN נחמן
Comforter.

NACHUM, NAHUM נחום
Comforted. A prophet in the 7th century B.C.E.

NADAV נדב
Benefactor.

NAMIR נמיר
Leopard.

NAOR נאור
Light.

NAPHTALI, NAFTALI נפתלי
To wrestle. Jacob's sixth son by Bilhah.

NATHAN נתן
He gave. Nathan was one of the minor prophets, who together with Zadok the priest, anointed Solomon king. In Yiddish, the name is Nusan.

NATHANIEL נתנאל, נתניאל
Gift of God. Nathaniel was David's brother.

NAVON נבון
Wise.

NEHEMIAH, NECHEMYA נחמיה
Comforted of the Lord. Nehemiah served as a governor of Judea and was in involved in rebuilding the walls of Jerusalem.

NIMROD נמרוד
Rebel.

NIR, NIREL, NIRIA, NIRIEL ניר, ניראל, ניריה, ניריאל
Plow or plowed field. Niriel means the tilled field of the Lord.

NISSAN ניסן
Flight, also emblem. Nissan is also the name of the lunar month in which Passover falls. Nisi is a popular nickname.

NISSIM נסים
Miracles. A name associated with Chanukah, popular among Sephardic Jews in Israel.

NITZAN ניצן
Bud.

NIV ניב
Aramaic and Arabic for speech.

NOAH נח
Rest, quiet, or peace. Noah, the only righteous man of his time, was selected to survive the great flood sent by God to punish an evil world. In Hebrew, it is pronounced Noach.

NOAM נעם
Sweetness, friendship.

NUR, NURI נור, נורי
Of Aramaic origin, fire. Also Nuria, Nurieh, and Nuriel, which means fire of the Lord.

O

OBEDIAH, OVADIAH, OVED עובדיה, עובד
Servant of God. Obadiah was one of the twelve minor prophets and the author of the Bible's shortest book. Oved was King David's grandfather.

OFER עפר
A young deer.

OMRI אמרי
From the Arabic, to live long. Omri was a king in Israel during the 800s B.C.E.

OREN, ORIN, ORRIN, ORON ארן
Fir tree, cedar. A popular Israeli name.

OZ עז
Strength.

OZNI אזני
A grandson of Jacob.

P

PALTI, PALTIEL, PILTAI פלטי, פלטיאל, פלטי
My deliverance. Palti was Michal's second husband. Piltai was a member of a priestly family.

PERETZ פרץ
Burst forth.

PESACH פסח
Pass over. A name given to boys born during Passover.

PINCHAS, PINCUS פנחס
Dark-complexioned. The priest Pinchas (Phineas in Greek) was a grandson of Aaron.

R

RAANAN רענן
Fresh, luxuriant.

RACHIM, RACHAMIM רחים, רחמים
Compassion. A common name among Sephardic Jews.

RANEN, RANON רנן, רנון
To sing.

RAPHAEL רפאל
God has healed. Raphael is one of the four archangels, who according to the Talmud was one of the the three messengers who visited Abraham and Sarah and told them they would have a son. Also spelled Rafael and Refael, Rafi is a popular nickname.

RAVID רביד
Ornament.

RAVIV רביב
Rain or dew.

RAZ, RAZI, RAZIEL רז, רזי, רזיאל
From the Aramaic for secret.

REUBEN, REUVEN ראובן
Behold, a son. Jacob and Leah's first son.

RIMON רימון
Pomegranate.

RON, RONEL, RONEN, RONI, RONLI רון, רונאל, רוני, רונלי
Song and joy, in various settings.

S

SAADIAH, SAADYA סעדיה
Aramaic for Ezra, meaning God's help. Saadiah ben Joseph was a great Egyptian-born scholar of the 9th century. A popular Sephardic name.

SAGI סגי
Strong.

SAMSON, SHIMSHON שמשון
Sun, signifying strength. Strong-man Samson, most famous for his betrayal by Delilah, was from the tribe of Dan.

SAMUEL, SH'MUEL שמואל
God has heard. Samuel, the son of Hannah, helped create a centralized monarchy in the 11th century B.C.E., and as prophet and judge, anointed King Saul and later King David. Samuel was the last of the judges.

SANDER סנדר
Yiddish for Alexander. (See above.)

SASHA
A Russian diminutive for Alexander, Sasha is also used as a girl's name.

SAUL, SHA'UL שאול
Borrowed. Saul was the first king of Israel, from the tribe of Benjamin.

SELIG סעליג
Yiddish for blessed. Also spelled Zelig.

SETH, SHET שת
Appointed. Seth was Adam's son, born after Abel's death.

SHAI שי
Gift.

SHALOM, SHLOMO, SHOLOM, SHLOMI שלום, שלמה, שלומי
Peace.

SHAMIR שמיר
Strong.

SHRAGA שרגא
Light, in Aramaic.

SIMCHA שמחה
Joy. Also a girl's name.

SIMON, SIMEON, SHIMON, SHIMEON שמעון
To hear or be heard. Shimon was the second son born to Jacob and Leah. (Simon is the Greek version.) Simi is a popular Israeli nickname for Shimon.

SIVAN סיון
The seventh month of the Hebrew calendar.

SOLOMON שלמה
Peace. Solomon, the son of David and Bathsheba, built the First Temple and is traditionally considered to have written Song of Songs, Proverbs, and Ecclesiastes. His reputation for wisdom is enshrined in the word *solomonic*. In Hebrew, Shlomo.

T

TABBAI טבאי
From the Aramaic word good. Names like Tov, Tovi, and Tavi share the root and the meaning.

TAL, TALOR טל, טליאור
Dew, dew of light. Also a girl's name.

TAMIR, TIMUR תמיר, תמור
Tall, like the tamar or palm tree.

TIVON טבעון
Student of nature.

TOBIAH, TUV'YA טוביה
God is Good. Toby is the popular nickname.

TZEVI צבי
Deer. Also spelled Tzvi and Zevi. Popular in Israel.

U

URI, URIEL אורי, אוריאל
From the root word light. Uriel is one of the four angels who
resides around God's throne.

UZI, UZIEL עזי, עזיאל
From the root for strength. Uzi means my strength; Uziel, God
is my strength.

W

WOLF, WOLFE וואלף
Yiddish for wolf. Variants include Vulf and Velvel. The Hebrew
is Ze'ev.

Y

YAKIR יקיר
Beloved, honorable.

YALON ילון
He will rest. A son of Caleb.

YAMIR ימיר
To change.

YANIR יניר
He will plow.

YARON ירון
To sing.

YAVNIEL יבניאל
God will build.

YEFET יפת
Beautiful. Also spelled Yafet, Yaphet. Yefet was one of Noah's sons.

YEHIEL יחיאל
May God live. Yehiel was chief musician in the court of King David.

YIFTACH יפתח
Open.

YIGAL יגאל
He will redeem. Popular in Israel.

YOAV יואב
God is father. King David's nephew and an officer in his army.

YOCHANAN, JOCHANAN יוחנן
God is gracious. There are more than fifty rabbis named Yochanan quoted in the Talmud.

YORAM יורם
God is exalted.

YORAN יורן
To sing.

YOTAM יותם
One of Gideon's sons.

Z

ZACH זַךְ
Pure or clean.

ZACHARY, ZACHARIAH זכריה
May God remember. The name of one of the minor prophets, and of a king of Judah and a king of Israel. Nicknames include Zack and Zeke.

ZALMAN זמלן, צלמון
Zalman is Yiddish for Shlomo. Tzalmon was a biblical warrior.

ZAMIR זמיר
Song, also nightingale.

ZAVDI, ZAVDIEL זבדי, זבדיאל
My gift, gift of God. An officer in David's army.

ZEBULON, ZEVULON זבולון
To exalt or honor. Zevulon was the sixth son of Jacob and Leah.

ZEDEKIAH צדקיה
God is righteousness. A king of Judah.

ZE-EV, ZEV, ZEVI, ZEVIEL זאב, זאבי, זאביאל
Wolf in Hebrew. (See Wolf.) Very popular in Israel.

ZEPHANIAH צפניה
God has treasured. A 7th-century prophet, Zephaniah belonged to the family of Judah.

ZERACH זרח
Light rising.

ZION, TZION צִיּוֹן

Excellent, a sign. A name for the Jewish people; also a mountain in Jerusalem.

ZIV, ZIVI זִיו, זִיוִי

To shine.

ZOHAR זֹהַר

Light, brilliance.

ZUSHYE, ZUSYA זושע, זוסע

Yiddish for sweet.

A Daughter!

A

ABIGAIL, AVIGAIL אביגיל
Father's joy. Abigail was an early supporter of King David, even before she became his wife. She was known for her beauty, wisdom, and powers of prophecy.

ABIRA אבירה
Strong.

ABRA אברה
From the Hebrew root Abba or father. A diminutive of Abraham.

ADA, ADI עדה, עדי
Ornament.

ADARA אדרה
Adar is the twelfth month in the Hebrew calendar.

ADENA, ADINA עדינה
Noble or adorned, gentle.

ADERET אדרת
A cape or outer garment.

ADIRA אדירה
Strong or mighty.

ADIVA אדיבה
Gracious, pleasant.

ADRA אדרה
From the Aramaic, glory or majesty.

ADVA אדוה
An Aramaic name that means wave or ripple.

AHARONA אהרנה
Feminine version of Aaron, which means teaching or singing. Variations include Arona, Arni, Arnina, Arnit, Arninit.

AHAVA אהבה
Love, beloved.

ALEEZA, ALIZA, ALITZA עליזה, עליצה
Joy or joyous one.

ALEXANDRA אלכסנדרה
Feminine of the Greek ruler Alexander. For a full explanation of the name, see Alexander. Queen Salome Alexandra was a ruler of Judea from 76 to 67 B.C.E.

ALIYA, ALIYAH עליה
To go up. Being called to the Torah during a synagogue service is known as being given an *aliyah*. Also, moving to Israel is called making *aliyah*.

ALMA עלמה
Maiden. In Spanish, it means soul.

ALONA אלונה
Oak tree. Alon is a popular boy's name.

ALUMA, ALUMIT עלומה, עלומית
Hidden.

AMALIA עמליה
The work of the Lord.

AMIRA אמירה
Speech. Ear of corn.

ANAT ענת
To sing.

ANNA, ANN חנה
These and many more (Annette, Annie, Anita, Anya) are all forms of the biblical name Hanna. Anna is the Hellenized version that inspired so many diminutives.

ARAVA ערבה
Willow.

ARELLA אראלה
Angel, messenger.

ARIELLA אריאלה
Lioness of god.

ARMONA, ARMONIT ארמונה, ארמונית
Castle or palace.

ARNA, ARNIT ארנה, ארנית
Cedar.

ARNONA, ARNONIT ארנונה, ארנונית
From arnon, a roaring stream.

ARZA, ARZIT ארזה, ארזית
Cedar beams.

ASHIRA עשירה
Wealthy.

ATALIA, ATALYA עתליה
God is exalted.

ATARA, ATARET עטרה, עטרת
Crown.

ATIRA עתירה
Prayer.

AVIELA, AVIELLA אביאלה
God is my father.

AVITAL אביטל
Dew of my father. Avital was one of King David's wives.

AVIVA אביבה
Spring. A popular Israeli name. Avivit and Avivi mean spring-like. Avivit also means lilac.

AVODA עבודה
Work.

AYALA אילה
Deer or gazelle.

AZA, AZAH, AZIZA עזה, עזיזה
Strong.

AZRIELLA עזריאלה
God is my strength.

B

BAILA, BAYLE ביילע
Yiddish form of Bilhah, one of the four women who gave birth to the tribes of Israel.

BASHA באשע
A diminutive of Batsheva.

BAT-AMI בת־עמי
Daughter of my people.

BATSHEVA בת־שבע
Daughter of the oath. The beautiful Batsheva was one of King David's wives and the mother of King Solomon.

BATYA בתיה
Daughter of God.

BELLA, BELLE
Americanized Yiddish derivatives of Bilhah.

BENYAMINA בנימינה
The feminine form of Benjamin.

BERIT, B'ERIT בארית
Well, a source of water.

BERURIA, BERURYAH ברוריה
Pure or clean. Beruriah, the daughter of Rabbi Haninah ben Teradyon and the wife of Rabbi Meir, lived in the second century, C.E. and was the only woman in Talmudic literature whose views were taken seriously by her contemporaries.

BINA בינה
Understanding, intelligence.

BIRA בירה
Capital.

BLUMA, BLUME בלומע
Yiddish for flower.

BONA בונה
Builder.

BRACHA ברכה
Blessing.

B'RINNA, BREENA ברנה
With joy.

BRINA בריינה
Based on the Yiddish for brown.

C

CARMEL, CARMELLE,
CARMELA, CARMELIT כרמל, כרמלה, כרמלית
Vineyard. A popular Israeli name with many variations: Carma, Carmit, Carmia.

CARNA, CARNIT קרנה, קרנית
Horn. Carniella means horn of God.

CHAVA חוה
Eve. Mother of life. A variant English spelling is Hava.

CHAYA חיה
Life.

CLARA כלרה
Yiddish for clean.

D

DAFNA דפנה
Laurel.

DALIA, DALIT דליה, דלית
Branch.

DANIELLA, DANIELLE דניאלה
God is my judge. The feminine version of Daniel has many derivatives: Dania, Dani, Danya, Danit.

DANYA דניה
Feminine of Dan.

DAVIDA, DAVITA דוידה
The feminine of David, meaning beloved or friend. Nickname, Davi.

DEBORAH, DEBRA, DEVORAH, DEVRA דבורה
To speak kind words or a swarm of bees. Devorah was a prophetess and judge who led a revolt against a Canaanite king. Her composition, the "Song of Deborah," is one of the oldest known Hebrew poems.

DEENA, DENA, DINA, DINAH דינה
Judgment. Deena was the daughter of Leah and Jacob—the only girl among his thirteen children.

DEGANIA דגניה
Corn. Also the name of the first *kibbutz*.

DELILA דלילה
Poor or hair. Samson's mistress Delila was a Philistine.

DERORA, DRORA דרורה
Freedom.

DIZA, DITZA דיזה, דיצה
Joy.

DODI דודי
Beloved, friend.

DORIT דורית
From this era. Very popular in Israel.

DORONA, DORONIT דורונה, דורונית
Aramaic for gift.

DORYA דוריה
Generation of God.

DOVA, DOVEVA, DOVIT דובה, דובבה, דובית
Bear.

E

EDNA עדנה
Delight, pleasure. Edna appears in the book of Tobit, which is part of the Apocrypha.

EFRAT אפרת
Honored, distinguished. The wife of Caleb.

EFRONA עפרונה
A songbird.

ELANA אילנה
Oak tree. Also spelled Ilana.

ELIANA אליענה
God has answered me.

ELINOAR אלינער
God of my youth.

ELIORA אליאורה
God is my light.

ELISHEVA אלישבע
God is my oath. Elisheva was Aaron's wife and thus the matriarch of the priestly caste. The Hellenized form is Elizabeth, which has many popular nicknames, among them: Ella, Elisa, Eliza, Elise, Elsie, Betsy, Liz, Libby, Bet, Beth, Betty, Elyssa. Elisheva Bikhowsky (1888–1949) was a Russian-born poet who settled in 1925 in Israel, where she wrote and published in Hebrew.

EMANUELLA עמנואלה
God is with us.

EMMA עמה
Originally from the Teutonic for grandmother or big one, the name was popular among Jewish immigrants to America at the turn of the century. Famous Emmas include the Russian-born anarchist writer and organizer Emma Goldman and the poet Emma Lazarus, who penned the verse on the Statue of Liberty.

EMUNA אמונה
Faith.

ESTHER אסתר
From the Persian for star. Esther is the heroine of the story of Purim. She, with help from her cousin Mordechai, averted the annihilation of the Jews in her community. The Hebrew name for Esther is Hadassah, which means myrtle. Variations include Esta, Essie, Estelle, and Estella. Etti is an Israeli nickname.

EVA, EVE חוה
Life. According to Genesis, Eve was the first woman, the mother of all human life. The Hebrew is Chava.

EZRAELA עזראלה
God is my help. The feminine for Ezra.

F

FREIDA, FRAYDE, FREYDEL פריידע, פריידעל
Yiddish for joy.

G

GABRIELLA, GAVRIELLA גבריאלה
God is my strength. The feminine version of Gabriel. Nicknames include Gabi and Gavi.

GALI, GALIT גלי, גלית
Fountain or spring.

GALYA גליה
God has redeemed.

GAMLIELA, GAMLIELLE גמליאלה
Feminine forms of Gamliel, a name common among talmudic
scholars.

GANIT גנית
Garden.

GAVRILLA גברילה
Heroine, strong.

GAYORA גיאורה
Valley of light.

GAZIT גזית
Hewn stone.

GILA גילה
Joy. Gilana and Gilat also mean joy. Gilia, a variant, means my
joy is in the Lord.

GILADA גלעדה
My joy is forever.

GINA, GINAT גנה, גינת
Garden.

GITTA, GITTLE גיטע, גיטל
Yiddish, good one. (See Tova)

GIVA, GIVONA גבעה, גבעונה
Hill.

GOLDA, GOLDE גולדה
Yiddish for golden. The Hebrew is Zehava.

GORNIT גרנית
Granary.

GURIT גורית
Cub.

H

HADARA, HADURA הדרה, הדורה
Splendid.

HADASS, HADASSAH הדס, הדסה
Myrtle tree, a symbol of victory. This is the Hebrew form of
the name Esther. Nicknames include Dass and Dasi.

HAGIT חגית
Festive, joyous.

HAMUDA חמודה
Precious.

HANNAH חנה
Gracious, merciful. In the Bible, Hannah was the wife of
Elkanah, the mother of Samuel, and the subject of a
heartbreaking tale of infertility and faith rewarded. (Samuel
means God has heard.) The Christian Bible refers to Hannah as
Anna, which means all its variations—Annie, Annette, Anita—
are rooted in Hannah.

HASIA חסיה
Protected of the Lord.

HASIDA חסידה
Pious one. Also, stork.

HAVIVA חביבה
Beloved.

HEDVA חדוה
Joy.

HEDYA הדיה
Voice of the Lord.

HEFZIBA חפצי־בה
My desire.

HEMDA חמדה
Precious.

HERZLIA הרצליה
Yiddish for deer. The feminine version of a masculine name, this is also the name of an Israeli city.

HILLA הלה
Praise.

HINDA הינדע
Yiddish for deer.

I

IDIT עדית
Choicest.

ILANA, ILANIT אילנה, אילנית
Oak tree. Also spelled Elana.

IRIT עירית
Daffodil. Popular in Israel.

ISAACA יצחקה
Laughter. The feminine of Isaac.

ISRAELA, ISA ישראלה, ישה
The name of the people, almost always used in the diminutive, Isa.

ITI, ITTI אתי
With me.

J

JACOBA, YACOVA יעקבה
To supplant. The feminine of Yacov.

JASMINE, YASMIN יסמין
Persian flower name.

JEMINA, YEMINA ימינה
Righthanded.

JESSIE, JESSICA, YISKA יסכה
God's grace.

JOHANNA, YOCHANA יוחנה
God is gracious. Feminine of Yochanan.

JONINA, YONINA יונינה
A dove.

JOSEPHA, YOSEFA יוספה
God will increase. The feminine of Joseph.

JUDITH, YEHUDIT יהודית
Praise. In the Apocryphal story, Judith was the heroine who saved Jerusalem by pretending to defect to General Holofernes' camp, where she beheaded him while he slept.

K

KADIA, KADYA כדיה
Pitcher.

KALANIT כלנית
Anemone.

KANARIT, KANIT כנרית, כנית
Songbird.

KARNA, KARNIT קרנה, קרנית
Horn, as in ram's horn.

KAYLA קיילע
Yiddish form of Kelila.

KELILA כלילה
A crown of laurel, symbolizing victory.

KETURAH קטורה
Perfumed.

KEREN קרן
Horn. Related to Karna. A popular Israeli name.

KETZIA, KEZIA קציעה
Fragrant. One of Job's daughters.

KINNERET כנרת
Hebrew name of the Sea of Galilee. Also, harp.

KIRYA קריה
Village.

KOCHAVA כוכבה
Star.

L

LAILA, LEILA, LILA לילה
Night.

LEAH, LEA לאה
In Hebrew it means weariness, but in Assyrian it means mistress or ruler. Leah, the daughter of Laban and Jacob's first wife, is one of the four matriarchs of Judaism. She gave birth to six sons: Reuben, Simeon, Levi, Judah, Issachar, and Zebulun, and one daughter, Deena.

LEEBA, LIBA ליבע
Yiddish for beloved. In Israel, the name also refers to the Hebrew root *lev,* which means heart.

LEORA, LIORA ליאורה
My light.

LEVANA, LIVANA לבנה
Moon, or white. Popular among Sephardic Israelis.

LEVONA לבונה
Spice or incense.

LIAN ליאן
My joy.

LIAT ליאת
You are mine.

LILY לילי
A favorite among Jewish-American immigrants in the early 20th century.

LIMOR לימור
My myrrh.

LIRON, LIRONA לירון, לירונה
My song.

LIVIA, LIVYA לויה
A crown. When the accent falls on the last syllable, Livia means lioness.

LUZA לוזה
Almond tree.

M

MAGDA מגדא
A high tower.

MAHIRA, MEHIRA מהירה
Energetic.

MALKA מלכה
Queen. A popular Sephardic name. (See Regina)

MARA מרה
Bitter.

MARGALIT מרגלית
Pearl. (See Penina)

MARNI, MARNINA מרני, מרנינה
Rejoice.

MARVA מרוה
Plant in the mint family.

MAXIMA מקסימה
Enchanter.

MAYA מיה
Modern Hebrew name based on a Roman mythological goddess.

MERI מרי
Rebellious.

MICHAELA מיכאלה
Who is like God. Feminine of Michael, one of the archangels.
Mia is a nickname.

MICHAL מיכל
Michal was King Saul's youngest daughter and one of King
David's wives. Also, a contraction of Michaela.

MILI מילי
Who is for me?

MIRA מירה
Light. Feminine of Meir.

MIRIAM, MIRYAM מרים
Sorrow or bitterness in Hebrew, but mistress of the sea in
Aramaic. Miriam was a prophetess, singer, and dancer, the sister
of Moses and Aaron. Nicknames include: Mim, Mindy, Minna,
Mira, Mirel, Miri, Mirit, and Mollie.

MIRIT מירית
Sweet wine.

MORIAH, MORIT מוריה, מורית
Teacher.

N

NAAMAH, NAAMIT נעמה, נעמית
Pleasant, beautiful.

NAAVA נאוה
Beautiful.

NADYA נדיה
From the word dowry. Common in Israel.

NAOMI נעמי
Beautiful, pleasant. In the Book of Ruth, Naomi was Elimelech's wife and Ruth's loving mother-in-law.

NASIA, NASYA נסיה
Miracle of God.

NATANIA, NETANYA נתניה
Gift of God.

NEDIVA נדיבה
Generous, noble.

NEHAMA נחמה
Comfort.

NEIMA נעימה
Pleasant.

NESYA נסיה
Yiddish for Nissan, the month of flowers.

NETTA, NETIA נטע, נטיעה
A plant.

NILI נילי
A plant.

NINA נינה
In Hebrew, the word for granddaughter.

NIRA נירה
Light.

NIRIT נירית
A flowering plant.

NITZA נצה
Bud.

NOA נועה
Tremble, shake. A biblical name popular in Israel today.

NURIT נורית
Buttercup.

O

ODELIA אודליה
I will praise God.

ODERA עודרה
Plow.

OPHIRA אופירה
Gold.

OPHRAH, OFRA עפרה
Young deer.

ORA אורה
Light.

ORLI, ORLIT אורלי, אורלית
My light.

ORNA, ORNIT ארנה, ארנית
Cedar.

P

PAZIT פזית
Gold.

PENINAH, PENINIT פנינה, פנינית
Pearl or coral. Elkanah's second wife. (See Margalit)

PERI פרי
Fruit.

PUAH פועה
A midwife during the Egyptian captivity, Puah and her colleague Shifra disobeyed Pharoah's order to kill all male Hebrews at birth.

R

RACHEL רחל
A ewe, symbol of gentleness and purity. Rachel was the best-loved wife of Jacob, who gave birth to Joseph and Benjamin. There have been many renowned Rachels, among them a wealthy woman who against her father's wishes married a poor and unlearned man named Akiva. He became the great Rabbi Akiva.

RAISA, RAIZEL רייזא, רייזעל
Yiddish for Rose.

RAKEFET רקפת
Cyclamen, a flower common in Israel.

RANANA רעננה
Fresh.

RANIT, RANITA רנית, רניתה
Joy or song.

RAPHAELA רפאלה
God has healed. Feminine of Raphael.

RAYNA, REYNA ריינע
Yiddish for pure or clean.

RAZI, RAZIA, RAZIELLA רזי, רזיה, רזאלה
Aramaic for secret. Razili means my secret.

REBECCA, REBEKAH רבקה
Beautiful, or to tie or bind. Rebecca, wife of Isaac, is the strong-willed matriarch who masterminded her son Jacob's deception of his father to gain the family blessing. Nicknames include Becky and Rikki.

REGINA
Sephardic name meaning queen in Latin. Malka in Hebrew.

RIMONA רמונה
Pomegranate.

RINA רנה
Joy or song.

RIVA ריבה
Young girl, also a diminutive of Rebecca.

RIVKA רבקה
The Hebrew form of Rebecca.

RONA, RONI, RONIT, RONIA רונה, רונית, רוניה
Joy or song.

ROSE, ROSA רוזה
The English translation of the Hebrew name Shoshana. Rose has been a popular name in many languages, including English, Yiddish, Ladino, and Hebrew. (See Raisel, Susan, Varda, Vered) Rose Schneiderman (1882–1972) was an American labor organizer and president of the Women's Trade Union League from 1918 to 1949.

RUTH רות

Friendship. The daughter-in-law of Naomi, who chose to stay with Naomi and the Jewish people after the death of her husband. Ruth, considered the model of the righteous Jew-by-choice, is an ancestor of King David, from whose line—says the tradition—the Messiah will come. Ruti is a popular nickname in Israel.

S

SAADA סעדה

Support or help.

SADIE

A diminutive of Sarah, Sadie was a popular name among Jewish immigrants to the United States.

SAMANTHA

Samantha is often given in memory of a grandfather Samuel, although there is no connection between the two names. It is not a Hebrew name.

SARA, SARAH שרה

Princess. Sarah was the first Jewish woman, the wife of Abraham, and, at the age of ninety, the mother of Isaac. Nicknames include Sari, Sarene, Sarina, Sarit. Yiddish versions include Sorale and Soralie.

SASHA

Variation on Alexandra, used as a proper name in the United States.

SERAFINA שרפינה

To burn. From the same root as the biblical seraphim, the angels surrounding God's throne.

SHALVIA שלויה

Peace, tranquility.

SHARON שרון
In the Bible, Sharon was a plain where roses bloomed, hence King Solomon's songs about the roses of Sharon. Sharona is a variation.

SHAYNA, SHAINA שיינע
Yiddish for beautiful.

SHELI, SHELLI שלי
Mine.

SHIFRA שפרה
Beautiful. Shifra the midwife, and her colleague Puah disobeyed Pharoah's order to kill all male Hebrews at birth. A popular Israeli name.

SHIRA, SHIRI שירה, שירי
Song. My song.

SHLOMIT שלומית
Peaceful.

SHLOMIYA שלומיה
Peace.

SHOSHANA שושנה
A lily or a rose.

SHULAMIT שולמית
Peace. Shula is a nickname.

SIDRA, SIDRAH סדרה
Torah portion.

SIMA סימה
Aramaic for gift.

SIMCHA שמחה
Joy. Also a boy's name.

SIMONA, SIMONE סימונה
To hear. The feminine of Simon, Simeon.

SIVANA סיונה
Sivan is the ninth month of the Hebrew calendar.

SIVIA, SIVYA, TZIVIA צביה
Deer.

SOPHIE
A popular name among Jewish-American immigrants.

SUSAN שושנה
Rose or lily. (See Rose, Shoshana, Varda) Susannah is a variation.

T

TAL, TALIA, TALYA, TALI טל, טליה, טלי
Dew.

TALMA תלמה
Hill.

TAMAR, TAMARA תמר, תמרה
Date palm. Also, righteous and graceful. A Yiddish variation is Tema.

TEMIMA תמימה
Honest.

TIFERET תפארת
Beautiful.

TIKVA תקוה
Hope.

TIRA טירה
Encampment.

TIRZA תרצה
Cypress, also desirable. Tirza was the biblical capital of Samaria.

TORI תורי
My turtledove.

TOVA טובה
Good one. Often Toby in English.

TZAFRIRA צפרירה
Morning breeze.

TZIPORA צפורה
Little bird. Moses' wife. Also spelled Zipporah. Tzipi is a common nickname.

TZURIA צוריה
God is strength.

U

UMA אמה
Nation.

URIT אורית
Light.

V

VARDA ורדה
Rose. (See also Susan)

VERED ורד
Rose.

VIDA, VITA וידה
Sephardic name meaning life. The equivalent of Eve, or the Hebrew Chava.

Y

YAEL, YAELA, YAALIT יעל, יעלה, יעלית
To ascend.

YAFFA יפה
Beautiful. Also the name of an Israeli city.

YAKIRA יקירה
Precious.

YARDENA ירדנה
Jordan River, to descend.

YARKONA ירקונה
Green. Also, a bird found in southern Israel and a river in northern Israel.

YEDIDA ידידה
Friend, beloved. The mother of Josiah, a king of Judah.

YECHIELA יחיאלה
May God live.

YEIRA יאירה
Light.

YEMIMA ימימה
Dove. A daughter of Job. Jemima in English.

YISRAELA ישראלה
Israeli or Jew.

YOCHEVED יוכבד
God's glory. Yocheved, an unacknowledged matriarch, was the
mother of Moses, Aaron, and Miriam.

YOELLA, YOELIT יואלה, יואלית
God is willing. Feminine version of Yoel or Joel.

YONA, YONINA, YONIT יונה, יונינה, יונית
Dove.

Z

ZAHARA, ZEHARI זהרה, זהרי
Brightness.

ZAHAVA, ZAHAVI, ZEHAVIT זהבה, זהבית
Golden.

ZARA זרה
Variation on Sarah. (See Zora)

ZE'EVA, ZEVA זאבה
Wolf.

ZIKIT זיקית
Longing.

ZILLA, TZILA צילה
Shadow.

ZIONA ציונה
Excellent, feminine of Zion.

ZIPPORAH צפורה
Little bird. Also spelled Tzipporah and Tzipora.

ZIVA, ZIVIT זיוה, זיוית
Splendid, radiant.

ZIVANIT זיונית
Mayflower.

ZORAH, ZORA זרה
A variation of Sarah. Arabic for dawn.

PART
3

Brit — Covenant

Covenants

B*rit,* the Hebrew word for covenant, is the way Jews describe and define their relationship to God. A covenant is a contract—an agreement between responsible parties, a two-way street. According to tradition, the document that spells out the rights and responsibilities for both sides in this agreement between God and the Jewish people is the Torah—the first five books of the Bible.

Four signs of covenants are mentioned in the Torah. The first, *Shabbat,* is a weekly reminder of the miracle of creation. The second, the rainbow, is the sign of God's promise, made after the great flood, that God would never again destroy the world. The third is the Torah itself, the "tree of life," in which people may find the answers to their most important questions. The fourth is *brit milah,* the covenant of circumcision. *Brit milah,* which the Talmud acknowledges is the most difficult of all the *mitzvot,* or sacred obligations, is how parents have passed on the contract from one generation to the next.

The covenant of circumcision is the oldest continuous Jewish rite, a ritual that unites Jews throughout ages and across cultures, and signifies the connection between individual human life and the Holy. With this ancient ceremony, parents announce their commitment to taking on the responsibilities and joys of raising a child according to the terms of the contract between God and the Jews. *Brit bat,* the act of welcoming infant daughters to this historic relationship, does the same with words and rituals that might involve water, candles, or touching the Torah.

In most regards, *brit milah* and *brit bat* are as different as two ceremonies can be. Bringing a son into the covenant of Israel is an ancient practice that leaves a permanent physical sign of the bond between each Jewish man and God. Bringing a daughter into the covenant with the intention and formality associated with *brit milah* is a relatively recent practice, and one that is still taking shape.

The historical absence of a covenant ceremony for daughters was interpreted in two radically different ways: as evidence that women were seen as second-class citizens who are not admitted to the covenant, or as proof that Judaism acknowledges women's spiritual superiority in that they do not need a physical reminder of God's presence. *Brit bat,* in its many forms, has become an accepted and expected rite of passage that reflects the overall change in women's status as full parties to the covenant between God and the Jewish people.

Brit bat is not an imitation of *brit milah.* Although there are some liturgical similarities between them, the two ceremonies are as different as male and female. What they do share, what all Jews share, is the covenant.

Brit Milah
The Covenant of Circumcision

> *"Such shall be the covenant between Me and you and your offspring to follow which you shall keep: every male among you shall be circumcised. You shall circumcise the flesh of your foreskin, and that shall be the sign of the covenant between Me and you."*
> —GENESIS 17:10–11

It's a boy!

After the initial rush of happiness and delight comes the realization: we've got to have a *bris*.★

The most ancient of all Jewish rituals, a *bris* is traditionally celebrated with feasting and song. It is, above all, a *simcha*—a cause for joy and celebration. But many American Jews approach *brit milah* with more confusion and fear than happiness.

Jews have performed the *mitzvah* of *brit milah* in an unbroken chain for 4,000 years, from the days of Abraham to the present. During that long history, observant Jews and secular Jews, rabbis and Jews with little or no understanding of the ritual have fulfilled this, perhaps the most difficult of all biblical commandments.

Even so, for many liberal Jews, *brit milah* is no longer entirely an automatic response but a decision made after considering a series of questions: Is it safe? Will my baby suffer? What is the best way to have it done?

Deciding to circumcise a son, especially in a traditional manner, announces your identification with Judaism in a powerful,

---

★ *The Hebrew word* brit *means covenant; a pledge or obligation.* Brit milah *is the covenant of circumcision, a physical sign of the unique relationship between the Jewish people and God. Sephardic Jews sometimes refer to the rite simply as* milah. *In America, the Ashkenazic Hebrew and Yiddish term* bris *is the most familiar name for the religious ritual of circumcision.*

unequivocal way. Most of all, it challenges you to ask Why? What does this mean to me as an individual and to us as a family? What do we hope it will mean to our son?

This chapter provides information to help you answer these questions. In the following pages, you will find an overview of *brit milah* that includes everything from the biblical roots of the ritual to advice about how to hire a *mohel,* a ritual circumciser. (The Yiddish pronunciation is "moil," the Hebrew is "mo-*hail.*") The more you know about the history and practice of *brit milah,* the less you will worry about your baby. Ideally, a *bris* is not a source of anxiety, but a cause for celebration.

Modern Questions

In the 1960s, ninety-five percent of all baby boys born in the United States were circumcised in the hospital within days of birth because doctors believed that the procedure was a boon to hygiene and health.[1] Many Jewish parents thus felt released from the need to "choose" circumcision, and many opted to have it done, without ritual, by a physician in the hospital.

But in 1971, the American Academy of Pediatrics announced that there was no medical reason for surgical removal of the foreskin, the sheath that covers the glans of the penis. By 1985, only fifty-nine percent of newborn boys underwent the procedure, which was no longer automatically covered by all medical insurance policies. The natural childbirth movement reinforced the growing reluctance to subject newborns to "unnecessary surgery," and a small but vocal anti-circumcision movement began to actively oppose the procedure, using words like "amputation" and "mutilation."

This debate has served to focus attention on the fact that Jews do not and have never circumcised their sons for medical reasons. In the words of Rabbi Moses Maimonides—the great 12th-century rabbi, philosopher, and physician—"No one should circumcise himself or his sons for any other reasons but for pure faith. Circumcision is the symbol of the covenant which Abraham made in connection with the belief in God's unity."[2]

Nevertheless, parents continue to ask questions about the safety and impact of circumcision.

What Are the Medical Risks of Circumcision?

According to a policy statement issued by the American Academy of Pediatrics in March 1989, "Newborn circumcision is a rapid and generally safe procedure when performed by an experienced operator." The incidence of complications is low, "approximately .2 percent to .6 percent," the pediatricians' task force on circumcision said. (*Mohels* claim that the circumcisions they perform, which are not included in the medical research, result in even fewer problems, but there are no scientific data to substantiate that claim.) The few complications that do occur tend to be limited to infection or bleeding. However, infection is very rare, at least in part because the site of the cut is so well supplied with blood.[3]

Jewish sons have survived circumcision for centuries. As many rabbis have pointed out, a tradition so meticulous about the sanctity of life and health would not require an act that might jeopardize either.[4]

Are There Any Medical Benefits to Circumcision?

The American Association of Pediatrics, while it does not recommend universal circumcision, does say that properly performed newborn circumcision prevents a variety of rare mechanical and inflammatory problems of the penis and has been shown to decrease incidence of cancer of the penis, which is also rare. New research also suggests that the procedure may protect against infections of the kidney and urinary tract.[5]

How Much Will This Hurt Him?

Until quite recently, the medical establishment dismissed the idea that newborns feel pain. Now, although that position has been widely discredited, there is no definitive answer about how much a baby suffers during a circumcision. People who have been to many *bris* ceremonies testify that babies usually start crying when they are exposed to the discomfort of being naked and placed flat on their backs. The procedure itself takes about thirty seconds. Afterward, babies are easily comforted and *mohels* report that infants rarely cry during the naming ceremony that immediately follows. Babies routinely nurse and fall asleep within minutes of the procedure.

Brit milah is generally performed without anesthesia. Use of a locally injected anesthetic—a dorsal penile block—is a recent development that is not well researched and involves some risk. Some *mohels* and doctors numb the area with a topical spray before cutting. However, the universal practice of giving the baby a little wine probably helps him relax and sleep.

There is, however, no minimizing the discomfort that parents feel on their son's behalf.

What's the Safest, Least Painful Way to Have My Son Circumcised?

Some Jews still choose to have their sons circumcised by a physician in the hospital before taking the baby home. Hospitals offer a professional, sterile environment, and parents are often reluctant to witness the procedure.

However, many factors argue in favor of a circumcision at home. Hospital "circs," as they are called, are performed in stark operating rooms where the newborn is strapped onto a board where he may be immobilized for as long as ten minutes. The baby is not permitted to eat for a few hours before the procedure, and afterward, he must be checked by a nurse before he can be returned to his mother.

At home, on the other hand, the room will be warm, the surroundings familiar. Few *mohels* insist the child have an empty stomach, and he may be given wine as a relaxant-anesthetic before the procedure begins. Loving hands hold him, and if a safety restraint is used, he will be immobilized for only a few moments. The circumcision itself is performed quickly, and the baby is swaddled and returned to his mother within minutes.

Another important difference between medical and religious circumcisions concerns timing. Medical circumcisions take place any time between the second and sixth day after birth, but *brit milah* is never performed before the eighth day. There is some evidence in favor of waiting the extra few days. In a full-term baby, substances that regulate blood coagulation and facilitate healing are slightly below normal at birth. A further decline in one of these substances occurs between the second and sixth day of life. However, a gradual increase begins after the sixth day, and by the eighth day its presence in the body is at above-normal levels.[6]

Finally, it is important to remember that a medical circumcision is *not a brit milah*. A *brit milah* is a ritual that includes prayers, is performed by a Jew, and expresses the deliberate intent of bringing a son into the covenant. According to *halachah* (Jewish law), a male who has had a medical circumcision without Jewish ritual is considered a Jew in need of a religious circumcision, called *hatafat dam brit* (see below).

What Is the Psychological Impact of Circumcision?

If God had asked Abraham to remove a flap of skin from his elbow and the elbows of all males of his household as a permanent sign of the covenant, the *bris* would not be the emotionally loaded commandment it is. Then again, had the request not been so awe-full, the sign of the covenant might well have been forgotten.

The fact that the mark of the covenant is surgically imprinted on the penis dramatizes the fundamental importance of the act. Certainly, Judaism ascribes enormous significance to circumcision. The Talmud, the compendium of traditional rabbinic thought and laws, states that "were it not for the blood of the covenant, heaven and Earth would not exist." And the philosopher Spinoza declared that the practice of *brit milah* alone would insure the survival of the Jewish people.

But ever since Sigmund Freud made the unconscious a subject of popular discussion, circumcision has been interpreted by some as symbolic castration. According to Freud, the Jewish father of psychoanalysis, male children are potential competitors for their mothers' affection. Sons thus pose a threat to their fathers, which places boys in danger of paternal hostility. From this perspective, circumcision can be seen as a ritual compromise—a symbolic castration.

Revisions of Freud aside, there seems to be little evidence that infants suffer psychological damage from the act of circumcision. Whether or not the pain is localized in the penis, and whether or not one so young has memory, the baby is certainly not carrying the complex cultural and sexual baggage that causes his elders so much discomfort. There is no question that *brit milah* is difficult for adults. It is, after all, an event focused on the penis, which recalls the act that gave him life and is a symbol of the baby's future sexuality.[7]

It is hard not to see *brit milah* as an essentially male ritual that connects fathers and sons to each other, and to hundreds of generations of Jewsh men before them. Observers have noted the relative lack of physical violence between Jewish fathers and sons. It is impossible to say whether the practice of *brit milah* contributes to this pattern, but as the first obligation of Jewish fathers to sons, it has certainly been a constant feature of Jewish family dynamics through the ages.

Why?

Parents who circumcise their sons cannot answer this question with strictly rational arguments. Every parent getting ready for a *brit milah* wishes, the week before, that the Jewish people had abandoned the practice. But the significance and ritual power of *brit milah* is not the stuff of reason, or even of language. This is a radical act of faith, as well as a tangible, physical, visceral connection to our most ancient past.

The simplest, most compelling answer to the question of why we do this to our sons is this: If we stop doing *brit milah* we stop being Jews. And that is a decision that even the most ambivalent is loathe to make.

In more affirmative terms, the ritual and celebration of *brit milah* demands a communal response to the miracle of every baby's birth. *Brit milah* is a dramatic gesture that makes the community stop and gather to wonder over the miracle of a new baby and the next generation.

The tension, release, and celebration that attend every *bris* reenact the drama of birth: the tension and worry of pregnancy, the life-and-death, blood-stained release of delivery, the wail and acclaim that announce a new life. At the heart of the ritual, *brit milah* is not about the circumcision; it is about the flesh and blood miracle of our lives as human beings.

Circumcision
in History and in the Bible

Jewish continuity is one of the most compelling reasons Jews continue to perform *brit milah,* but circumcision is not unique to Jews. It has been practiced by people all over the world for centuries. In the ancient world of the Hebrews, the Egyptians, Phoenicians, and Moabites also circumcised their sons.

Often, circumcision is performed at puberty as part of a rite of initiation to manhood and is a test of courage and fortitude. For

Jews, however, infant circumcision is an act of consecration, a sign of identity, and the first in a lifetime of religious obligations.

Brit milah is sometimes referred to as the covenant of Abraham because, according to the biblical story, Abram responded to God's command and circumcised himself (at the age of ninety-nine) and all the men of his household, including his thirteen-year-old son Ishmael. In accepting the terms of the covenant, Abram's name was changed to Abraham. (Sarai became Sarah without any special ceremony.) The practice of naming a son at a circumcision derives from Abraham's renaming at his *brit milah*. Isaac, the first son of a circumcised Hebrew, underwent *brit milah* on the eighth day, which is why the ritual has been performed eight days after birth ever since.

The importance of circumcision as a mark of peoplehood is a constant theme in the Bible. When Moses failed to circumcise his son, his wife Zipporah did it herself.[8] After the exodus from Egypt, the Hebrews who had suspended the practice during their forty years of wandering in the wilderness were circumcised before they could enter Canaan.

The covenant of circumcision has been a nearly non-negotiable test of Jewish commitment since biblical times. During the reign of Queen Jezebel, when many Israelites abandoned the covenant of Abraham, the prophet Elijah exhorted the people until they returned to the custom, which earned him the title, "Herald of the Covenant."

The fact that Jews consider *brit milah* so important has made it a target of anti-Semitic attack throughout history. The first recorded prohibition against circumcision was enacted by Antiochus Epiphanes, the villain of the Hanukkah story, who ordered the execution of mothers along with the sons they had defiantly circumcised. Later, one of the causes of the Bar Kochba rebellion in 132 C.E. was the Roman emperor Hadrian's proscription against *brit milah*.[9]

The Greeks, who revered the human body, thought circumcision a terrible desecration, and under Hellenistic rule, many Jews neglected the practice. Some Jews who wanted to participate in nude Greek athletic contests even underwent painful operations to obliterate evidence of the procedure.

During the 1st century C.E., there was heated debate among early Christians about whether conversion to Christianity required circumcision; in other words, whether a man had to be a Jew before he could become a Christian. When those who opposed circumcision prevailed, the two faiths split irrevocably. Later, Roman law made it illegal to perform circumcisions for the purpose of conversion to Judaism.

In the 19th century, some leaders of the early Reform movement suggested that *brit milah* be abolished. But that position never gained much support. As Leopold Zunz, a leading Reform scholar of the era, wrote, "To abrogate circumcision . . . is suicide, not reform."[10]

In the 20th century, stories from the time of the Holocaust and from the former Soviet Union testify to the steadfastness of Jewish practice of *brit milah,* no matter what the consequences. Despite all challenges, it remains a constant feature of the Jewish experience.

Traditional Interpretations

Brit milah was already an ancient custom by the time the rabbis were writing the Talmud and Midrash, the books that explain and expound upon the Torah. The rabbinical literature includes many laws regulating the practice—the who, where, and when of the ritual. There are many commentaries about the *whys* as well.

It was not enough, for example, to explain that *brit milah* be performed on the eighth day simply because that was Isaac's age at his circumcision. The rabbis went on to say that a child who lives for seven full days gains a measure of strength because he has encountered his first *Shabbat.*

The number eight is associated with things metaphysical. (The number seven is connected to the physical world—as in the seven days of the week and the seven stages of life.) According to the rabbis, the wisdom of the Torah puts *brit milah* on the eighth day to signify that a *bris* is the culmination of creation, the act that makes a baby *tamim* (perfect or complete), in the sense that Abraham was made a whole Jew by his circumcision.[11]

Every aspect of the biblical account of Abraham's circumcision was analyzed. In the Torah, God commands Abram to remove the *orlah,* a word that means not only foreskin but also any barrier standing in the way of a beneficial result. The word *orlah* is also used as a metaphor for obstructions of the heart that prevent a person from hearing or understanding God. Removing the *orlah* of the foreskin is interpreted as a permanent physical sign of dedication to the ongoing task of moving toward the Holy One.

The rabbis wrote that Abraham was selected to be the first man marked by circumcision precisely because he saw and heard God everywhere—because of the lack of barriers between him and the One. *Brit milah* affirms the human ability to change not only our habits but our very nature, in order to be closer to God.

In the Midrash the story is told that Adam was born without a foreskin, signifying the lack of obstacles between him and God. The appearance of the foreskin in later generations was interpreted as a reminder of Adam's purity and the subsequent distance between men and God. Thus, the tradition placed the day of Abraham's circumcision on the 10th of Tishri, the Day of Atonement when sins are forgiven.

The rabbis wrote that removing the foreskin was a way of sanctifying the act of procreation, and to them was also viewed as a means of curbing the sexual drive that might draw men away from God. (Whether circumcision limits sexual pleasure remains a subject of debate.)

Despite the tradition's reverence for and loyalty to *brit milah,* it also acknowledged it as a bittersweet, ambivalent rite of passage. Rabbi Shimon bar Yochai said, "Behold, a man loves no one better than his son, and yet he circumcises him!" To which Rabbi Nachman bar Shmuel responded, "He rejoices over the *mitzvah* even though he sees his son's blood being shed."[12]

Planning a *Bris*

Brit milah is regulated and elaborated by the laws of the Talmud, with a liturgy that was already old in the first century C.E. Jewish law clearly spells out the whos, hows, and whens of the *bris*. Nevertheless, customs vary around the world and change over time. Although the core of the ceremony is nearly universal, no two babies, no two families, and no two *bris* celebrations are quite the same.

You can, if you wish, have a great deal of say about the tone and even the content of the ceremony and celebration of your son's *brit milah*. Although you will find in this chapter most of the information you need for planning a *bris*, a *mohel*, rabbi, or cantor can answer any questions. If there are any medical issues, consult your pediatrician, your *mohel*, or both.

When and Where

Following the birth of a healthy boy, *brit milah* is scheduled eight days later, even if that day falls on *Shabbat* or a holiday—including Yom Kippur.* When counting, remember that days begin at sundown. A son born on a Thursday evening will be circumcised one week from the following Friday.

Despite the emphasis on the eighth day, however, Jewish law *requires* that the *bris* be postponed in case of illness or weakness of any kind. *Brit milah* is performed only when the pediatrician and *mohel* agree it's completely safe for the baby.

A *bris* may occur anytime before sundown, but it has long been customary to schedule the ceremony early in the day. The tradition explains the preference for a morning *bris* with the idea that Jews should rush to perform such a happy *mitzvah*. However, in the days before electricity, the need for bright daylight probably had something to do with the custom, too.

A *bris* may be held anywhere, but most are done in the family's home, which is where the ceremony was first performed. From the 9th century and into the 20th, however, *brit milah* was commonly observed in the synagogue immediately after morning

---

* *A* bris *may not be scheduled on a* Shabbat *or holiday, however, for the purpose of conversion, for babies born by Cesarean section, or if the* bris *was delayed for health reasons.*

prayers and became a community celebration. This is still the custom among some Orthodox Jews.[13]

Early morning continues to be a favorite time for a weekday *bris* because that allows guests to attend before going to work. Breakfast can serve as the *s'udat mitzvah,* the prescribed meal of celebration. But so can a brunch or late lunch.

The *Mohel*

A *mohel* is someone trained to perform *brit milah*—which means both the covenantal prayers (*brit*) and the surgical procedure (*milah*). Mohels (*mohalim* is the Hebrew plural) are not ordained as rabbis are. Traditionally, one becomes a *mohel* by apprenticeship with an accomplished, established practitioner.

The skills of *mohels* are legendary. It is said that non-Jewish doctors hire non-medically trained *mohels* to circumcise their sons, and according to reliable sources, the British royal family entrusts its sons only to the hands of London's most skilled *mohel.*

The status of the *mohel* as an important Jewish functionary has been acknowledged since at least the 1st century C.E.[14] But in fact, anyone can hang out a shingle and proclaim himself* a *mohel.* There is virtually no regulation or registration for American *mohels,* as there is in Great Britain.[15] In the United States, word-of-mouth recommendation is the only form of control or regulation.

There are very few full-time *mohels.* Most perform ritual circumcisions "on the side," both as a *mitzvah* and as an additional source of income. Jewish law permits *brit milah* to be performed by virtually any Jew, though the tradition is firm in its preference for pious male Jews, which is why, until recently, so many rabbis and cantors filled the role.[16] Since the late 1980s, the Reform and Conservative movements have recruited, trained, and certified

---

* *The Conservative and Reform movements both certify women as* mohels, *but the overwhelming majority are men.*

---

licensed physicians to serve as *mohels* for the liberal Jewish community.

Finding and Choosing a *Mohel*

Technical skills aside, the choice of a *mohel* is important for many reasons. Although he may share the honors with a rabbi, the *mohel* usually acts as the master of ceremonies at a *bris,* so he is the one who sets the tone. A *mohel's* style can be abrupt and businesslike, gently spiritual, musical, Borsht-belt funny, or any combination of these. The *mohel* can put people at ease, foster a spirit of celebration, inspire, and teach. Many do a fair amount of informal teaching about the history and religious significance of *brit milah* to insure that everyone present—Jews and non-Jews alike— understands the profound importance of the ritual.

Of course, in communities where there are only one or two practicing *mohels,* there is no question of choosing. But where there is some selection, most people make their choice based on recommendations. Because rabbis and cantors go to many *bris* ceremonies, they are the best people to consult, and most will gladly provide you with names and phone numbers. Feel free to call a local rabbi, even if you are not affiliated with his or her synagogue. Some *mohels* place advertisements in Jewish newspapers, though if you contact one through such an ad, be sure to get some references.

Also, contact more than one *mohel.* Given the busy schedules of physician-*mohels* in particular, it's a good idea to have at least one back-up.

Conversations with the *Mohel*

Your first contact with the *mohel* will probably be over the telephone. In the not-so-distant past, parents would call only after the baby was born, but it is increasingly common for parents to call

---

Questions for the *Mohel*

- Will you be around within a few weeks of our due date?
- How long have you been performing circumcisions?
- Do you use a restraint?
- Do you use any anesthetic?
- How do you feel about parents' participation?
- Can you help our guests understand the ritual? (You might want to inform the *mohel* if one of your families is not Jewish.)
- Can we call you after the *bris* with questions?
- What will we need to have ready?
- What is your fee?

---

much earlier in the pregnancy, whether or not prenatal tests indicate a male child.

A pre-birth call should, first of all, ascertain whether the *mohel* will be available around the due date. (*Mohels* take vacations, too.) Ask the *mohel* about his fee. Most charge a flat rate for the ceremony, adding travel expenses if any distance is involved. If you cannot afford the fee, let the *mohel* know; most are willing to reduce the price if there is a problem.

You should try to get a sense of the *mohel's* style. Is he jovial? Brusque? Willing to answer your questions about the ceremony? Is this someone you look forward to meeting?

Be prepared to answer some questions, too. A traditional *mohel* might ask about your Jewish status. While you may not want to discuss the volatile issue of "Who is a Jew?" at this moment in your life, the *mohel* has obligations beyond providing you with a service. He must remain faithful to his interpretation of Jewish law. Some Orthodox *mohels* may decline to do a *bris* on a baby born of a mother who was converted by a Reform rabbi, for example. But even a *mohel* trained by one of the liberal movements may ask if the mother is Jewish, so he knows whether to include the prayer for conversion at a *brit milah*.

Once your baby boy is born, your second or third phone call should be to the *mohel* to set up a date and time for the *bris*. You'll talk once again before the event, at which time the *mohel* will probably give you instructions about any items he wants you to have ready. At that point he may ask for your Hebrew names and the baby's Hebrew name. Do not leave the decision of a Hebrew name to the morning of the *bris*. If you need advice, consult a rabbi.

The *Mohel's* Responsibilities

The *mohel* generally leads the ceremony. He recites prayers, explains the procedure and its meaning, and informs the guests when the actual cutting is about to occur so they can choose to move away or gather near. Still, it is important to remember that the *mohel* is there to help *you* perform this *mitzvah*. According to Jewish law, the father is responsible for his son's *brit milah,* and technically the father performs the circumcision; the *mohel* acts only as his *shaliach* or representative. (This can be dramatized by having the father or both parents hand the *izmail,* or circumcision knife, to the *mohel,* just before the circumcision.)

On the day of your son's *brit milah,* the *mohel* will arrive a little before the ceremony is scheduled to begin, to examine the baby. If

---

Questions the *Mohel* May Ask You

- What is the baby's Hebrew name?
- What are your (the parents') Hebrew names?
- Who will act as *sandek?*
- Is the mother Jewish?
- Will a rabbi be co-officiating?
- Will you or other guests be participating in the ceremony, and how?
- Are there special things you would like me to say— or not say?

---

he has any questions about the baby's health, Jewish law obliges him to postpone the *bris*. Once he is satisfied that your son is fine, the *mohel* may discuss the ceremony with you and ask how you or other guests will participate. He will probably want to talk to the *sandek,* the person who holds the baby during the circumcision (more about the sandek below). If the *mohel* is to co-officiate with a rabbi, the two of them will need to confer.

After the circumcision, the *mohel* may or may not stay for the meal and celebration, depending on his schedule. An envelope containing his fee should be ready in advance and handed to him before he leaves.

Before the *mohel* leaves, he should examine the baby and give you complete instructions about taking care of the circumcision (see below). Some *mohels* make a follow-up phone call or two in the days after a *bris.* But you should feel free to call the *mohel* at any time with questions about your son's healing.

Guests and Participants

The only people who absolutely must be present at a *bris* are the baby, the *mohel* and the *sandek,* who assists by holding the baby.

However, because it is a *mitzvah* to attend a *bris,* it is also a *mitzvah* to welcome as many people as you can.

In general, you do not "invite" guests to a *bris,* and there certainly isn't time to mail formal invitations. Most parents simply call relatives and friends to tell them the date and time, and then they leave the front door open.

There are a few special honors, or *kibbudim,* that can be assigned to relatives and close friends at a *bris.* Customarily, grandparents are given the most important roles, including that of *sandek.*

The word *sandek* is probably derived from the Greek *syndikos,* meaning patron.[17] The *sandek* assists the *mohel* by holding the baby, who is lying on a table or on a restraining board, during the circumcision. Traditionally, the *sandek* wears a *tallit,* or prayer shawl. He is the only one who sits during the ceremony; everyone else stands. In some Sephardic communities fathers act as *sandek* for their own sons, though the custom in America has long been for grandfathers to fill this honored role.[18] (If you are fortunate enough to have both grandfathers present, the two men can share the honors of *sandek,* with one holding the baby during the circumcision and the other one doing the honors during the naming.) The term *sandeket,* the feminine version, is used to honor a female guest or relative who participates in the ceremony.

Elijah

The prophet Elijah, who preached about the importance of *brit milah,* has been linked to the ritual since biblical times. His presence is invoked by the *kisei shel Eliyahu,* the chair of Elijah. By the Middle Ages, Elijah's chair was a well-established custom at *bris* celebrations. In many European communities, the synagogue owned an elaborate throne used at all circumcisions. Today, any chair may be decorated or draped for the purpose, or a special pillow for the baby is used.[19]

Non-Jews in the Ceremony

There are other ceremonial roles that may be distributed to family and friends. In general, it is a considered a *mitzvah* to include as many people as possible, and it's a good way to affirm family unity. With the exception of the *sandek,* none of the roles or honors listed below need be limited to Jews. Non-Jewish grandparents, aunts, uncles, cousins, and friends can participate in many ways—depending on their comfort level, of course.

Among the honors you can give to guests at a *brit milah,* there are the roles of *kvatterin* (godmother) and *kvatter* (godfather), terms that come from eastern Europe. Unlike Christian godparents, the *kvatter* and *kvatterin* do not assume responsibility for the child's religious upbringing. Their roles are strictly ceremonial and limited to carrying the baby from the mother to the room where the *bris* takes place, and then to the ceremonial chair for Elijah, the legendary prophet who is a "guest" at every *bris.*

There are several other ways to include guests in the proceedings: Invite four friends to hold a prayer shawl on poles over the *bris*—a touch that recalls the parent's wedding canopy. (See *Hiddur Mitzvah—Beautiful Touches.*) Before the circumcision, pass the baby from the grandparents to the parents, or, if you are so blessed, from great-grandparents to grandparents to parents, a powerful visual tribute to your family's continuity. If a sibling is mature enough to participate, he or she might carry the baby into the room, light a candle, or read a blessing or poem. In some communities, it is customary to assign a role to a couple trying to conceive, invoking the luck and blessings of the new parents on them.

If these ideas sound too elaborate, it's fine to keep things very simple. You can always involve more people at the celebration afterward. (See *Simcha.*)

Women and *Brit Milah*

In the past, women had no active role in *brit milah,* and in some Orthodox communities, this is still the case. But women's participation in ritual life has widened across the spectrum of Jewish observance, and liberal Jews have expanded women's roles to include virtually all traditional honors. While some mothers participate fully, others find it too difficult to be in the room during the actual circumcision. Some women wait elsewhere, usually surrounded by supportive friends and family members, during the few minutes of the procedure. This is an entirely personal matter, and it is your choice.

A traditional prayer recited by new mothers at a *bris* is *birkat hagomel,* a blessing of thanks recited after recovering from an illness:

בָּרוּךְ אַתָּה יְיָ, אֱלֹהֵינוּ מֶלֶךְ הָעוֹלָם,
הַגּוֹמֵל לְחַיָּבִים טוֹבוֹת, שֶׁגְּמָלַנִי כָּל טוֹב.

*Ba-ruch a-ta Adonai, Eh-lo-hei-nu meh-lech
ha-o-lam, ha-go-mel l'cha-ya-vim to-vot,
sheh-g'ma-la-ni kol tov.*

Blessed are You Adonai Ruler of All, Who does
good to the undeserving and Who has dealt
kindly with me.

The community responds:

מִי שֶׁגְּמָלְךָ כָּל טוֹב, הוּא יִגְמָלְךָ כָּל טוֹב, סֶלָה.

*Mi sheh-g'ma-l'cha kol tov, hu yig-mol-cha kol tov,
seh-la.*

May the One Who has shown you kindness deal
kindly with you forever.

Liturgy and Ritual

As with most Jewish life-cycle rituals, the liturgy of *brit milah* is
very brief—no more than five or ten minutes long. It has three
basic parts: the circumcision; the *kiddush,* which includes the
baby-naming; and the celebratory meal. Although no two ceremonies are identical, what follows is a more-or-less generic outline
of a *bris.* At the end of this chapter, you will find two versions of
brit milah that elaborate on the basics.

Part One: Milah

The first part of the ceremony is as universal as anything in Jewish
religious life. As the baby is carried in, he is greeted with the

phrase: *Baruch haba,* which means "Blessed is the one who comes." "The One" refers both to the baby and the Holy One.

The baby may be taken to Elijah's chair for a moment, and may then be handed to the *sandek.* The *mohel* prepares the baby for the circumcision and may say a few words of introduction. He then recites the blessing:

בָּרוּךְ אַתָּה יְיָ, אֱלֹהֵינוּ מֶלֶךְ הָעוֹלָם,
אֲשֶׁר קִדְּשָׁנוּ בְּמִצְוֹתָיו, וְצִוָּנוּ עַל הַמִּילָה.

*Ba-ruch a-ta Adonai, Eh-lo-hei-nu meh-lech
ha-o-lam, a-sher ki-d'sha-nu b'mitz-vo-tav,
v'tzi-va-nu al ha-mi-lah.*

Blessed are You Adonai our God Ruler of the
Universe, Who sanctifies us with commandments
and commands us regarding circumcision.

The *mohel* removes the foreskin, making sure that at least one drop of blood is visible. Then the father or both parents recite this blessing, or repeat it after the *mohel:*

בָּרוּךְ אַתָּה יְיָ, אֱלֹהֵינוּ מֶלֶךְ הָעוֹלָם,
אֲשֶׁר קִדְּשָׁנוּ בְּמִצְוֹתָיו, וְצִוָּנוּ
לְהַכְנִיסוֹ בִּבְרִיתוֹ שֶׁל אַבְרָהָם אָבִינוּ.

*Ba-ruch a-ta Adonai, Eh-lo-hei-nu meh-lech
ha-o-lam, a-sher ki-d'sha-nu b'mitz-vo-tav,
v'tzi-va-nu l'hach-ni-so biv-ri-to shel Av-ra-ham
a-vi-nu.*

Blessed are You Adonai our God Ruler of the
Universe, Who sanctifies us with Your
commandments and commands us to bring our
son into the covenant of Abraham, our father.

Everyone says Amen, and the guests repeat the traditional wish:

כְּשֵׁם שֶׁנִּכְנַס לַבְּרִית, כֵּן יִכָּנֵס לְתוֹרָה וּלְחֻפָּה וּלְמַעֲשִׂים טוֹבִים.

K'sheim sheh-nich-nas la-b'rit, kein yi-ka-nes l'to-rah ul-chu-pah ul-ma-a-sim to-vim.

Just as he entered the covenant, so may he enter into the study of Torah, the wedding canopy and the accomplishment of good deeds.

Part II: Kiddush

As soon as the baby is dressed and swaddled, the second part of the ceremony begins with *kiddush,* the blessing over wine. After the *mohel* says the blessing, he drinks some wine and gives some to the baby. This is followed by a longer chanted prayer that includes the baby-naming.

> Blessed are You God, Source of Life, Who sanctifies your beloved from birth and who has impressed Your decree in his flesh, and marked this offspring with the sign of the holy covenant. Therefore, for the sake of this covenant, O living God, our portion, our rock, protect this child from all misfortune, for the sake of Your covenant that You have placed in our flesh. Blessed are You *Adonai,* Who establishes the covenant.
>
> Our God and God of our ancestors, sustain this child for his father and mother, and may he be called _____, son of _____ and _____.
>
> May his father rejoice in the issue of his loins and may his mother exult in the fruit of her womb,

as it is written, "Your father and mother will rejoice. She who bore you will exult."

And it is said, When I passed by you and saw you wallowing in your blood I said to you, "Because of your blood you shall live!" and I said to you, "Because of your blood you shall live!"[20]

And it is said, "God is ever mindful of God's covenant, the promise given for a thousand generations. That which God made with Abraham, swore to Isaac, and confirmed in a decree for Jacob, for Israel as an eternal covenant."

And it is said, "When his son Isaac was eight days old, Abraham circumcised him, as God had commanded him."

Praise God, for God is good. God's steadfast love is forever.

May this child, _____, grow into manhood. As he has entered the covenant, so may he enter the study of Torah, the wedding canopy, and the accomplishment of good deeds.

The ceremony may end here or continue with other prayers and blessings. The *mohel* may offer a traditional prayer that asks God to accept his work. The familiar words and melody of the *shehecheyanu,* the prayer of thanksgiving for new blessings, is often included. In Israel, *shehecheyanu* follows upon the father's blessing immediately after the circumcision.[21] Sephardic Jews follow the blessing over wine with the blessing for fragrant spices—Moroccan Jews use dried rose petals.

After the long *kiddush,* it has become customary for one or both parents to talk about how the name was chosen. If the baby has been named for a relative who has died, this is invariably a very moving moment. Typically, parents give voice to their hope that their son will grow up to be as learned, as quick to laugh, as devoted a friend and father as the man or men after whom he is named.

At this point, parents sometimes also add readings and prayers. Guests can offer impromptu blessings for the new baby, such as

"May he grow up in a world free of want and fear," or "May he inherit his mother's good looks and his father's appetite."

If this idea appeals to you, ask a few guests to think about a blessing in advance. Wishes like these can also be written in a guest book.

Some parents now provide a printed guide to explain the history and meaning of *brit milah* or provide responsive readings for the ceremony. This pamphlet traditionally includes the prayers recited after meals, which include blessings for a meal after a *bris*. (See *Hiddur Mitzvah—Beautiful Touches* for more on booklets.)

Part III: Celebration

Traditionally, the ceremony ends with the song, *Siman Tov Umazal Tov* (good fortune and good luck), a universal Jewish song of rejoicing, and a meal is served. This *s'udat mitzvah,* or meal celebrating the performance of a commandment, usually begins with a *motzi,* a blessing for bread, typically a specially made loaf of challah, a braided egg bread.

Variations

Most ceremonies follow this general order, but there are some striking exceptions. Probably the most radical departure from tradition is the custom of having the circumcision take place privately, with only the immediate family present. A "naming" then takes place a few weeks later at a larger celebration. This division of the ceremony into two parts is sometimes done because the mother is too ill to attend a *bris* eight days after the birth. But in some cases, parents feel strongly that the procedure should not be connected to a party. There is a biblical precedent for this choice, given that Abraham's celebration of Isaac's birth took place at his son's weaning, not at his circumcision.

Along the same lines, sometimes parents have the circumcision in a small room, away from most of the guests, and then move to a larger room where the company can witness the rest of the ceremony.

Parents who choose hospital circumcision sometimes request that a naming ceremony for their son be held later, in the synagogue. Responses to this request vary from rabbi to rabbi. The most traditional will insist on a *hatafat dam brit,* a ritual drawing of blood from the site of the circumcision, which fulfills the obligations of *brit milah,* before reciting the naming blessing. But some rabbis regularly officiate at such namings. Still others apply the Talmudic category of *l'chat'chilah la, di-avad in,* which means, "If you ask me before you do it, I'll say no; if you tell me after the fact, I'll say, All right." In such cases, a rabbi may insist on a private ceremony that will not encourage others to follow suit.[22]

Sample Checklist of Things You Need for a *Bris*

Diapers
Goblet for *kiddush*
Kosher wine
Yarmulkes (skullcaps)
Sturdy table and chair
Prayer shawl for the *sandek*
Kippah (skullcap) for the baby
Phone off hook

Candles and matches
Elijah's chair
Shawl to cover Elijah's chair
Tape recorder, camera, booklets
Cotton balls★
Gauze pads★
Petroleum jelly★
Ointment★

Payment for the mohel

★ *The mohel will provide you with specifics.*

Adoption, Conversion, and Rituals for Already Circumcised Sons

Brit milah for an adopted infant is not very different from *brit milah* for a son who is born to you. An adopted son is circumcised as soon as possible. If the baby was not born to a Jewish mother, tradition calls for a *beit din*, a court of three Jews, to be present to witness that the *bris* was performed for the purpose of conversion. The only differences in the ritual are in the *mohel's* prayers. Before the circumcision, he says:

בָּרוּךְ אַתָּה יְיָ, אֱלֹהֵינוּ מֶלֶךְ הָעוֹלָם,
אֲשֶׁר קִדְּשָׁנוּ בְּמִצְוֹתָיו, וְצִוָּנוּ לָמוּל אֶת הַגֵּרִים.

*Ba-ruch a-ta Adonai, Eh-lo-hei-nu meh-lech
ha-o-lam, a-sher ki-d'sha-nu b'mitz-vo-tav,
v'tzi-va-nu la-mul et ha-ge-rim.*

Holy One of Blessing Your Presence fills creation
You make us holy with Your commandments,
calling us to circumcise the convert.

During the longer blessing after the circumcision, the *mohel* says:

בָּרוּךְ אַתָּה יְיָ, אֱלֹהֵינוּ מֶלֶךְ הָעוֹלָם, אֲשֶׁר קִדְּשָׁנוּ
בְּמִצְוֹתָיו, וְצִוָּנוּ לָמוּל אֶת הַגֵּרִים וּלְהַטִּיף מֵהֶם דַּם
בְּרִית, שֶׁאִלְמָלֵא דַם בְּרִית לֹא נִתְקַיְּמוּ שָׁמַיִם
וָאָרֶץ, שֶׁנֶּאֱמַר: אִם לֹא בְרִיתִי יוֹמָם וָלַיְלָה חֻקּוֹת
שָׁמַיִם וָאָרֶץ לֹא שַׂמְתִּי. בָּרוּךְ אַתָּה יְיָ, כּוֹרֵת
הַבְּרִית.

Holy One of Blessing Your Presence fills creation
You make us holy with Your commandments,
calling us to circumcise the convert and to draw
the blood of the convert. Were it not for the

blood of the covenant, heaven and earth would
not have been fulfilled, as it is said, without My
covenant, I would not set forth day and night
and the laws of heaven and earth. Holy One of
Blessing, author of the covenant.

There are many ways to acknowledge the particular dimension
of adoption at a *bris*. For example, parents might recite this prayer,
or ask others to read from it with them:

We are grateful to God
Who has made this miracle of creation
And given us this baby boy.
His coming into our home has blessed us.
He is part of our family and our lives.
This child has now become our son.

Out of our love of God and Torah and Israel,
We wish to raise him up as a Jew.
We come now before a Jewish court of three
To begin his entry into the Jewish people
Through the *mitzvah* of *milah*.

Let this be the beginning
Of his living a life of *mitzvot*.
May we be privileged to raise him up
As a true and loyal son of Abraham and Sarah.
This child comes into the covenant in our
presence.
We welcome him with the words that God
spoke to Abraham our father:
Hit-halech l'fanai veh-yeh tamim
Walk before Me and be whole.[23]

According to Jewish law, the ritual conversion of a non-Jewish
boy includes not only *brit milah* but also *mikvah*—immersion in a
ritual bath. (See the chapter "Adoption" for a full discussion of
laws, customs, and ceremonies.)

According to *halachah,* the laws and rituals that apply to adopted sons also pertain to sons of Jewish fathers and non-Jewish mothers. At a *bris* for the son of a non-Jewish mother—even if she is committed to raising her child as a Jew—*mohels* may use the blessings for conversion. The question of *mikvah* can be dealt with later.

Of course, the children of a woman who has converted to Judaism are Jewish and undergo *brit milah* with the traditional prayers. However, it must be noted that Orthodox Jews and the state of Israel do not usually recognize conversions performed by Reform, Reconstructionist, or Conservative rabbis. Thus someday, in certain quarters, there may be a question as to the Jewishness of children born to a mother whose conversion was not supervised by Orthodox rabbis. Families with concerns about this matter should discuss them with a rabbi.

If an adopted child was circumcised by a physician without Jewish ritual, tradition also calls for a ritual called *hatafat dam brit*—the covenant of the drop of blood. This involves drawing a drop of blood from the site of the circumcision by a *mohel.* Technically, a *hatafat dam brit* does not require any blessings or a celebratory meal, but many adoptive parents choose to celebrate as they would for a *brit milah,* with *shehecheyanu, kiddush,* bestowal of a name, and other blessings and prayers.

For adopted sons, *hatafat dam brit* is performed as soon as possible. It involves very little pain and virtually no wound and is sometimes held at a *mikvah,* where the ritual of immersion follows. (Again, see *Adoption.*) *Hatafat dam brit* is sometimes performed on sons who were born to Jewish mothers but were circumcised without Jewish ritual.

Caring for the Newly Circumcised Baby

The *mohel* should provide you with information about the care of the circumcision wound. This advice will vary from practitioner to practitioner, but it is invariably simple.

Most *mohels* apply a Vaseline-saturated gauze bandage that should be taken off in a day or two. During those first few days, you might see a drop of blood or even blood stains on the baby's diapers, but this is usually no cause for alarm. The penis will be bright red at first and perhaps even a bit swollen, but this should subside within two weeks, at most. A mucus-like lymphatic secretion may appear on the shaft of the penis; this is no cause for alarm. Just leave it alone, and it, too, will go away.

Your *mohel* may give you specific instructions about applying an anti-bacterial salve or ointment, but generally, the less you do, the better. By the time of your first visit to the pediatrician— within a month—the penis should be completely healed.

Complications are extremely rare, but do not hesitate to call the *mohel* and/or your pediatrician immediately if the baby seems excessively fussy, has a fever, or develops an inflammation that surrounds the top of the penis. If you have any concerns or questions about how your son is healing, the *mohel* should be available and helpful.

Two Ceremonies for *Brit Milah*

In the past, most parents did not consider themselves active participants in a son's *brit milah*. The *mohel* would show up, do his job, and that would be that.

Given the power of the ancient ceremony and the anxiety associated with circumcision. many parents continue to follow the *mohel's* and/or rabbi's directions. But others have decided to personalize the ritual. This can be done very simply, with the addition of a poem or blessing or a short talk about the baby's namesake. Some parents are more ambitious and write ceremonies, complete with elaborate booklets that explain the ritual for their guests. Your own rabbi or *mohel* can help you design a *bris* that is right for you.

The following pages include two ceremonies that may be copied and used. These are intended as guides for you in designing your own ceremony. More poems, readings, and prayers are found in these chapters: *Hiddur Mitzvah, Brit Bat,* and *Adoption.*

Brit Milah Ceremony

As the baby is brought into the room, the parents, *mohel,* and/or rabbi say:

בָּרוּךְ הַבָּא.

Ba-ruch ha-ba.
Blessed are you who bear the divine presence.

Holding the baby, the mother says:

My son, my child, you have been as dear to me as my own breath. May I hold you gently now with the love to keep you close and with the strength to let you grow.

The father takes the child and says:

My son, my child, a piece of my life is you. You have grown to life apart from me, but now I hold you close to my heart and cradle you in my arms with my love.

Together the parents say:

We have been blessed with the gift of new life. We have shared love and pain and joy in bringing our son into life.

By the way we live, we aspire to teach our son to become a caring and loving person. We hope that in seeking to fulfill himself, he will accept his responsibilities to others and to his heritage. We dedicate ourselves to the creation of a Jewish home and to a life of compassion for others, hoping he will learn from our example.

God of our grandfathers, God of our grandmothers, we pray for covenant love, for life, for good. Keep us strong together.

This material is from The New Jewish Baby Book *by Anita Diamant, © 1993, published by Jewish Lights Publishing, P.O. Box 237, Sunset Farm Offices, Woodstock, VT 05091. The publisher grants permission to you to copy this ceremony for distribution to your guests. All rights to other parts of this book are still covered by copyright and are reserved to the publisher.*

Brit Milah Ceremony

בָּרוּךְ אַתָּה יְיָ, מְקוֹר הַחַיִּים מְשַׂמֵּחַ הַהוֹרִים עִם יַלְדֵיהֶם.

Ba-ruch a-ta Adonai, m'kor ha-cha-yim
m'sa-mei-ach ha-ho-rim im yal-dei-hem.
Blessed is the holy source of life,
who causes parents to rejoice with their children.

Parents:

We are ready to fulfill the *mitzvah* of circumcision, as it is written in the Torah, "Throughout your generations every male among you shall be circumcised when he is eight days old."

When the baby is placed on Elijah's chair, the *mohel* or rabbi says:

In Jewish folklore, Elijah is regarded as the forerunner of messianic days, the one who announces the advent of the Messiah. As we recall Elijah now, we rekindle our faith that every human life may yet bring about *y'mot hamashiach,* the era of harmony and peace for all people.

Mohel:

בָּרוּךְ אַתָּה יְיָ, אֱלֹהֵינוּ מֶלֶךְ הָעוֹלָם,
אֲשֶׁר קִדְּשָׁנוּ בְּמִצְוֹתָיו, וְצִוָּנוּ עַל הַמִּילָה.

Blessed by the Presence whose sanctity fills our lives,
we fulfill the *mitzvah* of circumcision.

Circumcision is performed.

Brit Milah Ceremony

Parents, repeating after the *mohel:*

בָּרוּךְ אַתָּה יְיָ, אֱלֹהֵינוּ מֶלֶךְ הָעוֹלָם,
אֲשֶׁר קִדְּשָׁנוּ בְּמִצְוֹתָיו, וְצִוָּנוּ
לְהַכְנִיסוֹ בִּבְרִיתוֹ שֶׁל אַבְרָהָם אָבִינוּ.

Ba-ruch a-ta Adonai, Eh-lo-hei-nu me-lech ha-o-lam,
a-sher ki-d'sha-nu b'mitz-vo-tav, v'tzi-va-nu
l'hach-ni-so biv-ri-to shel Av-ra-ham a-vi-nu.
Blessed by the Presence whose sanctity fills our lives,
we bring our son into the covenant of Abraham, our father.

Parents with *mohel,* rabbi, and/or guests:

זֶה הַקָּטֹן _____ גָּדוֹל יִהְיֶה.
כְּשֵׁם שֶׁנִּכְנַס לַבְּרִית,
כֵּן יִכָּנֵס לְתוֹרָה וּלְחֻפָּה וּלְמַעֲשִׂים טוֹבִים.

Zeh ha-ka-ton _____ ga-dol yih-yeh.
K'shem sheh-nich-nas la-brit,
kein yi-ka-nes l'to-rah ul-chu-pah ul-ma-a-sim to-vim.
As he has been brought into the covenant of our people,
so may he attain the blessings of Torah,
chupah, and a life of good deeds.

Raising the cup of wine, the *mohel* or rabbi says:

בָּרוּךְ אַתָּה יְיָ, אֱלֹהֵינוּ מֶלֶךְ הָעוֹלָם, בּוֹרֵא פְּרִי הַגָּפֶן.

בָּרוּךְ אַתָּה יְיָ, אֱלֹהֵינוּ מֶלֶךְ הָעוֹלָם, אֲשֶׁר קִדֵּשׁ יָדִיד מִבֶּטֶן, וְחֹק
בִּשְׁאֵרוֹ שָׂם, וְצֶאֱצָאָיו חָתַם בְּאוֹת בְּרִית קֹדֶשׁ. עַל כֵּן בִּשְׂכַר זֹאת,
אֵל חַי, חֶלְקֵנוּ צוּרֵנוּ, צַוֵּה לְהַצִּיל יְדִידוּת שְׁאֵרֵנוּ מִשַּׁחַת, לְמַעַן
בְּרִיתוֹ אֲשֶׁר שָׂם בִּבְשָׂרֵנוּ. בָּרוּךְ אַתָּה יְיָ, כּוֹרֵת הַבְּרִית.

Brit Milah Ceremony

אֱלֹהֵינוּ וֵאלֹהֵי אֲבוֹתֵינוּ וְאִמּוֹתֵינוּ, קַיֵּם אֶת הַיֶּלֶד הַזֶּה לְאָבִיו
וּלְאִמּוֹ, וְיִקָּרֵא שְׁמוֹ בְּיִשְׂרָאֵל _____ בֶּן _____ . יִשְׂמַח
הָאָב בְּיוֹצֵא חֲלָצָיו, וְתָגֵל אִמּוֹ בִּפְרִי בִטְנָהּ, כַּכָּתוּב: יִשְׂמַח אָבִיךָ
וְאִמֶּךָ, וְתָגֵל יוֹלַדְתֶּךָ. וְנֶאֱמַר: וָאֶעֱבֹר עָלַיִךְ וָאֶרְאֵךְ מִתְבּוֹסֶסֶת
בְּדָמָיִךְ, וָאֹמַר לָךְ בְּדָמַיִךְ חֲיִי. וְנֶאֱמַר: זָכַר לְעוֹלָם בְּרִיתוֹ, דָּבָר
צִוָּה לְאֶלֶף דּוֹר. אֲשֶׁר כָּרַת אֶת אַבְרָהָם, וּשְׁבוּעָתוֹ לְיִצְחָק.
וַיַּעֲמִידֶהָ לְיַעֲקֹב לְחֹק, לְיִשְׂרָאֵל בְּרִית עוֹלָם. וְנֶאֱמַר: וַיָּמָל
אַבְרָהָם אֶת יִצְחָק בְּנוֹ, בֶּן שְׁמֹנַת יָמִים, כַּאֲשֶׁר צִוָּה אֹתוֹ אֱלֹהִים.
הוֹדוּ לַייָ כִּי טוֹב, כִּי לְעוֹלָם חַסְדּוֹ. הוֹדוּ לַייָ כִּי טוֹב, כִּי לְעוֹלָם
חַסְדּוֹ.

_____ בֶּן _____ זֶה הַקָּטֹן גָּדוֹל יִהְיֶה. כְּשֵׁם שֶׁנִּכְנַס
לַבְּרִית, כֵּן יִכָּנֵס לְתוֹרָה, וּלְחֻפָּה, וּלְמַעֲשִׂים טוֹבִים.

Blessed is the presence whose sanctity fills our lives and ripens fruit on the vine.

You have sanctified your beloved from the womb, establishing your holy covenant throughout the generations. May devotion to the covenant continue to sustain us as a people. Blessed by the presence whose sanctity fills our lives, we give thanks for the covenant.

God of all life, sustain this child and the let him be known in Israel as _____ son of _____ and _____ .

May the father rejoice in his offspring and the mother be glad with her children. May you teach him through word and deed the meaning of the covenant forever, the word commanded to a thousand generations, the covenant made with Abraham, Isaac, Jacob, Sarah, Rebecca, Rachel, and Leah, an eternal covenant for Israel. As it is said, "And Abraham circumcised his son when he was eight days old, as God commanded." Give thanks to God for what is good, for covenant love that endures forever.

Brit Milah Ceremony

May this little child, _____ son of _____ and
_____ , grow into manhood as a blessing to his family, the
Jewish people and humanity. As he has entered the covenant of our
people, so may he grow into a life of Torah, *chupah,* and good
deeds.

Parents drink the wine the baby has already tasted. They explain
the baby's name. Other readings may be included here.

Rabbi or *mohel:*

יְבָרֶכְךָ יְיָ וְיִשְׁמְרֶךָ,
יָאֵר יְיָ פָּנָיו אֵלֶיךָ וִיחֻנֶּךָּ,
יִשָּׂא יְיָ פָּנָיו אֵלֶיךָ וְיָשֵׂם לְךָ שָׁלוֹם.

May God bless you and keep you.
My God be with you and be gracious to you.
May God show you kindness and give you peace.

Parents and guests:

בָּרוּךְ אַתָּה יְיָ, אֱלֹהֵינוּ מֶלֶךְ הָעוֹלָם,
שֶׁהֶחֱיָנוּ וְקִיְּמָנוּ וְהִגִּיעָנוּ לַזְּמַן הַזֶּה.

*Ba-ruch a-ta Adonai, Eh-lo-hei-nu meh-lech ha-o-lam,
sheh-heh-cheh-ya-nu v'ki-y'ma-nu v'hi-gi-a-nu la-z'man ha-zeh.*
Blessed be the Presence Whose sanctity fills our lives we give
thanks for life, for health and for this sacred moment.[24]

Covenant Ceremony

As the baby enters, all say:

בָּרוּךְ הַבָּא בְּשֵׁם יְיָ.

Ba-ruch ha-ba b'shem Adonai.
Blessed are you who comes in the name of the Eternal.

Parents:

הוֹדוּ לַייָ כִּי טוֹב, כִּי לְעוֹלָם חַסְדּוֹ.

Ho-du la-do-nai ki tov, ki l'o-lam chas-do.
Give thanks to the Eternal who is good,
whose goodness is everlasting.

Reader:

You are your parents' dream realized, their hopes fulfilled. You are
the latest and best chapter in the unfolding lives of your father and
mother.

Reader:

You are a bridge over which we who welcome you can gaze from
this day into future days, from our generation into yours. You are
the newest link in the endless chain of our people's history.

Grandparents:

Our God and God of all generations, we are grateful for new
beginnings, for the bond of new life that links one generation to
another. Thankful for the blessings of family, for the love and care
that brings meaning and happiness to our lives, we rejoice with
our children at the birth of our grandchild.

This material is from The New Jewish Baby Book *by Anita Diamant, © 1993, published by Jewish Lights Publishing, P.O. Box 237, Sunset Farm Offices, Woodstock, VT 05091. The publisher grants permission to you to copy this ceremony for distribution to your guests. All rights to other parts of this book are still covered by copyright and are reserved to the publisher.*

Covenant Ceremony

Reader:

If you hold a hand before your eyes, you can hide the tallest mountain. If we get caught up with what we do in our everyday lives, we can forget that miracles fill the world. You remind us of the many wonders that happen all around us.

All:

בָּרוּךְ אַתָּה יְיָ, אֱלֹהֵינוּ מֶלֶךְ הָעוֹלָם,
שֶׁהֶחֱיָנוּ וְקִיְּמָנוּ וְהִגִּיעָנוּ לַזְּמַן הַזֶּה.

Ba-ruch a-ta Adonai, Eh-lo-hei-nu meh-lech ha-o-lam,
sheh-heh-cheh-ya-nu v'ki-y'ma-nu v'hi-gi-a-nu la-z'man ha-zeh.
Blessed are You, O God, who gives us life, who sustains us,
and who brings us here to share in this occasion.

Reader:

A new son of Israel has come, and with him comes a great promise. In his soul is the potential to bring greatness into our world. He brings blessing to our lives, as he reminds us that the world is not yet complete. We each share in the task of perfecting this world.

Reader:

And so we set aside a chair for Elijah the prophet, may his memory be for a blessing. Recalling Elijah, we rekindle our faith that every human life has the potential to bring about an era of peace and harmony for all people.

Covenant Ceremony

Reader or *mohel:*

We welcome you to life with love. We rejoice in bringing this child into the *brit,* the covenant between God and the Jewish people.

Since the time of Abraham and Sarah, we Jews have been called to enter this covenant. As it says in Genesis, "I will establish My covenant between Me and you, to be God to you and to your offspring."

Parents:

We are ready to fulfill the *mitzvah* of circumcision as the Creator commanded us in the Torah. "Throughout your generations, every male among you shall be circumcised when he is eight days old."

Mohel:

בָּרוּךְ אַתָּה יְיָ, אֱלֹהֵינוּ מֶלֶךְ הָעוֹלָם,
אֲשֶׁר קִדְּשָׁנוּ בְּמִצְוֹתָיו, וְצִוָּנוּ עַל הַמִּילָה.

Blessed are You, Eternal Presence of the Universe, whose sanctified us with Your commandments and commanded us
concerning circumcision.

Circumcision is performed.

Covenant Ceremony

Parents:

בָּרוּךְ אַתָּה יְיָ, אֱלֹהֵינוּ מֶלֶךְ הָעוֹלָם,
אֲשֶׁר קִדְּשָׁנוּ בְּמִצְוֹתָיו, וְצִוָּנוּ
לְהַכְנִיסוֹ בִּבְרִיתוֹ שֶׁל אַבְרָהָם אָבִינוּ וְשָׂרָה אִמֵּנוּ.

Ba-ruch a-ta Adonai, Eh-lo-hei-nu me-lech ha-o-lam,
a-sher ki-d'sha-nu b'mitz-vo-tav, v'tzi–va-nu
l'hach-ni-so biv-ri-to shel Av-ra-ham a-vi-nu v'Sa-rah i-mei-nu.
Blessed are You, Eternal Presence of the Universe,
who has sanctified us with Your commandments and
commanded us to bring our son into the covenant of
Abraham our father and Sarah our mother.

All:

כְּשֵׁם שֶׁנִּכְנַס לַבְּרִית,
כֵּן יִכָּנֵס לְתוֹרָה וּלְחֻפָּה וּלְמַעֲשִׂים טוֹבִים.

K'shem sheh-nich-nas la-brit,
kein yi-ka-nes l'to-rah ul-chu-pah ul-ma-a-sim to-vim.
As he has entered the covenant,
so may he attain the blessings of Torah,
marriage, and a life of good deeds.

Reader:

May God who blessed our ancestors Abraham and Sarah, Isaac and
Rebecca, Jacob, Rachel, and Leah, bless this child who is circumcised and bring him speedily to full healing. May his parents
_____ and _____ fulfill the privilege of raising
him, educating him, and teaching him wisdom. May his hands and
heart be faithful in serving God.

Covenant Ceremony

Reader, rabbi or *mohel:*

בָּרוּךְ אַתָּה יְיָ, אֱלֹהֵינוּ מֶלֶךְ הָעוֹלָם,
בּוֹרֵא פְּרִי הַגָּפֶן.

Blessed is the Eternal Ruler of the Universe,
Creator of the fruit of the vine.

Father:

As we prepare to give you your name, we wrap you in this *tallit,*
the same *tallit* under which your mother and I were married.

Mother tells stories about the baby's namesake(s).

Rabbi or *mohel:*

אֱלֹהֵינוּ וֵאלֹהֵי אֲבוֹתֵינוּ וְאִמּוֹתֵינוּ, קַיֵּם אֶת הַיֶּלֶד הַזֶּה לְאָבִיו
וּלְאִמּוֹ, וְיִקָּרֵא שְׁמוֹ בְּיִשְׂרָאֵל _____ בֶּן _____. יִשְׂמַח
הָאָב בְּיוֹצֵא חֲלָצָיו, וְתָגֵל אִמּוֹ בִּפְרִי בִטְנָהּ. זֶה הַקָּטֹן גָּדוֹל יִהְיֶה.
כְּשֵׁם שֶׁנִּכְנַס לַבְּרִית, כֵּן יִכָּנֵס לְתוֹרָה, וּלְחֻפָּה, וּלְמַעֲשִׂים טוֹבִים.

Our God, God of our mothers and fathers, Sustain _____
through his parents' loving care. In the presence of loved ones, we
give this child the name _____ to be known in the Jewish
community as _____ *ben* _____ *v'*_____ . May
his name be source of joy.

All:

May this family grow together in health and strength, in harmony,
wisdom and love, their home filled with words of Torah and acts of
kindness. May we all share in the joy of seeing _____
grow into adulthood, a blessing to his family, his people, and all
humanity.

Covenant Ceremony

Parents, to their son:

יְבָרֶכְךָ יְיָ וְיִשְׁמְרֶךָ,
יָאֵר יְיָ פָּנָיו אֵלֶיךָ וִיחֻנֶּךָּ,
יִשָּׂא יְיָ פָּנָיו אֵלֶיךָ וְיָשֵׂם לְךָ שָׁלוֹם.

Y'va-reh-ch'chah Adonai v'yish-m'reh-cha,
Ya-eir Adonai pa-nav ei-leh-kha vi-chu-neh-ka,
Yi-sah Adonai pa-nav ei-leh-kha v'ya-seim l'chah sha-lom.
May God bless you and guard you.
May the light of God's Presence
shine on you and be gracious to you.
May the Presence of God lift you up
and give you a life of fulfillment,
contentment, wholeness and peace.[25]

Brit Bat
Covenant for a Daughter

> *"Go out and see what the Jews are doing."*
> —THE BABYLONIAN TALMUD[1]

American Jews are inventing ceremonies to celebrate the birth of their daughters. These ceremonies go by many names: *simchat bat* (rejoicing on account of a daughter), *brit chayim* (covenant of life), *brit kedushah* (covenant of sanctification), *brit bat Tziyon* (covenant for the daughters of Zion), *brit b'not Yisrael* (covenant for the daughters of Israel), *brit eidut* (covenant of witnessing), *brit ohel* (covenant of the tent), *brit haneirot* (covenant of candles), *brit Sarah* (covenant of Sarah), *brit r'chitzah* (covenant of washing), *brit mikvah* (covenant of immersion), and, most simply, *brit bat,* covenant for a daughter. Most of these rituals are still changing: Every ceremony that is written down—and many are not—is passed along to other parents, who almost always revise and reshape it for their own use.

This ferment of liturgical creativity has a number of sources from the 1960s, including a general openness to spirituality, ethnic back-to-roots movements, a renewed sense of Jewish identity after the 1967 war in Israel, and feminism. As Jewish feminists became parents in the 1960s and 1970s, they were dismayed by the disparity between the celebration surrounding the birth of a boy and the lack of ceremony to mark the arrival of a baby girl. The need to give Jewish expression to the joy that attends the birth of a daughter coincided with the Jewish renewal movement, which stressed a hands-on, home-style, learn-as-you-do attitude toward tradition. This approach was typified by *The Jewish Catalogs,* resource guides that offered a non-threatening doorway into Judaism and Jewish practice.[2]

Using *brit milah*—the covenant of circumcision—as a model, and with the experience of *bat mitzvah*—the coming-of-age ceremony for daughters—as a guide, parents began experimenting with covenant ceremonies for girls. What seemed experimental and tentative in 1975 is now mainstream. Most rabbis' manuals now include a naming or welcoming ceremony for daughters, and even in Orthodox circles, Jewish rites of passage for baby girls are no longer a novelty, especially because the lack of Jewish law on this subject frees traditionalists to improvise.

There can be no normative liturgy for a ritual as young as *brit bat*. Perhaps decades or even centuries from now, *brit bat* may develop into a ceremony as universal as *brit milah*. However, it is probably more likely that our great-great-grandchildren will continue to enjoy many choices when they welcome their daughters into the covenant and community of Israel. *Brit bat* may follow in the tradition of the Passover *hagaddah* (the book that contains the order of the *seder*), which is constantly being reinterpreted, even as it retains a distinctive core of symbols, stories, and blessings.

For now, *brit bat* continues to evolve. This chapter contains the basic building blocks for creating a ceremony for your daughter. Here you will find a menu of possibilities: blessings, prayers, readings, and symbols culled from dozens of *brit bat* ceremonies, as well as an outline and several examples to help you plan your own distinctive celebration.

History

Although *brit bat* seems a uniquely 20th-century celebration, it does have a long Jewish history. But because it was the history of women's lives, much of it went unrecorded. What remains are tantalizing remnants and hints.

The Torah records that all new mothers owed the Temple ritual thanksgiving offerings in the same amounts and of the same kinds, regardless of their baby's sex. The offering was due thirty-three days after birth for a boy, sixty-six days after birth for a girl, the difference representing the number of days of the mother's ritual "impurity" following the birth of a male or female child.[3]

What happened during those thirty-three or sixty-six days of separation from the community is the stuff of *Midrash*—the stories that fill in the spaces between words of Torah.[4] There may well have been ceremonies for baby daughters during those days apart, rites not shared with the men and therefore not recorded.

Similarly, there may well have been folk customs for naming, welcoming, and blessing daughters throughout the undocumented history of Jewish women's lives. In Yiddish, the unfamiliar word *brisitzeh* (a feminine Yiddish form of *bris*) remains, suggesting an Ashkenazic covenant ceremony.[5] *Hollekreish,* another naming ceremony based on non-Jewish folk customs (later described in the chapter *Celebrations and Customs*) may have had more significance for daughters than for sons.

The only formal acknowledgment of a daughter's birth in Ashkenazic tradition is the public naming in the synagogue. According to custom, the father is called to the Torah during the week after his daughter's birth, on *Shabbat* or on any day there is a Torah service. There, he offers the *mi shebeirach* blessing, an all-purpose special-occasion blessing in which his daughter's name is announced for the first time.

After the regular service is concluded, the family then provides food and drink for those present. Often, the mother and baby do not attend. If she is there, the mother may say the *birkat hagomel,* the prayer of thanksgiving for having survived an ordeal (see page 107).

The *mi shebeirach* blessing for naming a girl is:

> May the One who blessed our ancestors bless the mother _____ and her newborn daughter, whose name in Israel shall be _____ . May they raise her for the marriage canopy and for a life of good deeds.[6]

Sephardic tradition has much more to say about baby girls, but because most American Jews trace their ancestry and practice to eastern Europe, few people are familiar with the relative abundance of Sephardic rituals and customs that herald a daughter's birth. For example, when Syrian Jews name daughters in the synagogue, the congregation sings songs in the baby's honor and is then invited to attend a celebratory meal.[7] Moroccan Jews name their daughters at home in a ceremony led by a rabbi who holds the child, quotes from the bible, and pronounces a *mi shebeirach* that lists the names of the biblical matriarchs, Sarah, Rebecca, Rachel, and Leah. Songs are sung and during the naming, the women raise their voices in ululation as an expression of joy.

The Jews of Spain perform a ceremony at home, after the mother has recovered. It is called *las fadas,* a word probably based on *hadas,* which means fairies and suggests that the celebration was borrowed from a local non-Jewish custom of seeking the blessing of good spirits.[8]

In *las fadas,* the baby is brought into the celebration on a pillow. She is dressed in a miniature bridal gown and is passed around the room, and each guest gives her a blessing. When the baby reaches the rabbi, he recites a blessing for her health and happiness. Verses from *Song of Songs* are recited, songs are sung and a lavish feast follows.

The traditional Sephardic prayerbook includes a ceremony that contains the following readings and prayer:

FROM *SEDER ZEVED BAT*—
CELEBRATION FOR THE GIFT OF A DAUGHTER

O my dove in the rocky clefts,
In the shelter of terrace high
Let me see your face
Let me hear your voice
For your voice is sweet
And your face is beautiful.

One alone is my dove, my perfect one,
The darling of her mother,
The delight of her who bore her.
Daughters saw her—they acclaimed her,
Queens and consorts—they sang her praises.

May the One who blessed our mothers, Sarah, Rebecca, Rachel and Leah, Miriam the prophetess, Abigail and Esther the queen, bless also this darling baby _____. May the One bless her to grow up in comfort, health, and happiness. May the One give to her parents the joy of seeing her happily married, a radiant mother of children, rich in honor and joy to a ripe old age. May this be the will of God, and let us say Amen.[9]

Planning a *Brit Bat*

Although there are precedents, there are no rules for *brit bat*. The rest of this chapter offers many choices, beginning with consideration of where and when to hold your celebration. The ceremonies that appear at the end of this chapter are yours to use, in their entirety or as models for your own creative efforts. There is no right or wrong here—only opportunities for creativity and holiness.

Where

Brit bat can take place at home or in the synagogue, and there are pros and cons associated with either. Some people use a sanctuary or social hall because they need the space and also because they want to make this a community celebration. It may be simpler for you to hire a caterer and keep the commotion out of the house.

But others feel that home is the only place for a family occasion like *brit bat*. Some people find it easier to care for the baby, reassure older siblings, and host a celebration in the comfort of their own home.

When

Generally, parents schedule a *brit bat* on a day that is convenient for family and friends and when the mother feels well enough to enjoy the event. But some base their choice on Jewish criteria.

- *Eight days.* Having the ceremony on the eighth day taps into the ancient rite of *brit milah*. The same traditional explanations apply, such as the sanctity associated with the number eight, and the spiritual strength the baby derives from her first contact with *Shabbat*. (See *Brit Milah*)

  Holding the *brit bat* on the eighth day means that the miracle of birth is still very fresh in the parents' minds, and the ceremony will resound with the powerful emotions of labor and delivery. However, because many women often don't feel ready for a party so soon after giving birth, the eighth day is a relatively infrequent choice.

- *Fourteen days* has been advanced as another interval with traditional roots. In the Torah, after the birth of a daughter a mother's ritual impurity ends after fourteen days. Two weeks allows for the mother's recovery and, according to some pediatricians, is a reasonable amount of time to keep a newborn away from crowds.

- *Thirty days* is a popular choice because it allows the family enough time to recover, plan, and invite. It too has a basis in tradition, because the rabbis believed a child was viable only after thirty days.

- *Rosh Chodesh.* Some parents schedule the ceremony on the first day of the next new moon. A day for new beginnings, *Rosh Chodesh* is a semi-holiday which traditionally was a day of rest for women.

- *Shabbat.* Whether days or weeks after the baby is born, most *brit bat* ceremonies are scheduled for the Sabbath. Because *Shabbat* is itself a covenant between God and Israel, it seems an appropriate time for a covenantal ceremony.

A *brit bat* on *Shabbat* can take place at different times in the day and in a number of contexts. In some congregations, the custom is to take the baby up to the *bimah* (the raised platform in the synagogue) during services on Friday night or Saturday morning.

There the rabbi generally conducts a brief ceremony. Blessings such as the traditional *mi shebeirach* are offered, and the name is announced. Additional readings may be incorporated as well. Afterward, the *oneg Shabbat* or *Shabbat kiddush* is often sponsored by the new parents or in the family's honor.

Another option is to hold the *brit bat* immediately following the morning service, preceding *kiddush*. The celebration can coincide with the *Shabbat* midday meal, either in the synagogue or at home.

Brit bat is sometimes included in *havdalah,* the ceremony that marks the end of *Shabbat* and celebrates distinctions: *Shabbat* from the rest of the week, the mundane from the holy. A *havdalah brit bat* marks the separation between mother and baby, and the child's entrance into the community of Israel.

Guests and Participants

Once you've settled on where and when, there is the question of whom to invite and involve in the ceremony. Jewish tradition encourages us to include as many people as possible. Although some parents do mail invitations to their daughter's *brit bat* ceremony, most invite guests by telephone.

Although there are many exceptions, when *brit bat* takes place at home, the baby's parents usually lead the ceremony. When it is held in a synagogue, the rabbi officiates, although sometimes with a great deal of parental participation. You do not need a rabbi to perform a *brit bat* ceremony. The parents or any honored guest can serve as the ceremonial leader.

In general, it is considered a *mitzvah*—a good and holy deed— to include as many people as possible in a ritual such as this. Grandparents are usually given the most important *kibbudim* or honors, especially the roles and titles associated with *brit milah*— *kvatterin, kvatter* (godmother and godfather, respectively) and *sandek* (sponsor). The *sandek* or *sandeket* (the feminine version of *sandek*) holds the baby during the naming. The *kvatter* and *kvatterin* bring the baby into the room, hold her during some part of the ceremony, or perform other ceremonial tasks such as candle-lighting.

Non-Jews in the Ceremony

Non-Jewish grandparents, aunts, uncles, cousins, and friends can participate in many ways—depending on their comfort level, of course. Unlike godparents in Christian ceremonies, the *kvatter* and *kvatterin* do not assume responsibility for the child's religious upbringing; their roles are strictly ceremonial. The same holds true for the *sandek,* a word that probably derives from the Greek for "patron."

Blessings, poems, readings, or prayers can be distributed to any and to as many guests as you choose. People can be honored with tasks like reciting the *motzi,* the blessing over bread (traditionally a braided challah) before the meal or holding a prayer shawl over the *brit bat.* (See *Hiddur Mitzvah—Beautiful Touches* and *Simcha* for more about ways to enhance the ceremony and involve guests.)

The legend that the prophet Elijah attends all *brit milah* ceremonies has been attached to *brit bat.* The *kissei shel Eliyahu* (Elijah's chair) invokes the presence of the prophet, angel, protector, peripatetic guest, and harbinger of *y'mot hamashiach,* the days of the Messiah. (See page 105 in *Brit Milah* for more about Elijah.)

Booklets

Because *brit bat* ceremonies are still relatively new and because many guests—Jews and non-Jews alike—may not be familiar with the prayers and symbols, many parents prepare a printed guide to the proceedings. (For more about booklets, see *Hiddur Mitzvah—Beautiful Touches.*)

Elements of the *Brit Bat* Ceremony

Of the hundreds of *brit bat* ceremonies in circulation, some are short and simple, others long and elaborate. Although the ceremonies that appear at the end of this chapter provide some idea of their range, it is impossible to reproduce the variations. Nevertheless, a few elements seem nearly universal.

Brit bat tends to have a four-part structure: introduction, covenant, naming and conclusion, and celebration. As you assemble your own ceremony, keep this general structure in mind.

- *Part I: Introductory blessings and prayers.* Includes the greeting *brucha haba-ah* (blessed is she who enters) and prayers or readings by the parents and/or rabbi. *Kiddush* is sometimes recited here as well.

- *Part II: Covenant prayers or ritual.* Using blessings and/or symbolic actions, a baby daughter is entered into the covenant of the people of Israel. Generally, this is followed by the threefold wish that she will also take on the blessings of Torah study, marriage and a life of good deeds.

- *Part III: Naming and final blessings.* The name is announced and namesakes are lovingly recalled. Blessings, prayers, readings and wishes from the guests may be read and the ceremony ends with *shehecheyanu* and/or the priestly benediction.

- *Part IV: Celebratory meal.* The *s'udat mitzvah*—the meal in celebration of the fulfilling of a commandment—is part of all major life-cycle events.

The following "menu" explains this four-part structure in greater detail. Be advised, however, that traditional Jewish rituals are as powerful as they are brief. If you include every item on this menu in your *brit bat,* your liturgical "meal" will be too rich, and the ceremony will go on too long.

Part I: Introduction

BRUCHA HABA-AH "Blessed is she who enters." This greeting begins virtually all *brit bat* ceremonies. It not only recalls the beginning of *brit milah* (*baruch habah*—blessed is he who enters); it acknowledges the divinity of the female or the female aspects of the Divine.

CANDLE-LIGHTING can make a beautiful beginning. Another tradition associated with *brit milah,* lighting candles has an added dimension at a *brit bat* because the weekly honor of lighting *Shabbat* candles is traditionally given to women.

There are many ways to begin the *brit bat* with candles. The mother can light a single braided *havdalah* candle or a pair of white *Shabbat* candles. The female members of the family or all the women guests can be invited to bring their *Shabbat* candlesticks and light them together (traditional white or a rainbow of colored candles, as you wish). Seven candles, representing the days of creation, may be lit.

The baby's mother or her parents might use candlesticks that are a gift to the child. If a baby is named for a female relative who has died, using her candlesticks is a beautiful statement of continuity (see *Hiddur Mitzvah—Beautiful Touches*). Candles are sometimes also used as a covenantal "*brit* action."[10]

INTRODUCTORY READINGS AND PRAYERS. These words set the tone, and often explain the "theology" of the ceremony. One of the more popular stories used in *brit bat* is the following, which comes from the Midrash:

> When Israel stood to receive the Torah, the Holy One, Blessed be the One, said to them: I am giving you my Torah. Present to me good guarantors that you will guard it, and I shall give it to you.
>
> They said: Our ancestors are our guarantors.
>
> The Holy One, Blessed be the One, said, Your ancestors are not sufficient guarantors. Yet bring me good guarantors, and I shall give you the Torah.
>
> They said, Master of the Universe, our prophets are our guarantors.

The One said to them: The prophets are not
sufficient guarantors. Yet bring me good guarantors and I shall give you the Torah.

They said, Our children are our guarantors.

And the Holy One, Blessed be the One, said,
They certainly are good guarantors. For their sake,
I give the Torah to you.[11]

KIDDUSH. The blessing and drinking of wine is a part of
virtually every Jewish celebration. After the blessing, the baby is
given a drop to drink. The cup can then be passed to the parents,
grandparents, and other guests. It's nice to use a special *kiddush*
cup—an heirloom, a gift to the baby from a grandparent, or the
goblet used at the parents' wedding.

בָּרוּךְ אַתָּה יְיָ, אֱלֹהֵינוּ מֶלֶךְ הָעוֹלָם,
בּוֹרֵא פְּרִי הַגָּפֶן.

Ba-ruch a-ta Adonai, Eh-lo-hei-nu meh-lech
ha-o-lam, bo-rei p'ri ha-ga-fen.

Holy One of Blessing Your Presence fills
creation, forming the fruit of the vine.

Part II: Covenant

Daughters are most commonly entered into the covenant with a
bracha, a blessing, such as this one:

בָּרוּךְ אַתָּה יְיָ, אֱלֹהֵינוּ מֶלֶךְ הָעוֹלָם, אֲשֶׁר קִדֵּשׁ
יְדִיד מִבֶּטֶן. אֵל חַי חֶלְקֵנוּ צוּרֵנוּ, צַוֵּה לְהַצִּיל
יְדִידוּת שְׁאֵרֵנוּ מִשַּׁחַת, לְמַעַן בְּרִיתוֹ. בָּרוּךְ אַתָּה
יְיָ, כּוֹרֵת הַבְּרִית.

אֱלוֹהַּ כָּל הַבְּרִיאוֹת, קַיֵּם אֶת הַיַּלְדָּה הַזֹּאת
לְאָבִיהָ וּלְאִמָּא.

You have sanctified your beloved from the womb
establishing Your holy covenant throughout the
generations. May devotion to the covenant
continue to sustain us as a people. Praised are
You, Eternal God, who has established the
covenant. Blessed by the Presence whose sanctity
fills our lives, we give thanks for the covenant.[12]

However, many parents feel that *brit bat* requires symbolic
action as well as words.[13] Many lovely gestures can serve this
purpose, including candle-lighting, touching the baby's hand to a
Torah scroll, wrapping or covering the baby with a prayer shawl,
or some form of washing or immersion.

Water is probably one of the most-used covenantal symbols.
Washing the baby, usually just her feet or hands, is an earthy yet
gentle physical act that seems to have struck a responsive chord
among liberal American Jews. Since its first appearance in print, in
1983, *brit r'chitzah,* the covenant of washing, has become a primary
source and a touchstone for countless other ceremonies.[14]

Although some people are disconcerted by the similarity
between washing and Christian baptism, water rituals are very
much a part of Jewish practice. Observant Jews wash their hands
and say a blessing before meals, and *mikvah* marks the cycles of
women's lives. Indeed, the Talmud suggests that as Abram became
Abraham through the covenant of circumcision, Sarai became
Sarah through the ritual of immersion in water.

The Torah is rich with water imagery associated with women.
Sarah and Abraham welcomed the three guests who brought them
news of their son by bringing them water for washing. Rebecca
makes her biblical appearance at a well—as does Rachel. Miriam is
associated with a well of water that sustained the Hebrews in the
wilderness.[15]

The covenantal ritual act of *brit r'chitzah* involves the parents
washing their daughter's feet. As in *brit milah* there is a blessing
before the act of covenant, and another afterward. The well-
known Hebrew (and Jewish summer camp) song *Ma-yim* is a

wonderful accompaniment to any ceremony that involves water. Guests can hum the melody during the washing.

Before the washing, the rabbi or leader says:

בָּרוּךְ אַתָּה יְיָ, אֱלֹהֵינוּ מֶלֶךְ הָעוֹלָם,
זוֹכֵר הַבְּרִית.

*Ba-ruch a-ta Adonai, Eh-lo-hei-nu meh-lech
ha-o-lam, zo-cher ha-b'rit.*

Blessed are You, *Adonai* our God, Ruler of the Universe, Who is mindful of the covenant.

After the washing, the parents say:

בָּרוּךְ אַתָּה יְיָ, אֱלֹהֵינוּ מֶלֶךְ הָעוֹלָם,
זוֹכֵר הַבְּרִית בִּרְחִיצַת רַגְלָיִם.

*Ba-ruch a-ta Adonai, Eh-lo-hei-nu meh-lech
ha-o-lam, zo-cher ha-b'rit bir-chi-tzat rag-la-yim.*

Blessed are You, Adonai our God, Ruler of the Universe, Who is mindful of the covenant through the washing of the feet.

Here is part of one *brit* ritual that revolves around candle-lighting. Parents, grandparents, and special guests each light one of six candles, corresponding to the six days of creation. Each person reads a prayer, poem, or one of the following six verses:

Your word is a lamp unto my feet, a light for my path. (Psalms 119:105)

You are the One who kindles my lamp: the Lord my God lights up my darkness. (Psalms 18:29)

Arise, shine, for your light has dawned, God's radiance shines upon you! (Isaiah 60:1)

May the Lord continue to shine upon you and God's brilliant presence surround you. (Isaiah 60:2)

Lift up your eyes all about you and behold: They have all gathered around you; your sons shall be brought from afar, your daughters like babes on your shoulders. (Isaiah 60:4)

May God be gracious to us and bless us. May God's face shine upon us. (Psalms 67:2)

The parents lift the baby to the light. The parents or rabbi say:

Light was the first of God's creations; as light appeared, it brought with it the possibility of all the wondrous things to follow. We, too, kindle lights— of hope, of understanding, of celebration, of countless new possibilities. This little daughter with whom we (these parents) have been blessed has already brought light into our (their) lives. May God's radiance continue to shine upon us (them). May she grow to be a source of light to all those around her. May her radiance illuminate the world. May the light of Torah and *mitzvot* be reflected in her shining deeds. And my she help bring the light of redemption to the world. Amen.[16]

The Torah can be used as a central symbol for another covenantal gesture. During a synagogue service, the baby is taken up to the Torah where her hands are placed on the scroll. These verses—or other readings—can be distributed among parents and honored guests:

Teach me, O Lord, the way of Your laws, and I shall treasure them always. (Psalm 119:33)

Give me understanding and I shall treasure your Torah; I shall keep it whole-heartedly. (Psalm 119:34)

Your hands have made us and fashioned us. Give us understanding that we may learn your commandments. (Psalm 119:73)

I will lift up my hands and reach out to your commandments which I love. Your laws will be on my lips. (Psalms 119:48)

As this little child has touched the Torah, so may the Torah touch her life, filling her mind with wisdom, and her heart with understanding. May we (these parents) who have brought her here today always strive to bring her close to the ways of God and of our people. May we (they) teach her Torah every day through our (their) words and our (their) deeds. May we (they) raise our (their) daughter to a joyful life of learning, and to deeds of loving kindness.[17]

The *three-fold wish* for Torah, marriage and good deeds, which is traditional at a *bris,* often follows the covenant ritual. It expresses the communal wish that this daughter will fulfill the three requirements of all Jews, now that she has become a member of the people of Israel.

כְּשֵׁם שֶׁנִּכְנְסָה לַבְּרִית,
כֵּן תִּכָּנֵס לְתוֹרָה וּלְחֻפָּה וּלְמַעֲשִׂים טוֹבִים.

K'shem she-nich-n'sah la-brit,
kein ti-ka-nes l'to-rah ul-chu-pah ul-ma-asim to-vim.

As she has entered the covenant, so may she enter a life devoted to Torah, *chupah* and the accomplishment of good deeds.

The following reading, which expounds on the three-fold wish, is popular in *brit* ceremonies of all kinds:

> We dedicate our child to Torah—to a never-ending fascination with study and learning. With a book, she will never be alone.
>
> We dedicate our child to *chupah*—to never-ending growth as a human being, capable of giving and receiving love. With loving family and friends, she will never be alone.
>
> We dedicate our child to *ma-asim tovim*—to a never-ending concern for family and community, justice and charity. While she cares for others, she will never be alone.[18]

Part III: The Name, Readings, and Conclusion

The baby's name is given in both Hebrew and (if different) in English. Anything you say about how you chose your daughter's name will be meaningful. Because most American Jews name children to honor the memory of a family member who has died, the loved one is often described and remembered. The Hebrew meaning or biblical story associated with a name might suggest a comment on how, for example, you hope your baby Esther will grow up to be as loyal to her people as the Esther of the Purim story.

There is an old custom of making an acrostic poem using the first letters of the baby's name in Hebrew. Each Hebrew letter is matched with a phrase or line from the Bible that also begins with that letter. The most common source for this is Psalm 119, but you can also try Song of Songs, Proverbs, other Psalms and the weekly Torah portion closest to your baby's birth. Sometimes acrostics are calligraphed and made into beautiful wall-hangings.

Among the traditional blessings that are used are *birkat hagomel*, the blessing said after recovery from an illness; and *hatov v'hamativ*, another traditional prayer recited on the occasion of a great blessing (see page 107). The biblical poem, *Shir Hashirim*, Song of Songs, is often quoted at *brit bat* ceremonies—as it is at weddings.[19] Some couples use the theme of the seven wedding blessings, the *sheva brachot,* and recite seven blessings from the wedding liturgy and other sources. Similarly, you might include a song or reading from your wedding.

Contemporary and original blessings, prayers, poems, wishes, and readings are added here. Sometimes the parents read a letter they have written to their baby daughter—something to be saved and read again, perhaps at her *bat mitzvah.*

Siblings old enough to participate might read something to their new sister at this point. Participation by grandparents is always very meaningful. These lines are sometimes read by grandparents at *brit bat* ceremonies.

> The crown of the aged are children's children
> And the glory of children are their parents.
> (Proverbs 17:6)

> In the Talmud there is the story of an old man who was seen planting a carob tree as the king rode by. "Old man," the king called, "how many years will it be before that tree bears fruit?" The old man replied, "Perhaps seventy years." The king asked, "Do you really expect to be alive to eat the fruit of that tree?" "No," answered the old man, "but just as I found the world fruitful when I was born, so I plant trees that later generations may eat thereof." (*Taanit* 23a)

To add spontaneity and even a touch of humor to your *brit bat,* you can also invite the company to offer their prayers and wishes for your new baby: "May her life be filled with laughter and people who love her," or "May she sleep through the night soon." If the group is small and the baby placid, you could even pass her from person to person as they speak. (And make sure the tape recorder is on!)

The end of the ceremony is signaled by the following three prayers, in any order or combination:

Shehecheyanu. This prayer of thanksgiving may be the most common element of all *brit bat* ceremonies.

בָּרוּךְ אַתָּה יְיָ, אֱלֹהֵינוּ מֶלֶךְ הָעוֹלָם,
שֶׁהֶחֱיָנוּ וְקִיְּמָנוּ וְהִגִּיעָנוּ לַזְּמַן הַזֶּה.

Ba-ruch a-ta Adonai, Eh-lo-hei-nu meh-lech ha-o-lam, sheh-heh-cheh-ya-nu v'ki-y'ma-nu v'hi-gi-a-nu la-z'man ha-zeh.

Holy One of Blessing Your Presence fills creation, You have kept us alive, You have sustained us, You have brought us to this moment.

Traditional blessing for a daughter. On Friday night, after the *Shabbat* table blessings are made, many families add a blessing for their children. Reciting these words for the first time at *brit bat* can start that practice in your family.

יְשִׂמֵךְ אֱלֹהִים כְּשָׂרָה רִבְקָה רָחֵל וְלֵאָה.

Y'si-mech Eh-lo-him k'Sa-rah, Riv-kah, Ra-chel v'Lei-ah.

May God make you as Sarah, Rebecca, Rachel and Leah.
(Some families add the names of their grand-mothers and great-grandmothers to this list of biblical matriarchs.)

The priestly or three-fold benediction concludes all sorts of Jewish rituals and services, and some parents include it in the *Shabbat* blessing of their children. If a rabbi is officiating, he or she most often recites this. If not, the parents or the entire company can say:

יְבָרֶכְךָ יְיָ וְיִשְׁמְרֶךָ,
יָאֵר יְיָ פָּנָיו אֵלֶיךָ וִיחֻנֶּךָּ,
יִשָּׂא יְיָ פָּנָיו אֵלֶיךָ וְיָשֵׂם לְךָ שָׁלוֹם.

Y'va-reh-ch'cha Adonai v'yish-m'reh-cha,
Ya-eir Adonai pa-nav ei-leh-kha vi-chu-neh-ka,
Yi-sah Adonai pa-nav ei-leh-kha v'ya-seim l'chah
sha-lom.

May God bless you and protect you.
May God's presence shine for you and be
favorable to you.
May God's face turn to you and give you peace.

Part IV: *S'udat Mitzvah*

According to Jewish law, major life-cycle events are celebrated
with a *s'udat mitzvah,* or meal celebrating the performance of a
commandment. Such meals traditionally begin with the blessing
over challah (*motzi*) and end with the prayers sung upon comple-
tion of a meal (*birkat hamazon*). (See *Simcha,* for more on the meal
and party.)

Sample List of Things You Need for a *Brit Bat*

Kosher wine and goblet for kiddush
Yarmulkes (skull caps or *kippot*) for guests
Candles and candlesticks
Prayer shawl or scarf, for swaddling the baby
Elijah's chair
Tape recorder, camera
Booklets
Phone off the hook

Brit Bat

All:

בְּרוּכָה הַבָּאָה בְּשֵׁם יְיָ.

B'ruchah ha-ba-ah b'sheim Adonai.
May she who enters be blessed in the name of Lord.

Parents:

Through this covenant we affirm our daughter's part in the covenant, the *brit,* made between God and Israel at Mount Sinai.

According to our tradition, the entire Jewish people, women and men, children and infants, born and unborn, were included in the revelation of the Law and in its affirmation. It has always been the central endeavor of each Jew in every generation to understand this covenant and to live meaningfully by it. We give thanks for the opportunity to bring our daughter into the covenant, and we say:

בָּרוּךְ אַתָּה יְיָ, אֱלֹהֵינוּ מֶלֶךְ הָעוֹלָם,
אֲשֶׁר קִדְּשָׁנוּ בְּמִצְוֹתָיו, וְצִוָּנוּ
לְהַכְנִיסָהּ בִּבְרִיתוֹ שֶׁל עַם יִשְׂרָאֵל.

כְּשֵׁם שֶׁנִּכְנְסָה לַבְּרִית,
כֵּן תִּכָּנֵס לְתוֹרָה וּלְחֻפָּה וּלְמַעֲשִׂים טוֹבִים.

Ba-ruch a-ta Adonai, Eh-lohei-nu me-lech ha-o-lam,
a-sher ki-d'sha-nu b'mitz-vo-tav, v'tzi–va-nu
l'hach-ni-sah biv-ri-to shel am Yis-ra-el.

K'shem sheh-nich-n'sah la-brit,
kein ti-ka-nes l'to-rah ul-chu-pah ul-ma-a-sim to-vim.

Blessed are you Lord our God Ruler of the Universe who has made us holy through your commandments and commanded us to bring our daughter into the covenant of Israel. As our daughter enters the covenant, so may she attain love of learning through the study of Torah, happiness in partnership with another human being, and the capacity to act toward others in honest, respectful, and ethical ways.

At our marriage, seven blessings were recited. Today in celebration of our joy at the birth of our daughter, we ask loved ones to recite seven blessings over this *kiddush* cup filled with wine, the symbol of joy.

Rabbi or guest:

בָּרוּךְ אַתָּה יְיָ, אֱלֹהֵינוּ מֶלֶךְ הָעוֹלָם, בּוֹרֵא פְּרִי הַגָּפֶן.

Ba-ruch a-ta Adonai, Eh-lo-hei-nu me-lech ha-o-lam,
bo-rei p'ri ha-ga-fen.
Praised are You, Lord our God, Source of the Universe,
Creator of the fruit of the vine.

Guest:

בָּרוּךְ אַתָּה יְיָ, אֱלֹהֵינוּ מֶלֶךְ הָעוֹלָם, יוֹצֵר הָאָדָם.

Ba-ruch a-ta Adonai, Eh-lo-hei-nu me-lech ha-o-lam,
yo-tzer ha-a-dam.
Praised are You, Lord our God, Source of the Universe,
Creator of humanity.

Guest:

בָּרוּךְ אַתָּה יְיָ, אֱלֹהֵינוּ מֶלֶךְ הָעוֹלָם,
אֲשֶׁר יָצַר אֶת הָאָדָם בְּצַלְמוֹ, בְּצֶלֶם דְּמוּת תַּבְנִיתוֹ,
וְהִתְקִין לוֹ מִמֶּנּוּ בִּנְיַן עֲדֵי עַד.
בָּרוּךְ אַתָּה יְיָ, יוֹצֵר הָאָדָם.

Brit Bat

Ba-ruch a-ta Adonai, Eh-lo-hei-nu me-lech ha-o-lam,
a-sher ya-tzar et ha-a-dam b'tzal-mo, b'tzeh-lem d'mut tav-ni-to,
v'hit-kin lo mi-meh-nu bin-yan a-dei ad.
Ba-ruch a-ta Adonai, yo-tzer ha-a-dam.

Praised are You, Lord our God, Source of the Universe, Who created human beings in Your image and Your likeness. And out of their very selves You prepared for them a perpetual spiritual being. Praised are You, our Lord, Creator of humanity.

Guest:

בָּרוּךְ אַתָּה יְיָ, אֱלֹהֵינוּ מֶלֶךְ הָעוֹלָם,
אֲשֶׁר קִדְּשָׁנוּ בְּמִצְוֹתָיו,
וְצִוָּנוּ עַל קִדּוּשׁ הַחַיִּים.

Ba-ruch a-ta Adonai, Eh-lo-hei-nu me-lech ha-o-lam,
a-sher ki-d'sha-nu b'mitz-vo-tav, v'tzi–va-nu
al ki-dush ha-cha-yim.
Praised are You, Lord our God, Source of the Universe,
Who commands us to sanctify life.

Guest:

בָּרוּךְ אַתָּה יְיָ, אֱלֹהֵינוּ מֶלֶךְ הָעוֹלָם,
זוֹכֵר הַבְּרִית וְנֶאֱמָן בִּבְרִיתוֹ וְקַיָּם בְּמַאֲמָרוֹ.

Ba-ruch a-ta Adonai, Eh-lo-hei-nu me-lech ha-o-lam,
zo-cheir ha-brit v'neh-eh-man biv-ri-to v'ka-yam b'ma-a-ma-ro.
Praised are You, Lord our God, Source of the Universe,
Who remembers the covenant and Who is steadfastly faithful
in Your covenant, keeping Your promise.

Brit Bat

Guest:

בָּרוּךְ אַתָּה יְיָ, מְשַׂמֵּחַ הוֹרִים עִם יַלְדֵיהֶם.

Ba-ruch a-ta Adonai, m'sa-mei-ach ho-rim im yal-dei-hem.
Praised are You, Lord our God, Source of the Universe,
Who causes parents to rejoice with their children.

Guest:

בָּרוּךְ אַתָּה יְיָ, אֱלֹהֵינוּ מֶלֶךְ הָעוֹלָם,
שֶׁהֶחֱיָנוּ וְקִיְּמָנוּ וְהִגִּיעָנוּ לַזְּמַן הַזֶּה.

Ba-ruch a-ta Adonai, Eh-lo-hei-nu meh-lech ha-o-lam,
sheh-heh-cheh-ya-nu v'ki-y'ma-nu v'hi-gi-a-nu la-z'man ha-zeh.
Praised are You, Lord our God, Source of the Universe,
for giving us life, for sustaining us,
for enabling us to reach this day.

Rabbi or guest:

This baby is named in loving remembrance of _____.
She lives in her. Let her life make _____ known to all
who see her.

May the one who blessed our mothers, Sarah, Rebecca, Leah,
and Rachel, and our fathers, Abraham, Isaac, and Jacob, bless these
parents and their newborn daughter. Her name shall be
_____. May her parents rear their daughter with love of
Torah and the performance of good deeds, and may they be
privileged to bring her to the marriage canopy. Let us say Amen.

Brit Bat

Rabbi or parents:

יְבָרֶכְךָ יְיָ וְיִשְׁמְרֶךָ,
יָאֵר יְיָ פָּנָיו אֵלֶיךָ וִיחֻנֶּךָּ,
יִשָּׂא יְיָ פָּנָיו אֵלֶיךָ וְיָשֵׂם לְךָ שָׁלוֹם.

Y'va-reh-ch'chah Adonai v'yish-m'reh-cha,
Ya-eir Adonai pa-nav ei-leh-kha vi-chu-neh-ka,
Yi-sah Adonai pa-nav ei-leh-kha v'ya-seim l'chah sha-lom.
May God bless you and protect you.
May God's presence shine for you and be favorable to you.
May God's face turn to you and give you peace.

Parents:

Bread is the symbol of sustenance and honey the sign of sweetness.
We dip the bread in honey in hope that our daily strivings will be
sweetened by our love for each other.

בָּרוּךְ אַתָּה יְיָ, אֱלֹהֵינוּ מֶלֶךְ הָעוֹלָם,
הַמּוֹצִיא לֶחֶם מִן הָאָרֶץ.

Ba-ruch a-ta Adonai, Eh-lo-hei-nu meh-lech ha-o-lam,
ha-mo-tzi leh-chem min ha-a-retz.
Praised are You, Lord our God, Source of the Universe,
Who provides us with the staff of life.[20]

Brit Ohel Shel Sarah Immeinu

Covenant of the Tent of Sarah Our Mother

Song:

Ma to-vu

(How wonderful are your tents, Jacob, Your dwelling places, Israel!)

The baby is brought in and everyone says:

בְּרוּכָה הַבָּאָה.

B'rucha ha-ba-ah.
We welcome you into our midst,
We greet you as you enter into the covenant of Israel.

Rabbi or guest:

As Abraham was father to the Jewish people, so Sarah was its mother. Our sages say, Abraham dealt with the men, and Sarah dealt with the women.

Abraham would bring men into relationship with God and his people through *milah* and the covenant of religious circumcision. Sarah would bring the women into relationship with God and her people through their coming into her tent and taking formal residence there.

In Sarah's name, we now perform this ceremony of *brit ohel*, and bring this daughter of the Jewish people into her tent and into the covenant of Sarah our mother.

Brit Ohel Shel Sarah Immeinu

We thank you Adonai, our God and universal Sovereign, Who has made us holy by means of the *mitzvot,* commanding us regarding the covenant of the tent.

The *sandeket* is seated in the center of the room. Four friends raise a scarf, shawl, or *tallit* over her head. The parents hand the baby to the *sandeket* and say:

בָּרוּךְ אַתָּה יְיָ, אֱלֹהֵינוּ מֶלֶךְ הָעוֹלָם,
אֲשֶׁר קִדְּשָׁנוּ בְּמִצְוֹתָיו, וְצִוָּנוּ
לְהַכְנִיסָה לִבְרִיתָהּ שֶׁל שָׂרָה אִמֵּנוּ.

Ba-ruch a-ta Adonai, Eh-lo-hei-nu me-lech ha-o-lam,
a-sher ki-d'sha-nu b'mitz-vo-tav, v'tzi–va-nu
l'hach-ni-sah liv-ri-tah shel Sa-rah i-mei-nu.

We are grateful to You, Adonai, for You are our God and Ruler of the Universe. You have made us holy by means of the *mitzvot,* commanding us to bring our daughter into the covenant of Sarah our mother.

All:

כְּשֵׁם שֶׁנִּכְנְסָה לַבְּרִית,
כֵּן תִּכָּנֵס לְתוֹרָה וּלְחֻפָּה וּלְמַעֲשִׂים טוֹבִים.

K'shem sheh-nich-n'sah la-brit,
kein ti-ka-nes l'to-rah ul-chu-pah ul-ma-a-sim to-vim.
As she has entered into the covenant, so may she enter into Torah, *chupah,* and a life of good deeds.

Sandeket wraps the scarf around the baby and hands her to her mother.

Brit Ohel Shel Sarah Immeinu

Rabbi or parents:

בָּרוּךְ אַתָּה יְיָ, אֱלֹהֵינוּ מֶלֶךְ הָעוֹלָם, בּוֹרֵא פְּרִי הַגָּפֶן.

Ba-ruch a-ta Adonai, Eh-lo-hei-nu me-lech ha-o-lam,
bo-rei p'ri ha-ga-fen.
We praise you, Adonai, our God and universal Ruler,
Who creates the fruit of the vine.

בָּרוּךְ אַתָּה יְיָ, אֱלֹהֵינוּ מֶלֶךְ הָעוֹלָם,
אֲשֶׁר קִדֵּשׁ אֶת הָאֹהֶל וְכָל הַנִּכְנָסִים בּוֹ,
תַּפְרִיחַ אֹהֶל צַדִּיקִים שֶׁנֵּדַע כִּי שָׁלוֹם הוּא.
בָּרוּךְ אַתָּה יְיָ, מוֹשִׁיבֵנוּ בָּאֳהָלִים.

Ba-ruch a-ta Adonai, Eh-lo-hei-nu me-lech ha-o-lam,
a-sher ki-deish et ha-o-hel v'chol ha-nich-na-sim bo,
taf-ri-ach o-hel tza-di-kim sheh-nei-da ki sha-lom hu.
Ba-ruch a-ta Adonai, mo-shi–vei-nu b'o-ha-lim.

We praise you Adonai, our God and Ruler, who has sanctified the
tent and all who enter it. Cause the tent of the righteous to
flourish, that we may know that it is all peace. We are grateful to
you Adonai, for making us dwell in tents.

Eloheinu, our God and our ancestors' God, sustain this child who is
to known in Israel as _____ and referred to in the world
as _____.

Parents:

Help us nurture her and encourage her to fulfill the blessing in her
name.

Brit Ohel Shel Sarah Immeinu

All:

May her mother and father rejoice and find delight in their daughter. Let her coming into the covenant of the tent be at a favorable time for God and for Israel.

Parents:

May we find joy in this moment and pleasure in all that she becomes. May our tiny daughter grow to be great.

Rabbi or guest:

יְבָרֶכְךָ יְיָ וְיִשְׁמְרֶךָ,

יָאֵר יְיָ פָּנָיו אֵלֶיךָ וִיחֻנֶּךָּ,

יִשָּׂא יְיָ פָּנָיו אֵלֶיךָ וְיָשֵׂם לְךָ שָׁלוֹם.

May Adonai turn to each of you
and to all of us
and make for us a life
of wholeness and hopefulness and peace. Amen.[21]

This material is from The New Jewish Baby Book *by Anita Diamant, © 1993, published by Jewish Lights Publishing, P.O. Box 237, Sunset Farm Offices, Woodstock, VT 05091. The publisher grants permission to you to copy this ceremony for distribution to your guests. All rights to other parts of this book are still covered by copyright and are reserved to the publisher.*

Brit Eidut

Covenant of Witnessing

Parents:

We come together today to welcome our new daughter into our family and into the covenant of the Jewish people. More than 3,000 years ago, our ancestors stood at Mount Sinai and entered into a covenant with God. Men, women, children, officers, elders, hewers of wood, and drawers of water all stood before the Lord and proclaimed:

כֹּל אֲשֶׁר דִּבֶּר יְיָ נַעֲשֶׂה וְנִשְׁמָע.

Kol a-sher di-ber Adonai na-a-seh v'nishma.
All the words the Lord has spoken we will do.

The covenant that was established at Sinai was made not only with our ancestors but with those who would follow. This covenant has been reaffirmed throughout the millennia. Today we, too, are gathered: men, women, and children, our heads and our elders and a drawer of water. For Sarah, as she came into the world, drew out of her mother the waters that had sustained her before her birth.

We too, through our words today, with this drawer of water in our midst, reaffirm the pledge of our ancestors:

כֹּל אֲשֶׁר דִּבֶּר יְיָ נַעֲשֶׂה וְנִשְׁמָע.

Kol a-sher di-ber Adonai na-a-seh v'nishma.
All that the Lord has spoken we will do and obey.

Brit Eidut

All:

בְּרוּכָה הַבָּאָה.

B'ru-chah ha-ba-ah.
May she who comes before us today be blessed.

Parents:

When Abraham and Sarah dwelt at Mamre, three men appeared at the door of their tent. As a sign of hospitality, they offered these travelers water to drink and to wash their feet. In the same way that Abraham and Sarah welcomed the travelers, so do we welcome our daughter into this world, with food and drink and the washing of her feet.

All:

בָּרוּךְ אַתָּה יְיָ, אֱלֹהֵינוּ מֶלֶךְ הָעוֹלָם,
שֶׁהֶחֱיָנוּ וְקִיְּמָנוּ וְהִגִּיעָנוּ לַזְּמַן הַזֶּה.

Ba-ruch a-ta Adonai, Eh-lo-hei-nu meh-lech ha-o-lam,
sheh-heh-cheh-ya-nu v'ki-y'ma-nu v'hi-gi-a-nu la-z'man ha-zeh.
Holy One of Blessing, Your Presence fills creation,
You have kept us alive, You have sustained us,
You have brought us to this moment.

Father:

As you begin your journey through life, we pray that you will find sustenance in *ma-yim cha-yim,* the living waters which Judaism offers to all who draw from the well of our tradition.

(Baby's feet are washed.)

Brit Eidut

Mother:

As your father and I stood under the shelter of this *tallit* to be joined together as husband and wife, so now do we encircle you within it as you enter the circle of our family. As we wrap you in this *tallit,* so may your life be wrapped in justice and righteousness. As we embrace you today, so may you embrace your tradition and your people.

Guest:

As your eyes are filled with wonder when you gaze at the world, so, too, may you be filled with wonder at the everyday miracles of life.

Guest:

As you startle to the world around you, so may you remain ever open both to the happiness and to the pain of those you encounter in the world.

Guest:

As you cry for food and comfort now, so may you one day cry out to correct the injustices of the world, to help clothe the naked and feed the hungry.

Guest:

As your hand tightly grasps your mother's finger, so may you grasp hold of learning and grow in knowledge and in wisdom.

Brit Eidut

Rabbi or parents:

אֱלֹהֵינוּ וֵאלֹהֵי אִמּוֹתֵינוּ, קַיֵּם אֶת הַיַּלְדָּה הַזֹּאת לְאָבִיהָ וּלְאִמָּהּ,
וְיִקָּרֵא שְׁמָהּ בְּיִשְׂרָאֵל _____ בַּת _____. יִשְׂמַח הָאָב
בְּיוֹצֵאת חֲלָצָיו, וְתָגֵל אִמּוֹ בִּפְרִי בִטְנָהּ. זֹאת הַקְּטַנָּה גְּדוֹלָה
תִּהְיֶה. כְּשֵׁם שֶׁנִּכְנְסָה לַבְּרִית, כֵּן תִּכָּנֵס לְתוֹרָה, וּלְחֻפָּה,
וּלְמַעֲשִׂים טוֹבִים.

*Eh-lo-hei-nu vei-lo-hei i-mo-tei-nu, ka-yeim et ha-yal-dah ha-zoht
l'a-vi-ha ul-i-mah, v'yi-ka-rei sh'mah b'yis-ra-el _____ bat
_____. Yis-mach ha-av b'yo-tzeit cha-la-tzav, v'ta-geil i-mo
bif-ri vit-nah. Zoht ha-k'ta-nah tih-yeh g'dolah. K'shem sheh-nich-n'sah
la-brit, kein ti-ka-nes l'to-rah ul-chu-pah ul-ma-a-sim to-vim.*

O God, God of all generations, sustain this child and let her be
known in the house of Israel as _____. May she bring us
(her parents) joy and happiness in the months and years to come.
As we have brougt her into the covenant of Torah today, so many
she enter into the study of Torah, the blessings of marriage, and the
performance of good deeds.

Baby's namesakes are remembered.

Grandparents:

Our God and God of all generations, we are grateful for new
beginnings, for the bond of new life that links one generation to
another. Thankful for the blessings of family, for the love and care
that brings meaning and happiness to our lives, we rejoice with
our children at the birth of their child, our grandchild.

May they grow together as a family in health and in strength, in
harmony, wisdom and love, their home filled with words of Torah
and acts of kindness.

Brit Eidut

May we be enabled to share in the joy of seeing this child grow into adulthood, a blessing to her family, her people and all humanity.

All:

יְבָרֶכְךָ יְיָ וְיִשְׁמְרֶךָ,

יָאֵר יְיָ פָּנָיו אֵלֶיךָ וִיחֻנֶּךָּ,

יִשָּׂא יְיָ פָּנָיו אֵלֶיךָ וְיָשֵׂם לְךָ שָׁלוֹם.

Y'va-reh-ch'chah Adonai v'yish-m'reh-cha,
Ya-eir Adonai pa-nav ei-leh-kha vi-chu-neh-ka,
Yi-sah Adonai pa-nav ei-leh-kha v'ya-seim l'chah sha-lom.
May God bless you and protect you.
May God's presence shine for you and be favorable to you.
May God's face turn to you and give you peace.[22]

Brit Shomrei Hamachzorim

Covenant of the Guardians of the Sacred Cycles

Rabbi or guest, as baby is taken to the chair of Elijah:

In Jewish tradition, Elijah the prophet represents the coming of the Messianic time. Elijah is present at the covenant whose sign is circumcision, at the *Pesach seder,* at the weekly *havdalah* ceremony, and he is known as the guardian of young children. The presence of Elijah at this covenant ceremony bids us look through the life of one child to the fulfillment of all life.

Guest:

"When the men saw that Moses was so long in coming down from the mountain, they went to Aaron and asked him to make them a god. He said to them, 'Take off the gold rings that are on the ears of your wives, your sons, and your daughters, and bring them to me.'

"And the men took off the gold rings that were in their ears, too impatient to notice that the women refused their gold." (Exodus 32:1–3)

Guest:

And so, the Holy Ancient One made the special relationship of women to *Rosh Chodesh.* Celebrating the new moon, women became guardians of the cycles of sacred time. They watched the light grow bright and diminish, and with the light, welcomed holy days and *Shabbat* days in their order. And the ebb and flow of the cycles within their bodies made them watchful, mindful of the gifts of heaven and earth.

This material is from The New Jewish Baby Book *by Anita Diamant, © 1993, published by Jewish Lights Publishing, P.O. Box 237, Sunset Farm Offices, Woodstock, VT 05091. The publisher grants permission to you to copy this ceremony for distribution to your guests. All rights to other parts of this book are still covered by copyright and are reserved to the publisher.*

Brit Shomrei Hamachzorim

Today, we publicly announce the birth of our new daughter and sister, welcoming her into this covenant our mothers have guarded in secret for so long.

Guest:

Ever since Avraham and Sarah began helping people discover God, this has been our vision: a world of men and women acting together, sharing the tasks needed to nurture and teach, to sustain and develop, that we reach the sacred time for which we wait.

בָּרוּךְ אַתָּה יְיָ, אֱלֹהֵינוּ מֶלֶךְ הָעוֹלָם,
שֶׁהֶחֱיָנוּ וְקִיְּמָנוּ וְהִגִּיעָנוּ לַזְּמַן הַזֶּה.

Ba-ruch a-ta Adonai, Eh-lo-hei-nu meh-lech ha-o-lam,
sheh-heh-cheh-ya-nu v'ki-y'ma-nu v'hi-gi-a-nu la-z'man ha-zeh.
Let us bless the Source of All, Who has
breathed life into us, sustained us,
and brought us to this precious moment.

AWAKENING OF THE FIVE SENSES

The mother lights two *Shabbat* candles and says:

Jewish women have been guardians of the light, kindling the spiritual flame for home and community since ancient times. With every *Shabbat* and holy day we remember the spark of spirit within, and manifest its beauty and wonder through lighting the fire of enlightenment, love, and peace.

בָּרוּךְ אַתָּה יְיָ, אֱלֹהֵינוּ מֶלֶךְ הָעוֹלָם, בּוֹרֵא מְאוֹרֵי הָאֵשׁ.

Ba-ruch a-ta Adonai, Eh-lo-hei-nu me-lech ha-o-lam,
bo-rei m'o-rei ha-eish.
Let us bless the Source of All,
Who creates the illuminations of the flame.[23]

Brit Shomrei Hamachzorim

The baby is given a taste of wine as her father says:

Why do we make a blessing over wine rather than water? Water, after all, symbolizes purity and was created directly by God. But wine involves a partnership between people and God. God provides the fruit that we transform into wine, which in turn alters our awareness and lifts our spirit.[24] May _____ take what God provides and make it holy.

בָּרוּךְ אַתָּה יְיָ, אֱלֹהֵינוּ מֶלֶךְ הָעוֹלָם, בּוֹרֵא פְּרִי הַגָּפֶן.

Ba-ruch a-ta Adonai, Eh-lo-hei-nu me-lech ha-o-lam,
bo-rei p'ri ha-ga-fen.
Let us bless the Source of All, Who creates
the fruit of the vine, symbol of our rejoicing.

The mother introduces and then sings a *niggun,* a wordless melody. The guests join in, and she says:

May the sound of blessing caress her ears and fill her heart.

בָּרוּךְ אַתָּה יְיָ, אֱלֹהֵינוּ מֶלֶךְ הָעוֹלָם, שׁוֹמֵעַ תְּפִלָּה.

Ba-ruch a-ta Adonai, Eh-lo-hei-nu me-lech ha-o-lam,
sho-mei-ah t'fi-lah.
Let us bless the Source of All,
Who listens to prayer from the heart.

Flowers are held beneath the baby's nose:

The sense of smell unites us with our breath and reminds us of the soul. May the fragrance of beauty and peace surround _____ as she remembers the wisdom of her soul.

Brit Shomrei Hamachzorim

בָּרוּךְ אַתָּה יְיָ, אֱלֹהֵינוּ מֶלֶךְ הָעוֹלָם, בּוֹרֵא עִשְׂבֵי בְשָׂמִים.

Ba-ruch a-ta Adonai, Eh-lo-hei-nu me-lech ha-o-lam,
bo-rei is-vei v'sa-mim.
Let us bless the Source of All,
Who creates the sweet-smelling grasses.

The baby's hands are washed with water that was collected from rain, lake, river, or seawater:

Brit is the covenant of our separate male and female realities, united and transformed by an awareness of Spirit.

With the purifying water from the Garden of Eden do we wash, wake, and welcome you into the covenant of women, guarding the sacred cycles of time. From the Source of Oneness are we all born. Remember and return often to the pure spring of life. Immerse yourself in truth, joy, and hope.

בָּרוּךְ אַתָּה יְיָ, אֱלֹהֵינוּ מֶלֶךְ הָעוֹלָם,
אֲשֶׁר קִדְּשָׁנוּ בְּמִצְוֹתָיו, וְצִוָּנוּ עַל נְטִילַת יָדָיִם.

Ba-ruch a-ta Adonai, Eh-lo-hei-nu me-lech ha-o-lam,
a-sher ki-d'sha-nu b'mitz-vo-tav, v'tzi-va-nu
al n'ti-lat ya-da-yim.
Let us bless the Source of All, Who guides us
on the path of holiness and directs us
to lift up our hands through washing with water.

Naming:

מִי שֶׁבֵּרַךְ אִמּוֹתֵינוּ שָׂרָה, רִבְקָה, רָחֵל, וְלֵאָה
וּמִרְיָם הַנְּבִיאָה וַאֲבִגַיִל, וְאֶסְתֵּר הַמַּלְכָּה בַּת אֲבִיחַיִל
הוּא יְבָרֵךְ אֶת הַנַּעֲרָה הַנְּעִימָה הַזֹּאת

Brit Shomrei Hamachzorim

וְיִקָּרֵא שְׁמָה בְּיִשְׂרָאֵל _____ בַּת _____
בְּמַזָּל טוֹב וּבִשְׁעַת בְּרָכָה.
וִיגַדְּלָהּ בִּבְרִיאוּת, שָׁלוֹם וּמְנוּחָה
לְתוֹרָה וּלְחֻפָּה וּלְמַעֲשִׂים טוֹבִים.
וִיזַכֶּה אֶת אָבִיהָ וְאֶת אִמָּהּ לִרְאוֹת בְּשִׂמְחָתָהּ
בְּבָנִים וּבָנוֹת עֹשֶׁר וְכָבוֹד
דְּשֵׁנִים וְרַעֲנַנִּים יְנוּבוּן בְּשֵׂיבָה
וְכֵן יְהִי רָצוֹן וְנֹאמַר אָמֵן.

Mi sheh-bei-rach i-mo-tei-nu Sa-rah, Riv-kah, Ra-chel, v'Lei-ah
u-Mir-yam ha-n'vi-ah, va'A-vi-ga-yil, v'Es-ter bat A-vi-cha-yil
hu y'va-reich et ha-na-a-rah ha-n'i-mah ha-zoht
v'yi-ka-rei sh'mah b'Yisrael
_____ *bat* _____ *v'* _____
b'ma-zal tohv u-vish-at b'racha.
Vi-gad'lah biv-ri-ut, sha-lohm um-nu-chah
l'torah ul-chu-pah ul-ma-a-sim tovim.
Vi-za-keh et a-vi-ha v'et i-mah lir-oht b'sim-cha-tah
b'va-nim u-va-noht, oh-sher v'cha-vohd
d'shei-nim v'ra-a-na-nim y'nu-vun b'sei-vah
v'chein y'hi ra-tzohn v'no-mar a-mein.

May God Who blessed our mothers
Sarah, Rebecca, Rachel, and Leah
Miriam the prophet and Avigayil
bless this beautiful little girl
and let her name be called in Israel
_____ daughter of _____ and _____
at this favorable moment of blessing.
May she be raised in health, peace, and tranquillity
To study Torah
To stand under the *chupah* (if that is her choice)
To do good deeds.

_____

165

Brit Shomrei Hamachzorim

May her parents merit to see her happy
blessed with children, wealth, and honor
peaceful and content in their old age.
May this be God's will.
Amen.

Parents explain the meaning of the baby's name.

Let us bless the Source of All, Who has brought us to a life of
service and given us the opportunity to introduce our daughter to
the covenant of the sacred cycles.[26]

Brit Banot

As the baby is brought into the room all rise and say:

Who is she who shines through like the dawn, Beautiful as the sun, radiant as the moon? (Song of Songs 6:10)

The following lines may be read by the rabbi or leader, by selected guests, responsively, or by the entire company:

Look to Abraham your father and to Sarah who bore you. (Isaiah 51:2)

God appeared to Abram and said to him: I am *El Shaddai;* walk wholeheartedly before Me. Then I will establish a covenant between Me and you and your descendants who will come after you: A covenant in which I will be your God and your children's God, forever and ever. (Genesis 17:1, 7)

(The baby is held at the center of a large *tallit.* Each of the four corners is held by parents and honored guests and is folded around the baby.)

How precious is Your constant love, O God; You shelter us under Your wings. (Psalms 36:8)

Let all my being praise the Lord Who is clothed in splendor and majesty; wrapped in light like a garment, unfolding the heavens like a curtain. You send forth Your spirit and there is creation. You renew the face of the earth. (Psalms 104:1, 30)

O you who dwell in the shelter of the Most High and abide in the protection of Shaddai. My God, in Whom I trust, will cover you; you will find shelter under God's wings.

Rabbi or parents:

Brit Banot

Our God and God of our ancestors, we thank You for the gift of this child (our daughter) whom we welcomed into God's covenant today. May she grow to maturity embraced by God's love and the love of all who know her. May the *Shechinah*, God's sheltering presence, be with her always. May the words of Torah surround her. Clothed in majesty and honor, may she always look to the future with joy.

Parents:

בָּרוּךְ אַתָּה יְיָ, אֱלֹהֵינוּ מֶלֶךְ הָעוֹלָם,
אֲשֶׁר קִדְּשָׁנוּ בְּמִצְוֹתָיו, וְצִוָּנוּ
לְהַכְנִיסוֹ בִּבְרִיתוֹ שֶׁל אַבְרָהָם אָבִינוּ וְשָׂרָה אִמֵּנוּ.

Ba-ruch a-ta Adonai, Eh-lo-hei-nu me-lech ha-o-lam,
a-sher ki-d'sha-nu b'mitz-vo-tav, v'tzi–va-nu
l'hach-ni-so biv-ri-to shel Av-ra-ham a-vi-nu v'Sa-rah i-mei-nu.
O Lord our God, Ruler of the Universe, Who sanctifies us
with Your *mitzvot* and commanded us
to bring our daughter in to the Covenant of
Abraham our father and Sarah our mother.

All:

כְּשֵׁם שֶׁנִּכְנְסָה לַבְּרִית,
כֵּן תִּכָּנֵס לְתוֹרָה וּלְחֻפָּה וּלְמַעֲשִׂים טוֹבִים.

K'sheim sheh-nich-n'sah la-brit,
kein ti-ka-nes l'to-rah ul-chu-pah ul-ma-a-sim to-vim.
As she has entered the Covenant,
so may she attain the blessings of Torah,
marriage under the *chupah,* and a life of good deeds.

Brit Banot

Rabbi:

בָּרוּךְ אַתָּה יְיָ, אֱלֹהֵינוּ מֶלֶךְ הָעוֹלָם, בּוֹרֵא פְּרִי הַגָּפֶן.

Ba-ruch a-ta Adonai, Eh-lo-hei-nu me-lech ha-o-lam,
bo-rei p'ri ha-ga-fen.
Praised are You Lord our God, Ruler of the Universe,
Who creates the fruit of the vine.

Our God and God of our ancestors, sustain this child. We declare
that her name shall be _____ daughter of _____
and _____.

May the father rejoice in his offspring; may her mother delight in
the fruit of her womb. As it is written: Gladness and joy shall abide
with her; thanksgiving and happy song. (Isaiah 51:36)

God makes a covenant with her, a covenant of life and peace.
(Malachi 2:5)

As it is written: This is the child for whom I prayed; God has
granted my desire. (I Samuel 1:27)

O praise our God, Whose goodness endures forever

May this little one _____ become great.

As she has entered the Covenant, so may she attain the blessings of
Torah, marriage under the *chupah,* and a life of good deeds.

Let us say Amen.[26]

Hiddur Mitzvah
Beautiful Touches

The urge to decorate and beautify our surroundings—especially for celebrations—seems a basic human impulse. Jewish law codified this joyful instinct with a rabbinic principle. According to *hiddur mitzvah* (*hiddur* means beautifying) when a physical object is needed to fulfill a *mitzvah* or commandment, the object should be as lovely as possible. So although it is perfectly kosher to bless wine in a paper cup, it is considered praiseworthy to put the wine in a beautiful goblet that was made expressly for *kiddush,* or sanctification. In the past, communal ritual objects were used by individual families—synagogues had elaborate chairs used for the prophet Elijah's ceremonial seat, and even the clamps and knives used for *brit milah* were decorated. Today, the objects you use for your baby's *brit* ceremony can become family heirlooms that will recall powerful memories for you and hold a strong fascination for your child as he or she grows. Likewise, the songs and words you use and remember will always have a kind of magic.

Objects

BOOKLETS. It is becoming increasingly common to provide a printed guide or booklet to accompany your *brit,* or any of the other ceremonies mentioned in this book. The explanations, translations, responsive readings, poems, or prayers you provide can help make all your guests—regardless of their background—feel informed and involved. Copies of the booklet will become family treasures.

Booklets can be simple or elaborate, a single photocopied sheet or a pamphlet of many pages. Sometimes the cover is a copy of the birth announcement. The booklet can include the entire ceremony, or it can simply provide information about the baby's name or explanations of customs you have incorporated, including an announcement of *tzedakah* (righteous giving or charity) donated in honor of the birth. Often the booklet contains the *birkat hamazon,* the blessings that are sung after eating.

There is, however, a drawback to handing out booklets that are a complete "program" of the ceremony: The shuffling of paper and the act of reading can distance guests from the proceedings. Life-cycle rituals are not the same as worship services. They are once-in-a-lifetime events meant to be experienced and witnessed.

CANDLES. Although few Americans are familiar with the custom, lighting candles at a *brit milah* is a common practice in Jewish communities around the world. The practice may date back to times when circumcision was performed in defiance of anti-Semitic edicts, and candles burning in the window of a Jewish home signaled friends and neighbors to come celebrate a clandestine *bris.*[1] Because lighting *Shabbat* candles is traditionally a woman's *mitzvah,* candles seem appropriate at ceremonies for daughters as well (see *Brit Bat*).

Light, a universal symbol of both the divine presence and of the human soul, is used in many ways at ceremonies for new babies. Sometimes a single candle is lit for the baby—two for twins. But in some parts of the world, thirteen candles are lit, because there are thirteen references to *brit milah* in the book of Genesis.[2]

The mother and father might each light one candle, and then, using their lit tapers, light a third candle for the new life in their family. For some parents, this ceremony marks the addition of a new candle to their weekly Friday night *Shabbat* ritual.

Candles may be placed anywhere in the room. A circle of light surrounding the parents and baby makes a powerful visual statement, and the honor of lighting candles can be given to various family members or friends. Use white *Shabbat* candles, braided *havdalah* candles, or a rainbow of colored candles—whatever you like.

Candles can be lit in silence or with a reading, like this one for parents:

There is a new light in our hearts and in our
home.
These candles celebrate the birth of our child.
Out of the creative darkness of the womb s/he
has come.
These candles celebrate her/his emergence
into light.
Blessed is the woman who bears a child, for she
knows how love covers pain.
Blessed is the man who fathers a child, for he
makes a bridge between earth and heaven.
Child of light, you know not yet the love and
joy overflowing from our hearts.[3]

ELIJAH'S CHAIR. The decoration of the *kisei shel Eliyahu*—
Elijah's chair—is a *brit milah* custom practiced by Jews worldwide.
The prophet Elijah, who is associated with the coming of the
Messiah, is similarly welcomed at *brit bat* celebrations today.

Spanish Jews drape the prophet's chair with fabrics of purple
and gold and leave a prayer book or *chumash* (the book version of
the Torah) on it. In other nations, Jews place a beautiful pillow or
brightly colored scarves on the chair. Another option is to cover
Elijah's chair with a piece of cloth that will later be made into a
tallit or *wimpel* (Torah binder). Similarly, the baby can be brought
into the room wrapped in the *wimpel* fabric (see below). Other
coverings for the chair might include your *chupah* cover (the top of
the wedding canopy) or a shawl that belonged to a great-
grandmother or beloved aunt who did not live to see the birth of
your baby. (See *Brit Milah* for more about Elijah.)

CLOTHING. Some communities favor white clothing for the
baby, while others dress the baby in colorful attire—the choice is
yours. It is customary for baby boys to wear a tiny *kippah* (skull
cap), which might be a special gift from a relative or friend who
crochets. Because women in many liberal congregations now wear
kippot as well, the custom is sometimes used in ceremonies for
baby girls as well. If you wish your guests to wear *kippot,* as is
customary, have several on hand.

CHUPAH. Sometimes parents will raise their own marriage canopy to welcome the newest member of the family. Family members and special friends can be honored by holding the poles during the *brit*. The presence of older siblings under the canopy can provide a much-needed moment of recognition for older brothers and sisters who might feel lost in all the commotion surrounding the new baby.

KIDDUSH CUP. *Hiddur mitzvah* applies to any object used in the ceremony. Because wine is blessed at virtually all *brit milah* and *brit bat* ceremonies, a cup will be necessary—the more beautiful the better. A distinctive goblet, a gift for the baby, might be unveiled at the ceremony, or the *kiddush* cup you used at your wedding might be filled as the following words are recited:

> This cup is the vessel of our hopes. We first drank from it under our wedding *chupah*. Today, it is filled with the new wine of a life just begun and from it we taste the sweetness of the great joy that _____ has brought us.

WIMPELS. In Eastern Europe, the cloth used to wrap an infant at his *brit milah* was later cut and sewn into a long strip for use as a Torah binder—in Yiddish, *wimpel*, pronounced "vimpel." (The Hebrew is *mappah*.)

The *wimpel* was presented as a family's gift to the synagogue, usually in time for use on the *Shabbat* closest to the child's first birthday. The Torah binder then belonged to the synagogue and would be used when the child reached *bar mitzvah*. In Germany and Italy, *wimpels* were painted or embroidered with the child's name, his parents' names, the date of birth, and a Hebrew inscription and were lavishly decorated with all sorts of images, including (in some communities) the baby's zodiac sign.

The *wimpel* is enjoying a modest revival today, for daughters as well as for sons. To make one, use a piece of cotton, silk, linen, or wool as a swaddling blanket or as a covering for a table or pillow used at the *brit*. Later, create a strip seven to eight inches wide and nine to twelve feet long and decorate it as you wish, noting the child's name and birth date.[4]

Borrowing from the idea of the *wimpel,* a piece of fabric or clothing used during the *brit* ceremony can later be incorporated into an *atarah,* the neckpiece on a *tallit,* or prayer shawl. That *tallit* can be given to the child at the time of his or her *bar* or *bat mitzvah,* and perhaps (years later) even used for a *chupah.*

Music

Music, song, and dance are traditional at Jewish celebrations. Although the Ashkenazic repertoire is not nearly as rich as the Sephardic, there are particular melodies American Jews associate with baby rituals.

Siman Tov Umazal Tov (Good Fortune and Good Luck) is the all-purpose song of rejoicing, proclaiming the event as a source of joy for those gathered and for all Israel. Because of the prophet Elijah's association with *brit milah, Eliyahu Hanavi* is often sung during a *bris.* Now that Elijah's chair is a common feature at *brit bat,* it seems appropriate to sing the prophet's song there as well.

Hinnei Ma Tov Umah Na-im (How Good and Pleasant It Is) is another favorite at baby celebrations, because it extols the pleasure of community. *Yevarech'cha Adonai Mitziyon* (May the Lord Bless You from Zion) is popular because it includes the line, "May you see your children's children." Cantors are probably your best resource when researching music for a ceremony. Even if you do not belong to a synagogue, many cantors are glad to share their expertise. You might also ask people you know for the names of Jewish music professionals in your community.[5]

Words

It is customary in some circles to offer a *d'var torah,* a word of Jewish learning, on an occasion as important as a birth. Sometimes this is part of the ceremony and sometimes it is presented later, during the celebratory meal. Traditionally, such a *droshah* (teaching) is based on the baby's name, the weekly Torah portion, or a section from Proverbs, Song of Songs, or the Book of Psalms.[6] According to one tale, a Psalm is given to each Jew for every year of life. Thus, if you are thirty years old, Psalm 31 is yours to study and enjoy. The first Psalm is given to newborns.[7]

But for the *brit* ceremony itself, nothing is more meaningful or more powerful than your own thoughts and feelings about the birth of your child. The most common inspiration for parents' comments are stories and memories about the person or people for whom your baby is named. To recount these stories, you don't have to be a poet or a Jewish scholar. If you say what's in your heart, there won't be a dry eye in the house.

To help you find just the right words, this book contains dozens of prayers, poems, and creative translations of traditional texts. Several of these appear in the chapters on *Brit Milah, Brit Bat* and *Adoption.* So even if you are planning a *brit milah,* take time to glance through the other sections.

What follows are several original poems, as well as readings and prayers that have passed into common usage at *brit* ceremonies.

A BLESSING

May your eyes sparkle with the light of Torah,
and your ears hear the music of its words.
May the space between each letter of the scrolls
bring warmth and comfort to your soul.
May the syllables draw holiness from your heart,
and may this holiness be gentle and soothing
to you and all God's creatures.
May your study be passionate,
and meanings bear more meanings
until Life itself arrays itself to you
as a dazzling wedding feast.
And may your conversation,
even of the commonplace,
be a blessing to all who listen to your words
and see the Torah glowing on your face.

Danny Siegel[8]
Brachot 17a and Eruvin 54a

BLESSING THE CHILDREN

The mother and father place their hands on their
children's heads and recite:

For the boys—

May you be as Ephraim and Menasheh
    of whom we know nothing
    but their names
    and that they were Jews.
And may you be as all Jews
    whose names are lost
    as witnesses to God's care,
    love, and presence.
Remember them in your words,
    and live *Menschlich* lives
    as they lived *Menschlich* lives.

For the girls—

May you be as Sarah, Rivka, Rachel, and Leah,
    whose names and deeds
    are our inheritance;
    who bore us, raised us,
    guided and taught us
    that a touch
    is a touch of Holiness,
    and a laugh is prophecy;
    that all that is ours,
    is theirs;
    that neither Man or Woman alone
    lights the sparks of Life,
    but only both together,
    generating light and warmth
    and singular humanity.

Danny Siegel[9]

BLESSING THE CHILDREN

May you be as Henrietta Szold,
raising and building,
that your People
need not suffer
the loneliness of pain.

May you be as Herzl and Ben Yehuda,
stung and raving with visions
for the sake of Israel
and the Jews.

And may our family be together
as Sholom Aleichem and his children,
passing on our stories to each other
with a radiance of joy
and a laugh of love.

Danny Siegel[10]

ABOVE ALL, TEACH THIS NEWBORN CHILD

Above all, teach this newborn child to touch,
to never stop,
to feel how fur is other than the leaf or cheek
to know through these hands diamond from
    glass,
Mezuzah from anything else in the world
The same with *Challah* and a book.

As the baby grows,
teach this child to embrace the shoulders
    of another
before sadness brings them inhumanly low,
to stroke the hair softly of one younger who
    is weeping,
one older who cries.

Let these hands be a gentle Yes
When Yes is the Truth,
and gently, a No when No is right.
Whatever these fingers touch—
may they be for new holiness and blessing,
for light, life, and love.

Amen.

Danny Siegel[11]

On the Birth of a Brother or Sister

Welcome to the world!
You are so small and you cry so much.
People make such a fuss.
I don't know why.

I think I will take care of you
And play with you sometimes,
Because I am big.
I hope you like me.
I hope you learn to say my name.

Sometimes you will pull my hair
But I will not mind,
Unless you pull it very hard.
Sometimes I will fight with you
Because you want my toys.
I hope you will not mind.

Sometimes I will be angry at Mom and Dad
Because they spend too much time with you.
I hope you will forgive me.

Thank you, God, for little fingers and tiny toes
Just like mine.
Thank you God, for arms that are large enough
    to hold one more.

Thank you, God, for a love that is big enough
To include my brother/sister and ME!

Sandy Eisenberg Sasso[12]

So you have been born

So you have been born, ben Sarah★
your first great birth:

from water to air
from water to land
from the mikvah/womb to the midwife's hands.

The Great-Moon-Mother-of-Miracles
brought you to birth

(from the dark, where the secret light is sown)
to sunlight!
moonlight!
candlelight!!!

By this light, with God's aid be born
again and again
Shanah shanah [year after year]
chodesh chodesh [month after month]
chag chag [holiday after holiday]
shabbat shabbat [Sabbath after Sabbath]
nes nes [miracle after miracle]

Great-Moon-Mother-of-Miracles,
multiply miracles
bless with your light the *yoledet*,★★ her
child
With wave upon wave of your light,
renew, replenish your daughter,
your daughter's child.

Aviva bat Beilah/slr[13]

★ *For a daughter, "bat Sarah."*
★★ *A* yoledet *is a woman who has recently given birth.*

CHILD AT THE GATE OF COVENANT

So recently an expert
on the universe,
the furrow from his nose
down to his lips
drawn by an angel
at the gate of birth,
the child, ancient
as the earth, endowed
with words his mouth
can't yet pronounce,
watched by Elijah,
dabbed with wine,
a party to the covenant,
his parents' stories soon
to be like ancient history:
he is gently disengaged
from pleasures of eternity,
and entered in the rolls
of life, the surge
of worldly business
like a sea swell
rolling under him,
to bear him up,
the teaching life
will soon enough
extract from him
tucked almost inaccessibly
away, behind the furrow,
deep inside.

Joel Rosenberg[14]

For the Naming of a Girl-child

Between a boy-child and a girl-child,
  only the latter has the soul's shape.
  For he will grow up,
  huffing and thrusting,
  with a plate of armor
  'round his life-breath,
  and, if fortunate, will watch
  this outer veil grow limber
  and translucent, to reveal
  his true shape with advancing age.
  If not for circumcision,
  he would suffocate.

    But she
  was husked in heaven from the start.
  Her natural radiance will be
  tempered by the world.
  And she, more conscious of her exile,
  will accept the ring someday
  beneath the canopy, as if
  in willful diminution of her light
  (as once, of old, the moon),
  and she will take the future
  in her womb, as if in trust.
  And she, the nurse and blueprint
  of the universe, is Israel
  and the Presence quite enough,
  and so the contour of the soul,
  right from the first day of her life.
  No sign of covenant is made in her:
  she is a sign herself already,
  for, waxing and waning with the moon,
  she is the imprint of a world
  that breathes—her own small breath
  a tiny metronome by which
  the world is tuned.

Joel Rosenberg[15]

BRUCHA HABA'AH—BLESSED SHE COMES

Welcome Woman-Child
    Newborn guardian
    of the sacred gift
    of cycles and seasons.
Within and all around you
Be witness to the rhythms of
    surrender and renewal
    faith and love
Awaken intuition and knowledge
to the indwelling presence—*Shechinah*

We welcome you
    into the world
    into your family
    into your people

May you know from your early days
    how we travel through the dance
    of dark and light
    slavery and freedom
    wandering and revelation
    planting and harvest
    new moon and full moon
from the illumined place of now
    the sanctuary in time—*Shabbat*

Hanna Tiferet Siegel[16]

POEM OF THANKSGIVING

With all my heart, with all my soul, with all
    my might
I thank You, God, for the gift of this
    wonderful child.
I thank You for a healthy pregnancy, a safe
delivery and a speedy recovery.

With all my heart, with all my soul, with all
    my might
I pray for the continued health of this child.
I pray for her to be strong in mind and body,
To grow steadily and sturdily in a home filled
    with joy.
I pray for her to become a person who greets
    the world
With passion, courage, humility, humor
    and patience.

With all my heart, with all my soul, with all
    my might
I pray for God to watch over me and my family.
I pray for the ability to love and nurture
    this child
To provide for her and to educate her,
To understand her and to allow her the freedom
    to grow.

adapted by Rabbi Maggie Wenig
from the poem by Rabbi Judith Shanks[17]

Parents' Blessing

May you live to see your world fulfilled,
May your destiny be for worlds still to come,
And may you trust in generations past and
    yet to be.

May your heart be filled with intuition
and your words be filled with insight.
May songs of praise ever be upon your tongue
and your vision be on a straight path before you.
May your eyes shine with the light of holy words
and your face reflect the brightness of the heavens.
May your lips speak wisdom
and your fulfillment be in righteousness
even as you ever yearn to hear the words
of the Holy Ancient One of Old.

Brachot 17a[18]

Every person born into this world represents something new, something that never existed before, something original and unique. It is the duty of every person in Israel to know and consider that he is unique in the world in his particular character, and that there has never been someone like him before. For if there had been someone like him before, there would be no need for him to be in the world. Every single person is a new thing in the world and is called upon to fulfill his particularity in the world.

adapted from a passage by Martin Buber

BLESSINGS

In every birth, blessed is the wonder
In every creation, blessed is the new beginning
In every child, blessed is life.
In every hope, blessed is the potential.
In every transition, blessed is the beginning.
In every existence, blessed are the possibilities
In every love, blessed are the tears.
In every life, blessed is the love.[19]

PARENTS' PRAYER

We dedicate our child to Torah,
To a never-ending fascination with study
    and learning
With a book, s/he will never be alone.

We dedicate our child to *chupah,*
To never-ending growth as a human being
    capable of giving and receiving love.
With a loving mate, s/he will never be alone.

We dedicate our child to *ma'asim tovim,*
To a never-ending concern for family and
    community, justice and charity.
If s/he cares for others, s/he will never be alone.

We pray for wisdom to help our child achieve
    these things,
To fulfill the needs of his/her mind and body,
To be strong when s/he needs us to be strong,
To be gentle when s/he needs us to be gentle,
But always there when s/he needs us.
The birth of a child is a miracle of renewal.
We stand together this day, contemplating
    a miracle.[20]

PART
4

Simcha — Joy

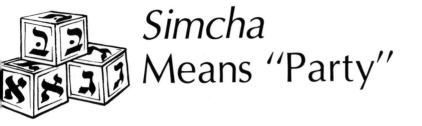

Simcha
Means "Party"

The birth of a Jewish baby is always occasion for a celebration. The word *simcha* means joy, and it also means party. If you're going to have a ceremony to welcome your new son or daughter to the Jewish people, you're going to have a party, a *simcha*, complete with food and drink.

Partying is not just part of Jewish culture; it is embedded in traditional Jewish law. Indeed, *halachah* requires that all major life-cycle events, including weddings, *bar* and *bat mitzvah*, and *brit milah*, feature a a *s'udat mitzvah*—a commanded meal. As *brit bat* has become a feature of Jewish observance in America, the tradition of the *s'udat* has been extended to include this celebration as well.

A meal to honor the birth of a new baby can be a lavish sit-down affair at a catering hall, but these days informal choices are more popular. A *s'udat mitzvah* can be a bagel-and-lox breakfast after a morning *bris;* dessert and coffee at the *oneg Shabbat* after a Friday night synagogue ceremony; or a buffet lunch after a *Shabbat* morning *brit bat*. Because of most new parents' states of mind and energy levels, this party is often quite simple.

A *bris* is held only eight days after birth, so formal invitations are very rare. Most parents call friends and relatives to let them know the time and place for the ceremony. For the most part, that same lack of formality also holds for *brit bat* ceremonies.

Food

It is customary to start the meal with a blessing over a large, braided loaf of *challah,* a rich egg bread served on *Shabbat* and other occasions. There is usually at least one ceremonial glass of wine for a blessing.

Traditional foods served to celebrate a birth all suggest fertility; chickpeas, eggs, and olives—round "seeds." The olive, which was also a source of heat and light in the ancient world, embodies the warmth and joy a baby brings. Parsley, or any green vegetable, signifies a wish for the earth's continued bounty; pastries, cakes and cookies signify the sweetness of the occasion. Persian Jews offer a plate of apples, a symbol of easy labor and delivery, to young couples in attendance at the meal.[1]

Some people bake and freeze all the goodies for their baby's *simcha* well in advance. For parents and grandparents-to-be who enjoy baking, this can provide a useful outlet for the nervous energy that comes with waiting. Likewise, if you plan to have a catered meal, you might want to contact a caterer and make menu selections in advance. (If you find yourself with time to spare before the baby comes, it's a good idea to compile a guest list complete with phone numbers, too.)

In the best of all possible worlds, new parents are not the ones to organize and host their own *s'udat mitzvah*. In Sephardic communities, paying for the food and drink at a *brit* is considered an honor assumed by the *sandek,* the person who holds the baby during the circumcision. Similarly, the *s'udat* is often a gift from grandparents.

Close friends and relatives may offer to bring food to the *s'udat mitzvah,* which can add a very *haimish,* or homey, touch to the gathering. But if you really prefer to do it yourself or let a caterer take care of everything, ask people who offer to help for a rain check in the form of a covered-dish meal, to be delivered during your first weeks at home with the new baby.

In any event, remember that your guests are coming to share your joy and see the baby—not to eat a gourmet meal.

Kashrut

Even for people who don't observe *kashrut* (the laws that govern what Jews eat), following its basic rules at the *simcha* can avoid embarrassment, discomfort, or hunger for observant guests—not to mention family feuds. The *mohel,* cantor, or rabbi who officiates at your ceremony may not be able to partake of the feast if you do not honor the dietary laws. Generally, if your party takes place in a synagogue, you will be required to serve a kosher meal.

Kashrut is not—as some people believe—an ancient health code. It is a way of sanctifying the basic human need for food. The laws of *kashrut* are based on specific proscriptions in the Bible against eating birds of prey and fish lacking fins or gills. The separation of fish and meat is an elaboration on the Torah's command not to "boil a kid in its mother's milk."

Briefly, *kashrut* permits the following foods: all vegetables and fruits, fish with fins and scales (no shellfish or bottom-feeding fish), domestic fowl, and animals that chew a cud and have split hooves. For meat to be kosher, the animal must also be killed according to specific ritual laws by someone who recites a blessing. Then the meat is soaked and salted to remove all traces of blood. Finally, meat and milk products are not eaten at the same meal and must be kept separate. Thus, *milchig* (dairy) and *fleishig* (meat) foods are not cooked in the same pots or served on the same dishes. The customary waiting period between consumption of meat and milk varies according to custom.

Probably the easier way to prepare or organize a kosher meal on your own is to keep it vegetarian, or *milchig.* To find a kosher caterer, ask for recommendations from friends, family, or your rabbi. Failing that, consult the "Yellow Pages" under "Catering." In larger cities and towns, there is usually a special listing of kosher services. "Kosher style" means the restaurant or caterer specializes in Jewish-identified foods, like knishes and lox, but it is usually a signal that the food is not really kosher.

Blessings and Toasts

Before beginning the meal, you can honor a special guest by asking him or her to say the *motzi,* the blessing over bread, traditionally made over a large braided loaf of *challah,* or the *kiddush,* the blessing over wine.

If your *brit* ceremony did not include an opportunity for guests to offer their blessings and wishes for the baby and family, the meal is a good time to do this. As always, it's a good idea to ask one or two guests to think in advance about what they might like to say. If there was no appropriate time for an older sibling to participate during the *brit* ceremony, the baby's brother(s) or sister(s) might be given a chance to shine here. If siblings are old enough, they could compose a few words of welcome for the new baby.

You can even appoint a "master of ceremonies" (perhaps an uncle or sister who has a snappy comeback for every occasion) to make merry, start songs, call on people to speak, make toasts, and and read telegrams or other messages from afar.

In some families, while everyone is finishing dessert and coffee, a friend or relative rises to deliver a *d'var Torah,* words of Torah or learning that are related to the baby's name, the weekly Torah portion, or some other aspect of the *simcha.*

The traditional ending for a *s'udat mitzvah* is the singing of the *birkat hamazon,* the blessings after eating. There is a special *birkat hamazon* for the meal following a *bris* that includes blessings for the baby, parents, *mohel,* and *sandek.* It is an honor to be asked to lead these prayers, which are printed in booklets called *bentshers.*[2]

Photography

Some parents, *mohels* and rabbis object to the presence of cameras during *brit* ceremonies, especially during a circumcision. Others welcome as much photography—video or still—as possible. A tape recorder is always an unobtrusive way to capture the spirit of the day.

Whatever your feelings about pictures at the ceremony, the *s'udat mitzvah* is a fine opportunity for recording the events of the day. In general, people don't hire professional photographers for such an intimate celebration, but it's a good idea to ask relatives or friends who are good with a camera to do the honors. Although candid pictures are wonderful, posed shots of proud grandparents holding the baby, and other family groupings will become treasured keepsakes.

Gifts

Jewish baby gifts range from the silly (bibs with Yiddish phrases like "*Bubbe's Fresser*"—Grandma's big eater) to the sublime (Grandpa's engraved *kiddush* cup). But there is also a middle path, filled with Jewish children's books, tapes and records, and art for the baby's room. For the pre-reader there are cloth, plastic, and cardboard books that feature the Hebrew alphabet, and baby blankets with the words *layla tov* (good night) woven into the design. Works of Jewish art for the nursery include bright posters of the *alef-bet,* special *tzedakah* (charity) boxes, and winsome *m'zuzot* for the doorpost to the baby's room. Calligraphers and artists have created special birth "certificates" and limited-edition prints especially for Jewish children. In some families, a hand-crafted silver, ceramic, or brass Chanukah *dreidl* (spinning top) has replaced the proverbial silver loving cup as the heirloom gift.[3]

Some gifts become heirlooms the moment they are given. A prayer shawl given by grandparents to a grandson becomes a tangible link to generations yet unimagined. Handmade gifts are always welcome. People who work in needlepoint have created hangings based on a baby's name, or made cross-stitch *alef-bets,* the Hebrew alphabet. People who work with wood might fashion wooden blocks with a baby's name painted in Hebrew and English on them. You can appliqué the letters of a baby's Hebrew name to a baby quilt or onto soft fabric blocks. Even something as small and simple as a hand-crocheted *kippah* for the baby to wear during the *brit* is a gift beyond price.

Although they are not exactly gifts, charitable contributions in honor of a baby's birth is a time-honored Jewish custom and a way of acting on your wish that this child inherit a better world. (See *Celebrations and Customs* for more about *tzedakah*)

Finally, thoughtful guests often bring a small gift for the baby's sibling(s), who invariably feel left out. It need not be a big present—just a token to help older kids know that they haven't been forgotten.

 # Announcements

A birth announcement may be the most welcome piece of mail anyone can receive, and the most joyful anyone can send. Although the printed birth announcement is a relatively new invention, its conventions seem written in stone, with the baby's weight and height noted along with the date of birth. But in recent years, Jewish parents have started a trend toward distinctive cards that celebrate the fact that a Jewish baby has been born.

In general, birth announcements tend to be simpler than wedding announcements, mostly because you want to get the news out as quickly as possible. They are usually sent out within a month of the baby's arrival. (Not everyone is able to meet that sort of deadline, and it really makes no difference when your cards go out; people are delighted to get the "official" news whenever it arrives.)

What to Say

There are no rules about what you should or should not say. Etiquette and tradition suggest nothing but the baby's name, the parents' names, date of birth, and the baby's size. Because few people stray from these basics, any personal message is sure to make an impact.

The presence of Jewish or Hebrew elements on your announcement makes a statement of Jewish identity and pride. The addition of the baby's Hebrew name—in English and/or with Hebrew letters—is the most common way to accomplish this. Similarly, you can give the birth date in both Gregorian and Jewish dates: 5 April 1993—5 Nisan 5753. You might also want to tell people if yours was a *Shabbat* baby, or if she was born during a holiday:

Hannah Yael enunciated her arrival
on the third day of Chanukah.
27 Kislev 5746—10 December 1985
Ellie, Jonathan & Aviva Kremer

Many announcements now mention the person or people in whose honor the baby was named. For example:

Karen Appel and Mark Fine
joyfully announce the birth of their son
Avi Appel Fine
May 25, 1984—23 Iyar 5744
Named after paternal grandfather Abraham Fine

We have a daughter!
Dory Rebecca is named after
Marty's grandmother Rivka
and Esther's grandfather Dov

While it has become customary to include the baby's weight and length at birth on the announcement, some parents omit this mundane information in favor of more personal and evocative details:

Leora was born with a full head of
soft, dark hair.

When Michael was born, he did not cry, but
opened his eyes and looked around the room
until he seemed to find our faces.

195

Ben has the long fingers and toes of his father's
family and shares the gift of healthy lungs with
his big brother Adam.

Mimi is a good eater, and thank God,
a good sleeper!

Parents often add a phrase from the Bible, in English and/or
Hebrew. If your baby has a biblical name, you might search out a
line that mentions it. For example, "He was called Solomon, and
the Lord loved him," or "Awake Devorah and sing." To find such a
quotation, check a biblical concordance or ask your rabbi or
cantor.

Psalms and the Song of Songs are full of graceful phrases, as are
the poems and prayers in this book's chapters *Brit Milah, Brit Bat,
Hiddur Mitzvah—Beautiful Touches,* and *Adoption.* A few favorites
from various sources follow:

For this child we have prayed.
Samuel 1:27

Light shine upon us
Our people have increased
And our joy is made great
For we have borne a child
May there be no end of peace
Isaiah 9

With each child, the world begins anew.
Midrash

By the breath of children God sustains the world.
Shabbat 119b

Today is the birthday of the world.
Rosh Hashanah liturgy

This little child, may he (she) grow big.
from the daily prayerbook

A good name is better than great riches.
Proverbs

How shall we bless her,
With what will this child be blessed?
With a smile like light,
With eyes, large and wide, to see every flower,
animal, and bird,
And a heart to feel all she sees.

The Adopted Baby

Adoption announcements bring the same good news as birth announcements—a new member of the family has arrived, and a new member of the Jewish people is here. The suggestions and quotations above all apply to the announcement of an adoption, including the custom of noting the baby's familial namesake(s).

Some adoption announcements do not make any mention of adoption at all, while others make a point of it. You can, for example, simply note two dates: the child's birthday and the date of his or her arrival home. If yours is an international adoption, place of birth might be included. And some parents incorporate names that were given to their children before adoption. A few examples follow:

Alexander Micah
Born: December 12, 1986, in Bogota, Columbia
Arrived home: February 18, 1987

Our daughter is home!
Rachel Susan Feldman-Bright
born
Seong Ae Han
(Beauty and Sincerity)

She is a gift and a wonder
Psalms

Not by our planting
But by heaven, our harvest

Nina Seong Mee Park (Beautiful Star) Gruber.

For this child we have prayed
Samuel 1:27

Alice and Philip Stein
joyfully announce the arrival of their son
Joshua Moshe
born June 15, 1990
adopted July 7, 1990

Design and Decoration

The creative possibilities are endless. Your wonderful news can be printed inside pink or blue cards from a stationery shop, or you can write personal notes inside museum art cards. You can compose an announcement on your computer and use press-apply Hebrew letters (available at most Judaica shops) or show off your Hebrew software. Many professional printers offer Hebrew lettering.

Calligraphers who work in Hebrew and English may be found in most American cities, and many of them advertise in Jewish newspapers. If your wedding invitation was the work of a calligrapher, this is a great time to get back in touch with him or her for another assignment. If you don't know where to begin looking for a calligrapher, your rabbi may be able to recommend someone.

If you opt for a calligrapher, it's a good idea to meet with the artist in advance of the baby's birth. Some couples who know their child's sex and have selected the child's name commission the whole announcement in advance and simply call the calligrapher with relevant details once the baby is born. Others select a design, give the artist a boy's name and a girl's name, and phone with the final outcome. (A list of the artists whose work appears in this book appears in the Appendix.)

Tzedakah (charity) boxes to honor the birth of a child
Artists: Leslie Gattman and Eugene Frank

Artist: Betsy Platkin-Teutsch

Artist: Peggy Davis

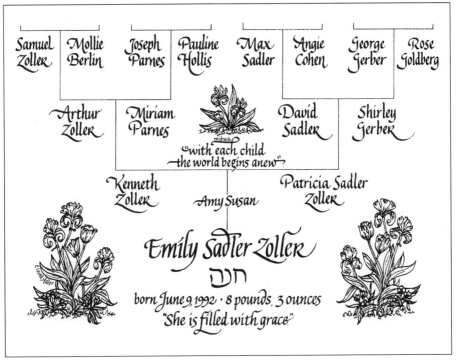

Samuel Zoller — Mollie Berlin | Joseph Parnes — Pauline Hollis | Max Sadler — Angie Cohen | George Gerber — Rose Goldberg

Arthur Zoller — Miriam Parnes | David Sadler — Shirley Gerber

midrash
"with each child the world begins anew"

Kenneth Zoller — Patricia Sadler Zoller

Amy Susan

Emily Sadler Zoller
חנה
born June 9, 1992 · 8 pounds, 3 ounces
"She is filled with grace"

Artist: Elaine Adler

elana miriam
stern

november 21, 1991 · יד כסלו תשנ"ב
7 pounds, 11 ounces

named for
toby's grandmother, edythe wiser
and hal's aunt, may abelson

toby & hal

אילת
מים

Artist: Elaine Adler

Artist: Betsy Platkin-Teutsch

Artist: Betsy Platkin-Teutsch

Celebrations and Customs

Some time-honored ways of marking the arrival of a Jewish baby, such as donating to charity, seem as relevant as today's headlines. Other are mostly unknown to American Jews and may seem downright quaint. All of them express the sense that a birth is proper cause for family and community celebration.

Tzedakah

Traditionally, Jews mark happy occasions like births, weddings, and *b'nai mitzvah* (*bar mitzvah* and *bat mitzvah* celebrations) with charitable donations or *tzedakah*—a word based on the Hebrew *tzedek,* which means justice. This is a way of sharing the joy of the occasion and of acknowledging that personal happiness is incomplete in a world so badly in need of repair. A donation made to honor of the birth of a child is a kind of investment in a happier, more just place we all wish for children. The act of giving in a child's name also expresses a hope that the child will grow up to give *tzedakah.*

Judaism does not view charity as an act of personal goodness but as a *mitzvah,* a holy obligation, and a privilege for the giver. The reason many Jews make contributions of $18—or some multiple of $18—is that the numerical value of eighteen is spelled out with the same Hebrew letters that mean life—*chai.*

Among Sephardic Jews, a large tray—the *senit Eliyahu hanabi* (tray of Elijah the prophet)—decorated with flowers and candles is passed at a *brit milah.* Guests are expected to fill it with gifts of money, and after the meal, the tray is auctioned off to the highest bidder, who distributes his bid, as well as the money on the tray, to charity.[1]

One way to make *tzedakah* an integral part of your *simcha* is to join the families and congregations that assess a voluntary "tax" of three percent on all food costs associated with Jewish celebrations. The money is sent to Mazon, an organization that helps soup kitchens, food pantries and other feeding programs in the United States and around the world. (Mazon, A Jewish Response to Hunger. 2940 Westwood Boulevard, Suite #7, Los Angeles, CA 90064–4120. 310-470-7769.)

Although it is customary to give money to Jewish organizations, donations can also be made to efforts and institutions that have meaning to your family—from the American Cancer Society to a rabbinical seminary, from AIDS research to Israel bonds.

Many people have trees planted in Israel in honor of a birth. This gesture has a centuries-old precedent: In ancient times, a cypress sapling was planted for the birth of a girl, a cedar for a boy. Later, branches would be cut from those trees for the child's wedding canopy. The Jewish National Fund (800-542-TREE) will take your order and send an announcement to the baby's family.

Although tradition teaches that *tzedakah* is best given anonymously, a simple announcement of charitable gifts given in the baby's name—as part of the *brit* ceremony, or in the ceremony's booklet, or in a birth announcement—may encourage others to make a contribution on this or a similar occasion. And that would be an extra *mitzvah*.

Pidyon Haben

Although every baby is cherished, the birth of a first child is an unparalleled experience that marks one of life's great passages: from adulthood to parenthood. *Pidyon haben,* the redemption of the first-born son, is one of the oldest of all Jewish rituals that marks this occasion.[2]

Until recently, liberal Jews abandoned the custom or observed it only perfunctorily. For many, the ceremony—in which parents buy their first-born sons back from a representative of the priesthood—seems hopelessly antiquated, legalistic, and devoid of spirituality. After all, it is a ritual that refers to a caste system and treats daughters as nonpersons. But the revival of interest in tradition has helped focus attention on the elements of *pidyon haben* that speak to the powerful feelings evoked by a first-born child.

In many ancient cultures, the first-born child, especially sons, enjoyed a special status—a fact that made the tenth plague visited upon the Egyptians in the story of Exodus, the killing of all first-born sons—a truly unspeakable punishment. The exemption of Jewish first-borns on that terrible night placed an obligation on all first-born Jewish sons thereafter, to serve God as members of the Temple priesthood.

Even when priestly service became limited to Levites and their descendants, all first-born sons were still seen as obligated and thus in need of a ritual release from their duty. This "redemption" was accomplished by asking a *kohane,* a priest or descendant of priests, to accept five shekels in exchange for the son's obligation.

According to *halachah, pidyon haben* must take place on the thirty-first day after birth and is required only when a Jewish woman's first pregnancy results in a baby boy.[3] If the mother has previously given birth to a girl, if she has miscarried, or if the delivery was by Cesarean section, the ceremony is not performed.[4]

Like all Jewish ceremonies, *pidyon haben* is very brief, consisting of a few exchanges between the father and a *kohane* or a rabbi. The father presents the baby and offers money, traditionally five silver dollars, as a substitute for giving up his son. The rabbi accepts the offer, announces the substitution ("This is instead of that; this is in exchange for that"), pronounces the threefold priestly blessing, and the company proceeds to eat, drink, and be merry.

New Forms

Recently, *pidyon haben* has been the inspiration and foundation for new ceremonies. Called by various names, *pidyon habat* (redemption of the first-born daughter), or *kiddush petter rechem* (sanctification of the one who opens the womb),[5] or *seder kedushat cha-yei hamishpachah* (ceremony of consecration to family life),[6] they all emphasize the unique experience of becoming parents for the first time. The new rituals are inclusive of all first-born children, girls as well as boys, children born by Cesarean section or after a miscarriage. The focus is not on redeeming a child from obligations but on sanctifying and dedicating the child for a life of service. (An example follows.)

Certain ritual elements of traditional *pidyon haben* are maintained, including the presentation of the child to the rabbi or ceremonial leader. The Passover story is also recalled, connecting the beginning of parenthood and the birth of the Jewish people. There is usually a dialogue between the rabbi and parents that includes an exchange of coins—now usually given to a Jewish charity. And, of course, there is a meal of celebration.

Because few people are familiar with the ritual, parents often distribute copies of the ceremony or some information explaining the ceremony and its significance.

Pidyon Ceremony

Parents present a gift of *tzedakah* and say:

For a son:

זֶה תַּחַת זֶה, זֶה חָלוּף זֶה, זֶה מָחוּל עַל זֶה.

Zeh ta-chat zeh, zeh cha-luf zeh,
zeh ma-chul al zeh.

For a daughter:

זֶה תַּחַת זֹאת, זֶה חָלוּף זֹאת, זֶה מָחוּל עַל זֹאת.

Zeh ta-chat zot, zeh cha-luf zot,
zeh ma-chul al zot.

This *tzedakah* instead of greed,
This gift in place of selfishness,
This commitment because of the blessing of new life.

May our son/daughter enter into life, Torah and a commitment to all that is Godly. As he/she has entered into the covenant, may he/she grow into a life of Torah, *chupah,* and good deeds.

Parents and guests recite the *shehecheyanu,* the prayer for new blessings. After *kiddush* (the blessing over wine) and *motzi* (the blessing over bread, which is dipped in honey for a sweet life), the *s'udat mitzvah* is served.[7]

Pidyon Ceremony

It is written: And when in time to come your child asks you, "What does this mean?" you shall say, "By strength of hand the Eternal brought us out of Egypt, from the house of bondage." (Exodus 13:14)

The experience of the Exodus from Egyptian bondage sensitized our people to the values of human freedom and dignity. May we exemplify these values as we grow together as a family, creating a home where love of Torah, awareness of that which is godly, and compassion for humanity always abide; where the hearts of the parents and the hearts of the children shall always be turned to one another.

Rabbi or leader:

Blessed with the sacred trust of new life, will you dedicate yourselves to the redeeming of life?

Parents:

We desire that the birth of our son/daughter inspire us to work for the redemption of all life. We express our partnership with that which is Godly in the process of *tikkun olam,* world redemption, as we, in honor of the birth of our child _____ *bat/ben* _____ *v'*_____, present a gift of *tzedakah.* May it be a symbol of our and his/her commitment to Torah, to involvement in the life of our people, and to the upholding of those values which make for human dignity, fellowship, and peace.

Blessed by the presence whose sanctity fills our lives, we redeem every first born and engage in *tikkun olam.*

Pidyon Ceremony

Parents present a gift of *tzedakah* and say:

For a son:

זֶה תַּחַת זֶה, זֶה חָלוּף זֶה, זֶה מָחוּל עַל זֶה.

Zeh ta-chat zeh, zeh cha-luf zeh,
zeh ma-chul al zeh.

For a daughter:

זֶה תַּחַת זֹאת, זֶה חָלוּף זֹאת, זֶה מָחוּל עַל זֹאת.

Zeh ta-chat zeh, zeh cha-luf zeh,
zeh ma-chul al zeh.

This *tzedakah* instead of greed,
This gift in place of selfishness,
This commitment because of the blessing of new life.

May our son/daughter enter into life, Torah and a commitment to all that is Godly. As he/she has entered into the covenant, may he/she grow into a life of Torah, *chupah,* and good deeds.

Parents and guests recite the *shehecheyanu,* the prayer for new blessings. After *kiddush* (the blessing over wine) and *motzi* (the blessing over bread, which is dipped in honey for a sweet life), the *s'udat mitzvah* is served.[7]

First Days

In the tight-knit communities of the past, and in some traditional circles today, the first days of a child's life, especially of a son, were marked by ritual visits to the family's home by relatives, friends, and neighbors. Some of these customs may seem antiquated or even intrusive. However, they provide a reminder of life and offer models for communal celebration and observance.

Sh'lom Zachar (well-being of the son) was celebrated on the first Friday night after the birth of a son. If the baby was born on a Friday evening after *Shabbat* candles had been lit, people would arrive, unannounced but expected, that very night. Guests assembled in the new baby's home to recite psalms, sing songs, and discuss Torah. Little children were invited to recite the *Sh'ma* (the prayer that declares God's unity) near the cradle. Adult visitors offered prayers on behalf of the new arrival and his mother, tuning the baby's ears to the sound of Hebrew from his first days on Earth.

Legend has it that, while in the womb, babies learn the entire Torah, but just before birth an angel causes the infant to forget all he or she knows. *Sh'lom Zachar* was considered an opportunity to console the baby for this loss.[8]

In addition to gifts of food, friends would bring charms and amulets to banish evil spirits, especially Lilith (she was supposedly attracted to newborns, who were thought to be especially vulnerable before their *brisses*).

In our day, the first *Shabbat* of a baby's life may be spent in the hospital, and even if the baby is home, the family may prefer privacy to a house full of guests. For families who feel ready to handle a more concentrated expression of welcome, a *Sh'lom Zachar* or a *Sh'lom N'keivah* (well-being of the daughter) ceremony can be organized by relatives or friends as an hour-long coffee-and-dessert event. A blessing over wine, a *shehecheyanu,* a chorus of *Siman Tov Umazal Tov* and voilà! You have a Jewish celebration.

Sh'lom Zachar/N'keivah can also provide a model for welcoming an adopted child or a baby brought home after a hospital stay necessitated by medical complications. The first *Shabbat* evening at home might be an appropriate time for a simple gathering. A shared meal, song, candlelight, and loving support can make an auspicious beginning and a cherished memory.

Whether your home is quiet or filled with friends and relatives, the first Shabbat with your newborn is precious. When you light Sabbath candles, show them to the baby, and then read this poem to each other:

For All Newborn Children on Their First Shabbat

When the sun sets
And the stars pull an evening blanket
    across the sky
    coaxing the world to rest and sleep
    and us—to dream
We kindle lights
    Eternal light
    Remembrance light
    Shabbat light
The light in children's eyes
Hands cupped over candle's flame
Drawing setting sun inside our souls
We build a memory and a home for light
We bless this moment
    and give thanks.

Paused between day and night
We breathe a new soul into the world
We take a breath and sing.

Rabbi Sandy Eisenberg Sasso[9]

Another celebration held the night before a *bris* was called *Vach Nacht*, watch night, or *Leil Shimurim*, the night of the vigil. Newborn sons and their mothers would not be left alone for an instant on this night, when they were perceived to be in mortal danger from Lilith and other demons. To protect the little one, a mixture of magic and piety was employed; a *minyan* (a prayer quorum of ten men) surrounded mother and child, and a chalk circle was drawn on the floor to keep out the demons.

Sephardic Jews celebrate a similar custom called *Zocher Habrit,* "remembering the *bris,*" but without the preoccupation with demons and darkness. In some communities, the night before a *bris* is celebrated with a festive meal in the grandfather's home, complete with dancing and singing. Elsewhere, the celebration is held at the home of the *sandek* and then moves in a torch-lit, singing procession to the home of the new baby.[10]

Parents who view the *mitzvah* of *brit milah* with trepidation report that the presence of sympathetic friends the night before the *bris* is a comfort—especially when the company includes parents who lived through it all recently.

Another eastern European custom, *Hollekreish,* was borrowed from Christian neighbors and based on ancient pagan custom. The original meaning of the name is obscure. *Kreisch* comes from the German for "scream" or "shriek." And although some rabbis trace "*Holle*" to the Hebrew *chol* ("profane" or "secular"), it more likely refers to an ancient Teutonic goddess Holle or Holda, who played the part of Lilith in the pantheon of German mythology. *Hollekreish* was probably meant to scare the demon Holle away from a baby and mother until baptism would protect them.[11] In some communities, *Hollekreish* was celebrated only for boys, and elsewhere the practice included girls.[12]

The children of the community were invited to the new baby's home on the fourth *Shabbat* of his or her life, where they assembled around the baby's cradle. The father, cantor, or the children themselves would read selected biblical verses. Then the cradle would be lifted into the air three times, and three times the same question would be asked:

Hollekreish, Hollekreish; wie soll das kindchen heissen.
What should the little child be called?

The children would shout the baby's name each time and then be rewarded with sweets.

The Evil Eye

Fear of the evil eye and of dark and malicious spirits prompted many customs. In some communities, packets of nuts and sweets were attached to the cradle to keep the spirits occupied. Elsewhere, red ribbons were tied around the crib. Biblical verses were sometimes posted around the baby's room.[13] The pervasive dread of the *ayn horeh,* evil eye, also made for a strange baby etiquette. For example, one would never extol the beauty of a baby, at least not without mentioning some "flaw," spitting three times, or at least saying, *kayn ayn horeh,* lest you attract the jealousy of the demon world.

As absurd as these beliefs may seem today, the unspoken awe and fear that surrounds the mystery of birth is still with us. Many Jews will not buy a layette, have a crib in the house, or allow a baby shower before the birth. When asked why, we claim that our reticence is based on concern that something might, God forbid, happen to the baby and then it would be too painful to have all that paraphernalia around. But then, even thinking such a thought requires that you spit three times to dispel the evil eye. Old superstitions die hard.

PART

5

Modern Life

Infertility and
Genetic Testing

The Talmud says, "One who does not partici-
pate in 'Be fruitful and multiply' causes God's presence to vanish."[1]
Judaism's fierce pro-natalism has long been a source of pain to
those who cannot fulfill the commandment because of infertility.
Even in the Bible, barrenness afflicts a striking number of the
matriarchs, including Sarah, Rebecca, Rachel, and Hannah.
Rachel's anguished cry, "Give me children, or I shall die," sounds
all too familiar to infertile couples today.

Divine intervention was the cure for biblical infertility, but
today we seek solutions in doctors' offices and hospitals. And
there, Jewish law enthusiastically applies the biblical imperative of
healing the sick to fertility problems.

There is near-universal Jewish support for virtually all technologies in which the parents are the sources of egg and sperm, from
testing and drug treatments to surgery that clears blocked fallopian
tubes, to *in vitro* fertilization. The only Jewish caveat about
aggressive medical intervention is a concern for the privacy of
individuals and couples.

Judaism has always viewed the act of lovemaking as sacred and
private, and the Talmud stresses the importance of modesty,
decorum, and respect in sexual relationships. Couples undergoing
the embarrassing and physically and emotionally taxing procedures
of infertility testing and treatment should recall Judaism's insistence
on compassion and consideration for those who endure this
invasion of privacy.

When infertility technology moves beyond the closed system
of a married couple, Jewish law is not so clear about what is
permissible. Present-day Jewish physicians, rabbis, and ethicists
respond to developments such as sperm and egg harvesting and
transplantation with a wide range of opinions. You can find Jewish

support for artificial insemination with donor sperm and surrogate mothers as legitimate "last resorts" for infertile couples. But you'll also find Jewish voices decrying these practices as destructive of families, as adulterous, and as fundamentally unethical. It is beyond the scope of this book to resolve these issues, or even to discuss them in detail. The ethical dimensions of new technologies deserve careful consideration. Consultation with a sympathetic rabbi, as well as physicians, may help in your deliberations.[2]

Tay-Sachs and Allied Diseases

Tay-Sachs disease is an inherited disorder of the central nervous system that is 100 times more common in Jewish children than in non-Jewish children. By the age of about six months, a baby with Tay-Sachs disease loses physical skills, sight, and the ability to eat or smile. There is no known cure for the disease, and death usually occurs by five years of age.

The cause of Tay-Sachs disease is the absence of a vital enzyme called Hexosaminidase A (Hex A), which the body uses to break down fatty substances (lipids) in the brain. Without the Hex A enzyme, lipids accumulate and eventually destroy brain function.

Carriers of the Tay-Sachs gene do not have the disease themselves, but if they marry another carrier, there is a one-in-four chance that a pregnancy will result in an afflicted baby. A simple blood test determines whether an adult is a carrier. Couples who find out that both partners carry the Tay-Sachs gene may choose to adopt rather than try to conceive. Others decide to use artificial insemination with sperm from a confirmed noncarrier. Still others conceive and use prenatal testing as a second line of prevention.

Amniocentesis, removal of a small quantity of fluid from the uterus early in the second trimester of pregnancy, can determine whether the fetus has Tay-Sachs. If the child is found to have the disease, a couple may choose to terminate the pregnancy.

Jewish law sanctions the practice of abortion in some cases. Even the most conservative interpretation of Jewish law allows abortion to save the life of the mother, and more liberal positions permit abortion if the birth would cause the mother mental anguish and suffering. In cases where there is evidence of prenatal defects or genetic disease, Jewish law sanctions abortion not from the perspective of the child, but in order to spare the mother's pain at the inevitable loss of the child.

For more information about Tay-Sachs and the other rare genetic lipid storage diseases that affect Jews, contact: The National Tay-Sachs and Allied Diseases Association, 2001 Beacon Street, Brookline, MA 02146, 617-277-4463.

Grief and Healing

Sometimes there are happy endings to sagas full of doctor visits, surgeries, amniocentesis, and the emotional rollercoaster of fertility treatment and genetic counseling. Sometimes the happy ending is a birth, sometimes an adoption.

But even with the best outcome, infertility and pregnancy loss can leave wounds that take time to heal. The following prayers were written to help in that process.

PRAYER ON THE OCCASION OF A MISCARRIAGE OR ABORTION

May the One who shares sorrow with Your creation be with us now as we experience the loss of potential life. We are sad as we think of our hopes for this unborn one, as in our minds we imagine what might have been.

Life is a fabric of different emotions and experiences. Now, while we experience life's bitterness and pain, be with us and sustain us. Help us to gather strength from within ourselves, from each other, and from our friends.

Blessed are You, O Divine Presence, who shares sorrow with Your creation.

Rabbi Rebecca T. Alpert

יחידו של עולם *Y'chido shel olam,* Holy One of Being, Source of all life and destiny of all souls, receive the soul of this one that was not-yet-a-life but only a dream. Send us healing in our grief and confusion. Give us strength and the ability to look for a future again filled with new life and new dreams. Let hopeful parents everywhere, who have known the agony of loss, be soon comforted by the sounds of a baby's cry.

Rabbi Lawrence Kushner

ON ACCEPTING INFERTILITY

God, as I let go of the sorrow from the past,
　　grant me relief, and bless me with hope;

Restore tender loving to my marriage
　　even as You graced Adam and Eve
　　with perfect pleasure in Gan Eden so
　　long ago.

God, grant me release and bless me with healing;
Make these scars of barrenness
　　Turn into banners of abundance for those
　　around me.

God grant me release and bless me with peace.
May my husband (my wife) and I learn to share
　　our lives with others as if they were our own.

God, grant us release and bless us with love.
May once again sounds of joy and gladness,
　　delight and rejoicing be heard in this
　　household of Israel.

Blessed are You, our God, who creates joy
　　between husband and wife.

Rabbi Nina Beth Cardin

This prayer is part of a longer ceremony on accepting infertility. For a copy, send a stamped, self-addressed envelope to Rabbi Nina Beth Cardin, c/o Jewish Theological Seminary, 3080 Broadway, New York, NY 10027.

Adoption

ADOPTION

We did not plant you, true.
But when the season is done,
When the alternate prayers
For sun and for rain are counted,
When the pain of weeding
And the pride of watching are through,
I will hold you high,
A shining sheaf
Above the thousand seeds grown wild.
Not by our planting,
But by heaven,
Our harvest.
Our own child.

author unknown[1]

If you turned to this chapter first, you probably already know the statistics: as many as one in six American couples may have difficulty conceiving, which explains why more and more Jews are turning to adoption.

If you did start reading on this page, remember that the rest of this book is for you, too. While this chapter focuses on issues specific to adoption, the sections on names, covenant ceremonies, celebrations, and announcements apply to all new parents, whether you meet your bundle of joy in a delivery room, at an airport, or in an office.

For many people, adoption is a difficult choice, a last resort. The decision may represent a great loss that some compare to the pain of losing a loved one. Adopting may mean acknowledging that you do not expect to ever have a child of your own flesh, which can be a heart-breaking conclusion. Thoughtful adoption professionals believe that many people need to mourn that loss before looking ahead to adoption (see pages 211–212).

The process of adopting is anything but simple. It begins with questions: International or domestic? Through an agency or privately? Infant or older child? Then comes the paperwork, the home study, and the waiting. Fortunately, you do not have to go through any of this alone. There are welcoming networks of people who have been there before you and can guide and comfort you through the process.

Adoption is no longer a rarity in the Jewish world, nor is it a shame or stigma kept secret from the child and the community. The emerging Jewish view of adoption is best put by Rabbi Daniel Shevitz, the father of two adopted sons, whose writings and comments inform this chapter: "As long as there are children in need of homes, and loving homes in need of children, adoption should be encouraged as an act of piety and love."[2]

And as any adoptive parent can tell you, there is no difference between *nachas* (the special joy children give their parents) from adopted children and *nachas* from biological children.

Judaism and Adoption

Neither biblical nor rabbinic Judaism provides much guidance for modern couples considering adoption. Jewish law on adoption is sketchy, lacking any mention of specific rules or legal procedures. Still, *halachah,* traditional Jewish law, did address the care of needy children, and the rabbis looked kindly on the actions of Pharaoh's daughter, who adopted Moses. It has always been considered a *mitzvah*—a good and holy act—to take orphaned children into one's home, and foster or adoptive parents were expected to assume all the burdens and the rewards of parenthood. The Talmud says, "Those who raise a child are called its parents, and not the ones who conceived it."

What little Jewish law exists on the subject of adoption relates to Jewish orphans, who, in the past, were most likely to require assistance from the Jewish community.³ Today, however, the release of Jewish children for adoption is quite rare, and most adoptions involve non-Jewish children.

Conversion

Adopting a non-Jewish child raises the issue of conversion. Some parents feel that their commitment to raising the child as a Jew is sufficient and that the laws and formal conversion rituals are irrelevant, especially for infants. However, many others feel it is important to follow the spirit and even the letter of Jewish law, as a way of declaring this child one of their own and as a way of affirming their commitment to Jewish family life.

According to *halachah,* conversion to Judaism requires *mikvah* (ritual immersion) for both girls and boys, and *brit milah* for boys. Both are traditionally done in the presence of a *beit din,* a rabbinical court of three.

An uncircumcised adopted male newborn is given a *brit milah* on the eighth day after birth, or as soon as possible thereafter, in the presence of a *beit din,* one of whom is generally the *mohel,* the person who performs the circumcision. For a baby adopted at three months of age or older, it is common to have the procedure done in a hospital, under a physician's care and with anesthesia.

If a baby was circumcised without religious ceremony, the Jewish ritual is reenacted in a ceremony called *hatafat dam brit,* in which the *mohel* draws a drop of blood from the site of the circumcision and recites the prayers of *brit milah.* This ceremony is easily done in the home or synagogue, regardless of the child's age. The chapter on *brit milah* contains a full discussion of the practice, laws, and customs pertaining to circumcision, including a special section on *bris* for conversion and adoption.

Mikvah is required of all converts to Judaism, male and female, adults and children of all ages. Immersion in a *mikvah* is an act of renewal and rebirth. The water of the ritual bath recalls the mystical source of all water and thus all life—the river whose source is Eden.⁴ The *ma-yim cha-yim,* or living water, of *mikvah* also represents the physical source of human life, the waters of the womb.

Immersion must be total, as it was in the womb. The naked child is held loosely and lowered into the water, where one of the child's adoptive parents or a relative or friend "births" the baby as a Jew.

If you live in a temperate climate or if the adoption of your child occurs during the summer, it is perfectly kosher to do *mikvah* in any body of *ma-yim cha-yim*, living or running water. Ponds, lakes, rivers, and oceans are natural *mikvaot*. For many people, natural bodies of water provide a more spiritually satisfying experience; for others, weather, family custom, or rabbinical preference may discourage this option.

Your rabbi can convene a *beit din*, a court of three rabbis, to witness the immersion. When the child is raised from the water, the following blessing is recited by one of the rabbis or by a family member:

בָּרוּךְ אַתָּה יְיָ, אֱלֹהֵינוּ מֶלֶךְ הָעוֹלָם,
אֲשֶׁר קִדְּשָׁנוּ בְּמִצְוֹתָיו, וְצִוָּנוּ עַל הַטְּבִילָה.

*Ba-ruch a-ta Adonai, Eh-lo-hei-nu meh-lech
ha-o-lam, a-sher ki-d'sha-nu b'mitz-vo-tav,
v'tzi-va-nu al ha-t'vi-lah.*

Praised are you, Adonai, God of all creation who
sanctifies us with your commandments and
commands us concerning immersion.

The *shehecheyanu* is then recited.

For boys, a *mikvah* appointment is scheduled sometime after the circumcision has healed. However, *brit milah* or *mikvah* are delayed if there is the least suspicion of a health risk.

For girls, *mikvah* is the only ritual requirement. Traditionally, girls are named after *mikvah*, either immediately following immersion or sometime later in a ceremony at a synagogue or at home. The chapter on *brit bat* contains many suggestions for celebrating the arrival of a daughter into your lives and into the covenant of the Jewish people.

Although circumcision is performed at the earliest possible date, there is some difference of opinion regarding *mikvah*. It is not uncommon to take newborns to the *mikvah*. One father counsels blowing into the baby's face as she is dunked, which he claims makes the child hold her breath for the few seconds of immersion. However many parents and rabbis prefer to wait until the child is old enough to hold his or her breath.[5] Some even suggest that *mikvah* take place when the child is preparing for his or her *bar* or *bat mitzvah* so it becomes an intentional rite of passage for a young person preparing to receive and accept the responsibilities of the Torah.

This approach dovetails with Talmudic law regarding converted children. When a child not born to a Jewish mother reaches adulthood (traditionally, thirteen years old for boys, twelve for girls) he or she has the right to affirm or renounce his or her Jewish identity. Legally, the right to renounce expires when a child reaches adulthood.[6]

There are serious objections to the idea of waiting so long, on both *halachic* and psychological grounds. Without *mikvah,* an adopted child is not legally Jewish. And formally reminding a child who is twelve or thirteen that she or he is not "really" Jewish could cause real distress. This is often a time when identity issues are coming to the fore; adoption, some people say, creates enough cause for ambiguity that conversion should not be added to it. A simple declaration of one's Jewish identity at *bar mitzvah* or *bat mitzvah* is sufficient acknowledgment of the Talmudic right to renounce.

Whatever you decide to do about *mikvah,* there is widespread support among adoption professionals, Jewish and non-Jewish, for full disclosure about your child's origins. In the case of international or interracial adoption, there is often no question of concealment; but the same principles apply even if the child resembles his or her adoptive parents. The story of how Mommy and Daddy waited and hoped for little Sarah's arrival, complete with pictures of their airport meeting can easily become part of a child's sense of who she is and how she belongs.

Who Is a Jew?

Although the tradition views *mikvah* and *milah* as essential for all converts, some liberal rabbis dispense with ritual circumcision in the case of already circumcised boys, and others disapprove of immersion for infants and children altogether. These positions are controversial in the larger American Jewish community and in Israel. The debate is an old one and rests on the authority of Jewish law.

But even if your Reform, Conservative, or Reconstructionist rabbi follows Jewish law, Orthodox rabbis still may not recognize your son or daughter as a Jew. (This is true for adult conversions as well.) Unless the rituals are supervised and witnessed by Orthodox rabbis, your child's conversion may be challenged as inauthentic by the Orthodox community. Given the on-going debate on this matter in the state of Israel, a non-Orthodox conversion may, at some point, impugn your child's status as a Jew and a citizen there. For this reason, some liberal Jews seek out Orthodox rabbis to oversee the conversion of their children, just to make sure that nobody, in any Jewish community anywhere, can question the children's identity. This is an issue worth discussing with a rabbi.

The overwhelming majority of Jews have their sons circumcised as infants, a practice that is followed with adopted infant sons. However, if the child is much older, circumcision is a far more difficult decision to make and explain. The fear and pain associated with having the procedure done on a school-age boy cannot be wished away, and some parents refuse to subject a new son to such a bewildering operation. But for others, a decision not to circumcise seems just as wrong. One adoptive parent wrote eloquently of her decision to have two sons, ages seven and eleven, circumcised: "We considered letting the boys grow up and make the decision for themselves. It would have been an easier way out for us as parents," she wrote. However, she and her husband decided to go ahead with the procedure, despite her fears that "it might make them hate Judaism, not to mention make them hate us. I could only say to them that if I did not have them circumcised, I would not be treating them like my true sons . . . the same as if they had been born to me as babies."[7]

Challenges and Services

In certain periods of Jewish history, the biological or racial aspect of Jewish peoplehood was considered paramount. The same racial definition of Judaism that has been the pretext for so much anti-Semitism has not yet disappeared from the Jewish community. Although overt racism is, by and large, socially unacceptable, some Jews fear and reject people—even children—who look "different." This fear finds expression in everything from the garden-variety cruelty that kids display on the playground, to the grandmother who worries that her granddaughter might one day grow up to marry the Korean-born Rosenbloom kid.

But the Jewish people is a changing people, and as it changes, the old prejudices are withering. Just as the Jewish population in Israel includes black-skinned Ethiopians and blue-eyed redheads from the former Soviet Union, the American Jewish community of the twenty-first century will include members who are tall and blond, as well as those who are dark-skinned and almond-eyed. Besides, the Jewish people is not a race but a people who choose to enter into a special relationship with God. As Rabbi Daniel Shevitz has written, the most important aspect of Jewish self-definition has always been the covenant, "the bonds of promise, service, and expectation between God and Israel, that make one a true member of the Jewish community."[8]

While all Jewish parents worry about their children's commitment to Judaism as adults (Will they identify as Jews? Will they intermarry?) adoptive parents may be particularly sensitive to the difficulties their kids may face as adolescents and later in life. Indeed, some parents feel guilty about asking a child to assume the burden of belonging to a minority group. One adoptive parent writes, "I'm sure that little voices inside each of them were saying something to the effect, 'Millions of American families, and we had to get Jews.'"

Although the first line of support for any major life change is your community of family and friends, professional services tailored to meet the specific needs of Jewish adoptive families are coming of age. Jewish family agencies vary greatly in terms of sensitivity and expertise, but most now acknowledge the particular concerns of adopting couples, and some provide a spectrum of support services, from help with special-needs children to family counseling to *Chanukah* parties.

All members of adoptive families benefit from contact with other parents and children who share similar histories, questions, and challenges. Just being part of a group of families who look like yours is an important form of validation.

Stars of David is a national nonprofit information and support network for Jewish adoptive families that was founded in 1984 and grew from one to 500 families in less than three years. Chapters have formed in many states around the country, linked by a national newsletter, *Star Tracks*. However, local Stars of David groups are autonomous and run programs that are responsive to the needs of their members. For more information about Stars of David—which is *not* an adoption agency—contact Susan M. Katz, 3175 Commercial Ave., Suite 100, Northbrook, IL 60062-1915, (708) 205-1200; (800) STAR349. http://www.webassist.com/stars-of-david/.

Names

There is virtually no difference in the ways adoptive parents and birth parents select names, which means that when American Jews adopt, they tend to name their children in memory of family members who have died. Typically, a child's full Hebrew name includes his or her parents' names as well, as in *David ben Mosheh v'Rivka,* David the son of Moses and Ruth; or *Gila bat Rafael v'Leah,* or Gila, the daughter of Raphael and Leah. It is much rarer to follow the custom for adult converts, in other words, *David ben Avraham Avinu v'Sarah Immeinu,* David the son of Abraham our father and Sarah our mother. This "generic" convert's name was more common in the past, when adopted children were likely to be Jews by birth (see *A Jewish Name*).[9]

Announcements

The announcement of an adoption is wonderful news and an opportunity to answer questions about your new baby. For suggestions about creative and thoughtful ways to word an adoption announcement, see the chapter on *Announcements.*

Ceremonies

The adoption of a child is a rite of passage as momentous as a birth and merits the same attention and care we lavish on all joyous life-cycle events. Any and all ceremonies related to adoption—*brit milah, mikvah, brit bat*—may be the occasion for a meaningful, personal celebration. The poem at the beginning of this chapter and the prayer given here are ways to acknowledge the path that brought this child to your arms.

> We have been blessed with the precious gift of this child. After so much waiting and wishing, we are filled with wonder and with gratitude as we call you our son/daughter. Our son/daughter, our child, you have grown to life apart from us, but now we hold you close to our hearts and cradle you in our arms with love. We welcome you into the circle of our family and embrace you with the beauty of a rich tradition.
>
> We pledge ourselves to the creation of a Jewish home and to a life of compassion for others, hoping that you will grow to cherish and emulate these ideals.
>
> God of new beginnings, teach us to be mother and father, worthy of this sacred trust of life. May our son/daughter grow in health, strong in mind and

kind in heart, a lover of Torah, a seeker of peace. Bless all of us together within Your shelter of Shalom.

Rabbi Sandy Eisenberg Sasso[10]

Some parents prefer to hold a Jewish ceremony that sanctifies the act of adoption itself. The following is a model of a simple, moving Jewish adoption ceremony. The chapters on *brit milah, brit bat,* and *hiddur mitzvah* contain rituals, prayers and poems that can help you modify this one or can serve as models for a ceremony of your own creation.

מָתָה הָיְתָה זֹּאת הִיא נִפְלָאת בְּעֵינֵינוּ

She is a gift from God and a wonder in our eyes

Sima Shapiro & Adam Rubin
joyfully announce
the arrival of their daughter
Dina Perl
דינה פערל
born June 21, 1992
adopted August 8, 1992

ב״ה

Artist: Peggy Davis

Brit Immuts

Covenant of Adoption

The baby is escorted into the room by one or more grandparents and then is handed to other relatives or friends. The parents explain the ceremony and tell the story of the baby's name.

The baby is given to the parents, who take the following oath.

For a boy:

נִשְׁבָּעִים אֲנַחְנוּ בְּשֵׁם מִי שֶׁשְּׁמוֹ רַחוּם וְחַנּוּן שֶׁנְּקַיֵּם אֶת הַיֶּלֶד הַזֶּה כְּאִלּוּ הָיָה מִזַּרְעֵנוּ יוֹצֵא חֲלָצֵינוּ. וּנְגַדְּלוֹ וְנַחֲזִיקוֹ וְנַדְרִיכוֹ בְּדַרְכֵי תוֹרָתֵנוּ, כְּכֹל מִצְווֹת הַבֵּן עַל הָאָב וְהָאֵם. יְהִי יְיָ אֱלֹהֵינוּ עִמּוֹ בְּכֹל מַעֲשֵׂי יָדָיו. אָמֵן, כֵּן יְהִי רָצוֹן.

Nish-ba-im a-nach-nu b'sheim mi sheh-sh'mo ra-chum v'cha-nun sheh-n'ka-yeim et ha-yeh-led ha-zeh k'i-lu ha-yah mi-zar-ei-nu yo-tzei cha-la-tzei-nu. Un-ga-d'lo v'na-cha-zi-ko v'nad-ri-cho b'dar-chei to-ra-tei-nu, k'chol mitz-vot ha-bein al ha-av v'ha-eim. Y'hi Adonai Eh-lo-hei-nu i-mo b'chol ma-a-sei ya-dav. A-mein, kein y'hi ra-tzon.

For a girl:

נִשְׁבָּעִים אֲנַחְנוּ בְּשֵׁם מִי שֶׁשְּׁמוֹ רַחוּם וְחַנּוּן שֶׁנְּקַיֵּם אֶת הַיַּלְדָּה הַזֹּאת כְּאִלּוּ הָיְתָה מִזַּרְעֵנוּ יוֹצֵאת חֲלָצֵינוּ. וּנְגַדְּלָה וְנַחֲזִיקָה וְנַדְרִיכָה בְּדַרְכֵי תוֹרָתֵנוּ, כְּכֹל מִצְווֹת הַבַּת עַל הָאָב וְהָאֵם. יְהִי יְיָ אֱלֹהֵינוּ עִמָּה בְּכֹל מַעֲשֵׂי יָדֶיהָ. אָמֵן, כֵּן יְהִי רָצוֹן.

Nish-ba-im a-nach-nu b'sheim mi sheh-sh'mo ra-chum v'cha-nun sheh-n'ka-yeim et ha-yal-dah ha-zoht k'i-lu ha-y'tah mi-zar-ei-nu yo-tzeit cha-la-tzei-nu. Un-ga-d'lah v'na-cha-zi-kah v'nad-ri-chah b'dar-chei to-ra-tei-nu, k'chol mitz-vot ha-bat al ha-av v'ha-eim. Y'hi

Brit Immuts

Adonai Eh-lo-hei-nu i-mah b'chol ma-a-sei ya-deh-ha. A-mein, kein y'hi ra-tzon.

We solemnly swear, by the One Who is called loving and merciful, that we will raise this child as our own. We will nurture him/her, sustain him/her, and guide him/her in the paths of Torah, in accordance with the duties incumbent upon Jewish parents. May God ever be with him/her. We pray for the wisdom and strength to help our child _____ become a man/woman of integrity and kindness.

For a boy:

הַמַּלְאָךְ הַגֹּאֵל אֹתִי מִכָּל רָע יְבָרֵךְ אֶת הַנְּעָרִים, וְיִקָּרֵא בָהֶם שְׁמִי וְשֵׁם אֲבֹתַי אַבְרָהָם וְיִצְחָק, וְיִדְגּוּ לָרֹב בְּקֶרֶב הָאָרֶץ.

Ha-mal-ach ha-go-eil o-ti mi-kol rah y'va-reich et ha-n'a-rim, v'yi-ka-rei va-hem sh'mi v'sheim a-vo-tai Av-ra-ham v'Yitz-chak, v'yid-gu la-rov b'keh-rev ha-a-retz.

May the One Who saved me from all evil bless this boy, and let him be called by our name and the names of our ancestors, and may he multiply throughout the land. (Genesis 48:16)

For a girl:

בְּרוּכָה אַתְּ לַיְיָ בִּתִּי, וְעַתָּה בִּתִּי אַל תִּירָאִי, כֹּל אֲשֶׁר תֹּאמְרִי אֶעֱשֶׂה לָךְ כִּי אֵשֶׁת חַיִל תִּהְיִי.

B'ru-chah at la-do-nai bi-ti, v'a-ta bi-ti al ti-ra-i, kol a-sher to-m'ri eh-eh-seh lach ki ei-shet cha-yil tih-yi.

Be blessed of the Lord, daughter! And now, daughter, have no fear. I will do in your behalf whatever you ask, for you will be a fine woman. (based on Ruth 3:10–11)

Brit Immuts

Parents:

יְבָרֶכְךָ יְיָ וְיִשְׁמְרֶךָ,
יָאֵר יְיָ פָּנָיו אֵלֶיךָ וִיחֻנֶּךָ,
יִשָּׂא יְיָ פָּנָיו אֵלֶיךָ וְיָשֵׂם לְךָ שָׁלוֹם.

Y'va-reh-ch'chah Adonai v'yish-m'reh-cha,
Ya-eir Adonai pa-nav ei-leh-kha vi-chu-neh-ka,
Yi-sah Adonai pa-nav ei-leh-kha v'ya-seim l'chah sha-lom.
May God bless you and protect you.
May God's presence shine for you and be favorable to you.
May God's face turn to you and give you peace.

All:

בָּרוּךְ אַתָּה יְיָ, אֱלֹהֵינוּ מֶלֶךְ הָעוֹלָם,
שֶׁהֶחֱיָנוּ וְקִיְּמָנוּ וְהִגִּיעָנוּ לַזְּמַן הַזֶּה.

Ba-ruch a-ta Adonai, Eh-lo-hei-nu meh-lech ha-o-lam,
sheh-heh-cheh-ya-nu v'ki-y'ma-nu v'hi-gi-a-nu la-z'man ha-zeh.
Holy One of Blessing, Your Presence fills creation,
You have kept us alive, You have sustained us,
You have brought us to this moment.

Guests offer personal blessings and prayers.

Kiddush is recited and the meal is served.[11]

The Changing Jewish Family

It's hard to make generalizations about *the* Jewish family in America because Jewish families now come in all shapes, sizes, and color combinations. However, now that conversion to Judaism is commonplace and the intermarriage rate nationally is more than 50 percent, most Jewish families today probably include non-Jewish relatives.[1] If this is a reality in your family, a Jewish birth celebration can raise a host of issues and opportunities.

Inviting non-Jewish family members to your baby's *brit* ceremony may pose no problem. Some couples who decide to raise Jewish children enjoy the full support of both extended families. For many new grandparents, the joy of having a new baby in the family far outweighs any other consideration.

But in some cases, a Jewish ceremony for a new baby raises difficult issues for non-Jewish family members. These can surface even in families where a conversion or a Jewish wedding ceremony preceded the baby's birth. And oftentimes, when one of the parents is not Jewish, the baby's ceremony may be the first public announcement—and demonstration—of a decision to raise the children as Jews.

Addressing Your Non-Jewish Family's Concerns

A public ceremony to announce that a grandchild will be raised as a Jew can stir strong feelings. *Brit milah,* the covenant of circumcision, is an emotionally loaded subject for many Jews, and it can be even more disturbing to non-Jews who have never attended a *bris* and may harbor fears and misconceptions about what's going to happen to the baby.

New parents, already overwhelmed by the responsibilities of taking care of a newborn, can be hurt and angered when family members talk about their concerns. But parents and others should also try to remember that a grandparent's (or sister's or uncle's) lack of enthusiasm may not reflect latent anti-Semitism. Sometimes hesitancy or distress may reflect nothing more than a sense of being left out, or fear for a baby boy's well-being. Your Jewish ceremony may also remind non-Jewish family members of religious or family traditions that have great meaning for them, but that you are not going to pass on to this baby. Some family members may see your decision as a personal rejection of them and all they stand for. In some cases, people may even fear, from a Christian perspective, for the fate of an unbaptized baby's soul.

It's important to be sensitive and show respect for such concerns. To make things easier for everyone, you might ask non-Jewish family members to participate in the ceremony in ways that are appropriate and comfortable for them and for you. Invite questions and explain the meaning of the planned ritual, both in terms of its Jewish content and how it speaks to you personally. And always, keep your shared joy about the new baby paramount in your conversations.

If grandparents or other relatives voice reservations about your decision to celebrate your child's entry into the Jewish community, you may feel hurt. But try not to get angry. If a family member says something that seems anti-Semitic, confront the issue head-on, but lovingly. Perhaps there has been some misunderstanding. Maybe there are unspoken fears that need to be discussed. This is not to say that you should tolerate bigotry. Try a firm but positive statement such as: "I'm really surprised to hear you talk that way about Judaism. You raised us to be tolerant."

Remember to be clear about what you are doing and why: You are announcing to the world that you have decided to raise your child as a Jew. But also, take the time to reassure your non-Jewish family that this decision is not intended to hurt them in any way and that your affirmation of the Jewish tradition is not a repudiation of them. Let them know that you want to share your joy with them. Grandparents may need to hear you say the obvious: that you want them to play an important part in your baby's life.

Provide information and offer reassurance about the ritual. People are often afraid that they will say or do something wrong at a religious ceremony that is new to them. The more you let your non-Jewish family know about what to expect, the better. Giving non-Jewish grandparents this book to read before the ceremony—before the birth of your baby, if possible—can prepare them for what's going to happen, and why. The book's appendices for non-Jewish guests at *brit milah* and *brit bat* offer concise introductions to the ceremonies.

You might even try to think of your ceremony as a new beginning for your entire extended family. Sometimes, when a new baby is born, family structures that have been stuck in old patterns can loosen up. As children become parents and parents become grandparents, the constellation of the family may realign in new ways. This may be a good moment to begin an honest, respectful dialogue about religious differences and religious decisions.

Participation by Non-Jewish Relatives and Guests

There is a wide range of opinion and practice regarding non-Jewish participation in *brit* ceremonies, but by and large, there is plenty of room for inclusion.

The limits to participation vary. In general, it seems only appropriate that the leader of any Jewish ritual be a Jew. Likewise at a *bris*, the role of the *sandek*, the one who holds the baby during the circumcision, traditionally goes to a Jewish man who himself underwent the procedure while being held by another Jewish man. Hebrew prayers and blessings that invoke the idea of being commanded (*asher kid'shanu*, "Who has commanded us") are usually recited only by non-Jews who are "commanded" to perform ritual deeds, or *mitzvot*.

For ceremonies held in a synagogue, the customs of the congregation should be honored. Thus, if non-Jews are not called up to the Torah on other occasions, they probably will not be called up for yours. But because many ceremonies for new babies are held at home, participation tends to be very much a matter of parental discretion. If a rabbi or *mohel* (someone trained in the ritual of circumcision) is involved in planning and leading a home ceremony, it's probably a good idea to discuss the honors you plan to bestow on non-Jews with him or her.

There are many ways for non-Jewish relatives and friends to join in the ceremony. Grandparents and others may offer personal prayers, or may read from non-religious texts or sources that have meaning to Jews and Christians. They can offer toasts, sing songs, hold or carry the baby into the room, and give treasured gifts. Virtually all the ceremonies that appear in this book include readings and prayers that can be read by any honored guest.

The Role of Godparents

One important difference between Jewish and Christian birth rituals concerns godparents. In many Christian churches, godparents speak on behalf of the child at a baptism or christening and sometimes agree to act as the child's spiritual guides in the future, especially if the parents cannot. In the Jewish tradition, however, godparents (*kvatter* and *kvatterin* in Yiddish) play a strictly honorary role at the ceremony. There is no real religious significance attached to them.

Celebrating Your Family's Diversity

Although the ceremony itself should be unambiguously Jewish, the celebration that follows is a good time to honor all the important aspects of your baby's birthright, from both sides of the family. By featuring distinctive elements from the non-Jewish family—food, music and dance, songs from another language, ceremonial clothing and gifts, family toasts—you send a clear signal of respect for their traditions. You also demonstrate your intention to teach your child to be proud of the extended family's varied heritage.

For the Non-Jewish Parent of a Jewish Child

Although you and your spouse may have long ago agreed to raise your child as a Jew, the ceremony that makes this decision public may leave you feeling awkward or confused. You might worry about saying or doing something inappropriate during the ritual, or you may be concerned about how your family is reacting. You might wonder how you can affirm a religious tradition that is generally unfamiliar to you.

It is important to talk to your spouse about these feelings and to know that you are not alone. Many non-Jews have made the same decision and are now fully engaged in the task of raising Jewish children, by supporting their Jewish education and by making Jewish ritual a part of family life. Some congregations run support groups for interfaith families that help non-Jews feel more connected to the community.

To become comfortable with the ceremony itself, you should learn as much as possible about the Jewish history and traditions that surround it. Then make it as personally meaningful as you can. During the ritual, or at the meal afterwards, read a poem or non-sectarian prayer or even part of a children's book that you love. Play a favorite piece of music. Make sure the food being served satisfies your tastes and celebrates your ethnic and cultural tradition. (There was no mention of herring or bagels at Mt. Sinai.)

Finally, remember that your decision to raise your child as a Jew doesn't obligate you to become an expert on Judaism. You and your child have a lifetime in which to explore the tradition, the languages, the history, the lore, the customs—together. Most important, remember that choosing to give your child a sense of identity, history, and community is the act of a loving parent—which is what Jewish children, like all children, need more than anything.

PART
6

The First Year

The First Year

For all parents, the first year of a child's life is a series of milestones. The first smile, the first step, the first word, are all breathlessly reported to doting grandparents and half-interested friends alike.

The first year of a Jewish baby's life is also a series of occasions for *shehecheyanu*—the prayer of thanksgiving that greets all sorts of milestones—from the first full night's sleep to your child's first Passover *seder*. As the seasons change during your child's first year, Jewish holidays are experienced and remembered differently: giving Jonathan his first applesauce on *Rosh Hashanah;* trying to get Dan to look at all the candles on the eighth night of *Chanukah;* hauling Shira's diaper bag and playpen to a *Purim* party.

Babies change your life forever, and that includes your idea of rest and relaxation. If you were accustomed to *Shabbat* as an island of rest and peace in a busy week, you almost certainly will miss a measure of quiet and calm.

Shabbat

The Sabbath provides ways to celebrate your newly reconstituted family with simple, sweet rituals that will stay with your children as long as they live. Many families have rediscovered the custom of adding a candle for each child on Friday night. And reciting the traditional *Shabbat* blessing for children reminds everyone—no matter how tired or aggravated—of the love that makes you a family.

The *Shabbat* blessing of children takes place after candle-lighting. Either or both parents say:

For girls:

יְשִׂמֵךְ אֱלֹהִים כְּשָׂרָה רִבְקָה רָחֵל וְלֵאָה.

*Y'si-mech Eh-lo-him k'Sa-rah, Riv-kah, Ra-chel
v'Lei-ah.*

May God make you as Sarah, Rebecca, Rachel
and Leah.★

For boys:

יְשִׂמְךָ אֱלֹהִים כְּאֶפְרַיִם וְכִמְנַשֶּׁה.

Y'sim-chah Eh-lo-him k'Ef-ra-yim v'chim-na-sheh.

May God make you as Ephraim and Menasheh.★★

Some parents add the priestly benediction:

יְבָרֶכְךָ יְיָ וְיִשְׁמְרֶךָ,
יָאֵר יְיָ פָּנָיו אֵלֶיךָ וִיחֻנֶּךָּ,
יִשָּׂא יְיָ פָּנָיו אֵלֶיךָ וְיָשֵׂם לְךָ שָׁלוֹם.

*Y'va-reh-ch'chah Adonai v'yish-m'reh-cha,
Ya-eir Adonai pa-nav ei-leh-kha vi-chu-neh-ka,
Yi-sah Adonai pa-nav ei-leh-kha v'ya-seim l'cha
sha-lom.*

May Adonai bless you and protect you. May
Adonai shine the countenance upon you and be
gracious to you. May Adonai favor you and grant
you peace.

★ *The matriarchs of Judaism.*
★★ *The sons of Joseph and Osenath.*

In some families, parents take the opportunity to tell their children how proud they are of something the children learned or did or said in the past week.

First Birthday

Some parents celebrate their child's first birthday by planting a tree or by making a donation of *tzedakah*—righteous giving, or charity. If you created a *wimpel*, or Torah binder, to honor your child's *brit*, it is customary to take the completed band to your synagogue on or near the child's first birthday as a gift to the congregation (see page 173).[1]

Weaning

Nursing is a powerful connection between mother and child, and its end is a milestone for both. Recently, weaning has become the occasion for Jewish celebrations that hearken back to Judaism's first baby and also reflect contemporary Jewish women's spirituality.

In the past, when infant mortality was a terrible fact of family life, weaning may have been celebrated with more ceremony than birth or circumcision. There is no mention of a celebration in honor of Isaac's *brit;* the Torah says, "And the child grew and was weaned and Abraham made a feast on the day Isaac was weaned." In the Bible, Hannah's prayer of thanksgiving was offered after Samuel's weaning.

Even rabbinic literature notes the importance of the nursing relationship, using it as a metaphor for the bond between God and the people of Israel. Indeed, the Midrash compares the giving of the Torah at Sinai to a nursing mother.[2]

Contemporary weaning celebrations tend to be brief and simple, consisting of a series of prayers, personal reflections and commentary, and a meal. Because weaning often takes place over the course of weeks or months, a celebration like this will occur sometime during the process, whenever you feel it is time to observe this very personal rite of passage.

Commonly, weaning celebrations are held at home, either as part of a *Shabbat* lunch or incorporated into the ceremony that ends the Sabbath, *havdalah*. *Havdalah,* which means separation, is a recurrent theme of weaning celebrations. As the weekly *havdalah* ceremony sanctifies and celebrates the difference between sacred and secular time, weaning marks a physical separation of mother and child.

It is customary to begin the meal at a weaning celebration by having someone other than the mother feed the child his or her first solid food. (A symbolic "first" is fine, too. If your baby has already tasted rice cereal, offer a first taste of barley cereal or *challah*.) The honor of feeding the baby might be given to the father, a sibling, or a grandparent. Another custom associated with this rediscovered rite of passage is the giving of *tzedakah* in the amount of the baby's weight, often to a charity having to do with hunger or children or both.

Weaning celebrations can be as simple as the addition of a *shehecheyanu* at the first *Shabbat* night meal after which the baby has not nursed for a full week. Or you can make weaning a more public milestone, complete with a printed program of readings, songs, and blessings.

The ceremony might reprise lines or readings from your child's *brit* ceremony, reflecting on the distance between that day and this. The familiar lines from Ecclesiastes seem particularly appropriate at weaning.

> A season is set for everything, a time for every experience under heaven:
> A time for being born and a time for dying,
> A time for planting and a time for uprooting the planted;
> A time for slaying and a time for healing,
> A time for tearing down and a time for building up;
> A time for weeping and a time for laughing,
> A time for wailing and a time for dancing;

A time for throwing stones and a time for gathering stones,
A time for embracing and a time for shunning embraces;
A time for seeking and a time for losing,
A time for keeping and a time for discarding;
A time for ripping and a time for sewing,
A time for silence and a time for speaking;
A time for loving and a time for hating;
A time for war and a time for peace.

Some parents use white wine, to symbolize mother's milk, for the *kiddush*. If the baby has not already been given a *kiddush* cup, this might be a nice occasion to buy one for your son or daughter and offer him or her a sip from it. The ceremony that follows has a big, fun finish.

Weaning Celebration

Parents:

Just as Abraham and Sarah rejoiced at the weaning of their son Isaac, our hearts, too, are glad that our child has grown into full childhood, sustained in good health by God's gift of milk.

Mother:

בָּרוּךְ אַתָּה יְיָ, אֱלֹהֵינוּ מֶלֶךְ הָעוֹלָם,
אֲשֶׁר פָּתַח אֶת שַׁדַּי וְהֵנַקְתִּי אֶת פְּרִי רַחְמִי.

Ba-ruch a-ta Adonai, Eh-lo-hei-nu meh-lech ha-o-lam,
a-sher pa-tach et sha-dai v'hei-nak-ti et p'ri rach-mi.
Blessed are You, God, Ruler of the Universe,
Who opened my breasts to nurse the fruit of my womb.

Father:

בָּרוּךְ אַתָּה יְיָ, אֱלֹהֵינוּ מֶלֶךְ הָעוֹלָם,
מְשַׂמֵּחַ הוֹרִים עִם יַלְדֵיהֶם.

Ba-ruch a-ta Adonai, Eh-lo-hei-nu meh-lech ha-o-lam,
m'sa-mei-ach ho-rim im yal-dei-hem.
Blessed are You, God, Ruler of the Universe,
Who enables parents to rejoice in their children.

Together:

In love, we will continue to give sustenance to our child and provide for her/his physical needs. May we also provide her/him with spiritual sustenance through examples of lovingkindness and through the teaching of Torah and the traditions of our people.

This material is from The New Jewish Baby Book *by Anita Diamant, © 1993, published by Jewish Lights Publishing, P.O. Box 237, Sunset Farm Offices, Woodstock, VT 05091. The publisher grants permission to you to copy this ceremony for distribution to your guests. All rights to other parts of this book are still covered by copyright and are reserved to the publisher.*

Weaning Celebration

A donation of $_____$, two times _____'s weight, has been made to _____ (name of a charity).

Today, we present _____ with a *kiddush* cup, symbolizing her/his independence from the breast and the hope that she will grow to participate in the *mitzvah* of *kiddush*.

The blessings over wine and bread are recited, and the baby is given a piece of *challah*.

Parents break a baby bottle.

All:

Mazel Tov![3]

Appendix I
What Non-Jews Should Know about *Brit Milah*

This appendix, intended for non-Jewish guests who will attend the ceremony, restates some of the material found in earlier chapters and provides a general explanation of the ritual and its meaning.

Jews and Christians look at many things differently. We have different theologies, different liturgies, different holiday cycles, and different ways of celebrating the life cycle. Nevertheless, Jews and Christians share many things, and what we share is no less profound than our differences.

We share a belief in a God who can be approached through prayer and worship, a God who loves and is revealed in the Bible and in history. We share a book, the Hebrew Bible, which most Christians call the Old Testament. Both Jews and Christians celebrate religious rituals at the beginning of life.

In virtually all cultures, rituals for babies are moments of sacred initiation, and many share certain elements—especially joy and gratitude for the gift of a new person in the world. Most Jewish and Christian birth rituals also bestow a name upon a new baby. By doing this within a religious framework, both traditions give a spiritual dimension to the child's identity; hence the term "christening."

But there are important differences between the rites of the two faiths. The Christian ritual of baptism uses water as a sign of identification with the death and resurrection of Jesus, and as a sign of welcome into the Christian community. Jewish baby ceremonies, including those that use water, all signify a child's entry into the Jewish covenant with God. The Hebrew word for covenant is *brit*.

Brit refers to the relationship between the Jewish people and God. A covenant is a contract—an agreement between responsible parties, a two-way street. Circumcision is one of the terms of that agreement set forth in the Bible. Since the beginning of the Jewish people, starting with Abraham and Sarah, Jewish parents have been called to welcome their eight-day-old sons into this covenant with a ceremony that is also called *brit*.

Girls are welcomed into the covenant with a ceremony called *brit bat*. Rituals for daughters are a relatively new addition to the life cycle, and feature some of the same prayers, songs and traditions found in *brit milah*.

The covenant of circumcision (*brit milah, brit*, or *bris*) is the oldest continuous Jewish rite, a ritual that unites Jews throughout ages and across cultures and signifies the connection between individual human life and the Holy. With this ancient ceremony, parents announce their commitment to taking on the responsibilities and joys of raising a Jewish child.

The procedure itself may be unsettling to some people, and at most *bris* ceremonies, guests who do not wish to watch the removal of the foreskin from the baby's penis simply keep their distance during the procedure. However, the circumcision itself is not the core element of the service. It is the blessings and intention to bring the child into what is also known as "the covenant of Abraham" that give the ritual its religious significance. A Jewish male who has not been circumcised is still Jewish—he is considered simply a Jew in need of a *bris*. Likewise, a Jewish male who was circumcised without Jewish rites is considered in need of a ceremonial *bris*.

Circumcision itself has been deemed safe by the American Academy of Pediatrics. Circumcision in the home, rather than in the hospital, is also safe and, by all accounts, much easier on the baby. Although the baby feels some pain, his discomfort is very brief (the procedure takes only a few seconds) and he is readily soothed afterward.

The person who performs circumcisions for the purpose of bringing a child into the Jewish covenant is called a *mohel* (pronounced mo–*hail* or *moil*). *Mohels* are not ordained: They are Jews who are trained in the procedures and blessings of *brit milah*. Many American *mohels* today are also physicians.

Names

As at a christening, a Jewish boy receives his name at a *bris*. A Hebrew name, which may or may not be different from his English name, will be announced. The Hebrew name is used on religious documents, and is the name by which Jews are called when they are summoned in the synagogue to read from the Torah scroll, which contains the first five books of the Hebrew Bible. Names are most often given in memory of a loved one who has died, as a tribute.

Godparents

One important difference between Jewish and Christian birth rituals concerns godparents. Christian godparents often have an important religious function, speaking on behalf of the child at a baptism or christening, and sometimes agreeing to act as the child's spiritual guides in the future. In the Jewish tradition, however, godparents (*kvatter* and *kvatterin* in Yiddish) play a strictly honorary role at the ceremony, which often entails little more than bringing the baby into the room or holding him or her during some part of the ritual.

Joy

The Hebrew word for joy, *simcha,* is also the Hebrew word for party. According to Jewish law and tradition, all life-cycle events must include a meal of celebration and expressions of happiness. A joyful heart is the most important gift you can bring to a *bris.*

Appendix II
What Non-Jews Should Know about Brit Bat

This appendix restates some of the material found in earlier chapters and provides a general explanation of celebrations that welcome baby girls into the Jewish people.

Jews and Christians look at many things differently. We have different theologies, different liturgies, different holiday cycles, and different ways of celebrating the life cycle. Nevertheless, Jews and Christians share many things, and what we share is no less profound than our differences.

We share a belief in a God who can be approached through prayer and worship, a God who loves and is revealed in the Bible and in history. We share a book, the Hebrew bible, which most Christians call the Old Testament. Both Jews and Christians celebrate religious rituals at the beginning of life.

In virtually all cultures, rituals for babies are moments of sacred initiation, and many share certain elements—especially joy and gratitude for the gift of a new person in the world. Most Jewish and Christian birth rituals also bestow a name upon a new baby. By doing this within a religious framework, both traditions give a spiritual dimension to the child's identity; hence the term "christening."

However, there are important differences between the rituals of the two faiths. The Christian ritual of baptism uses water as a sign of identification with the death and resurrection of Jesus, and as a sign of welcome into the Christian community. Jewish baby ceremonies, including those that use water, all signify a child's entry into the Jewish covenant with God. The Hebrew word for covenant is *brit*.

Brit refers to the relationship between the Jewish people and God. A covenant is a contract—an agreement between responsible parties, a two-way street. Boys become part of the covenant through the ancient ritual of *brit milah,* the covenant of circumcision. *Brit bat*—which means covenant for a daughter—is how parents welcome their infant daughters to this historic holy relationship. The ceremony is also a way of announcing a family's commitment to taking on the responsibilities and joys of raising a Jewish child.

Brit bat ceremonies have a long history among Mediterranean and Middle-eastern Jews. However, until recently, this tradition was unknown to most American Jews, whose ancestry is Ashkenazic, or eastern European. The desire to celebrate the birth of a daughter with the same purpose and joy that is traditional for the birth of a son, has prompted a new ritual that has become, within a single generation, very much a part of the Jewish life cycle.

Brit bat has inspired a great deal of creativity and liturgical variety. Although there is no standard or required ceremony for daughters, nearly all rituals include blessings and prayers, songs and wishes, and a convenant prayer or gesture that enacts the baby's entry into the Jewish people.

Names

One of the most important moments at the ceremony is the announcement of the baby's name. As at a christening, a Jewish girl receives her name at a *brit bat.* Indeed, many ceremonies are called "namings." A Hebrew name, which may or may not be different from her English name, will be announced.

The Hebrew name is used on religious documents, and is the name by which Jews are called when they are summoned in the synagogue to read from the Torah scroll, which contains the first five books of the Hebrew Bible. Names are most often given in memory of a loved one who has died, as a tribute.

Godparents

One important difference between Jewish and Christian birth rituals concerns godparents. Christian godparents often have an important religious function, speaking on behalf of the child at a baptism or christening, and sometimes agreeing to act as the child's spiritual guides. In the Jewish tradition, however, godparents (*kvatter* and *kvatterin* in Yiddish) play a strictly honorary role at the ceremony, which often entails little more than bringing the baby into the room or holding her during some part of the ritual.

Joy

The Hebrew word for joy, *simcha,* is also the Hebrew word for party. According to Jewish law and tradition, all life-cycle events must include a meal of celebration and expressions of happiness. A joyful heart is the most important gift you can bring to a *brit bat.*

Jewish Resources for New Parents

Giving your baby a Jewish name and celebrating with a Jewish ceremony that welcomes him or her to the covenant of Israel is just the beginning. The following books can help you in the lifelong work of raising a Jewish child and living a Jewish life that has meaning and value to you. You are your child's most important teacher.

Books for Children and Parents

Jewish children's literature is flourishing, with new titles in every category, from books for pre-readers to mysteries for young adults. Here are a few classics to enjoy together.

Gellman, Marc. *Does God have a Big Toe?* New York: Harper & Row, 1989. Bible stories with an attitude.

Kar-Ben Copies, Inc., Rockville, Md. publishes indestructible little "board books" for pre-readers about many of the Jewish holidays and the Hebrew alphabet.

Kushner, Lawrence. *The Book of Miracles: Jewish Spirituality for Children to Read to their Parents and for Parents to Read to Their Children.* New York: Union of American Hebrew Congregations Press, 1987. Jewish spirituality while standing on one foot.

Kops, Simon. *Fast, Clean, and Cheap (or everything the Jewish teacher and parent needs to know about art)*. Los Angeles: Torah Aura Productions, 1989. Hands-on projects for every occasion.

Sasso, Sandy Eisenberg. *God's Paintbrush*. Woodstock, Vt.: Jewish Lights Publishing, 1992. Beautifully illustrated theology.

Schwartz, Howard. *Elijah's Violin and Other Jewish Fairy Tales*. New York: Harper & Row, 1983. A collection of classic tales.

Shaffer, Patricia. *Chag Sameach: A Jewish Holiday Book for Children*. Berkeley, Ca.: Tabor Sarah Books, 1985. This book is noteworthy for its depiction of multi-racial Jewish families.

Family Resources

Books to help you think about Jewish family life.

Bell, Roselyn, ed. *The Hadassah Magazine Jewish Parenting Book*. New York: The Free Press, 1989. An anthology of articles that have appeared in the magazine.

Diamant, Anita and Howard Cooper. *Living a Jewish Life: Jewish Traditions, Customs and Values for Today's Families*. New York: HarperCollins, 1991. A how-to that explains why-to.

A "*tzedakah*-master," Danny Siegel has written books full of ideas to inspire you to make charity a part of your family's daily life.

Siegel, Danny. *Gym Shoes and Irises: Personalized Tzedakah* (Books 1 and 2). Pittsboro, N.C.: The Town House Press, 1982, 1987.

Siegel, Danny. *Munbaz II and Other Mitzvah Heroes*. Pittsboro, N.C.: The Town House Press, 1988.

Siegel, Danny. *Mitzvahs*. Pittsboro, N.C.: The Town House Press, 1990.

The following three publishers produce excellent hands-on material:

Behrman House Publishing Co., West Orange, N.J. *Home Start Kits.* A series of booklets for pre-schoolers and one for first and second graders.

Melton Research Center of the Jewish Theological Seminary, New York, N.Y. *Together.* A series of books on holiday and subjects such as Israel, Torah, and *Shabbat.*

Torah Aura Productions, Los Angeles, Calif. *Building Jewish Life.* A lively, inviting series of books about the holidays for children, with more sophisticated explanations for parents.

General Jewish Reference

Books for looking up everything you always wanted to know but didn't know where to look.

The Encyclopaedia Judaica. Jerusalem: Keter Publishing Co., 1972. The "EJ," as it is known, is the Britannica of Judaism. This is a major financial investment, but there is little this sixteen-volume work does not cover.

Klein, Isaac. *A Guide to Jewish Religious Practice.* New York: Jewish Theological Society of America, 1979. The standard reference book on *halachah,* or Jewish law. Published by the Conservative movement; this is where you go to look up the law on just about anything.

Rosten, Leo. *The Joy of Yiddish.* New York: McGraw-Hill, 1968. This is more than just a funny dictionary of English, Yiddish and "Yinglish" words. It's a guide for people who are exploring and discovering Yiddishkeit—Jewishness.

Siegel, Richard, and Michael and Sharon Strassfeld. *The Jewish Catalog, Vols. I, II, and III.* Philadelphia: Jewish Publication Society, 1973, 1976, and 1980). A trove of Jewish information in a do-it-yourself format. Note: *The Jewish Catalogs* assume that readers are Hebrew-literate and somewhat familiar with Jewish law and observance.

Telushkin, Joseph. *Jewish Literacy: The Most Important Things to Know about the Jewish Religion, Its People, and Its History.* New York: William Morrow and Co., 1991. A great one-volume resource.

The Jewish Holidays and Life-Cycle

Hows and whys.

Cardozo, Arlene Rossen. *Jewish Family Celebrations: The Sabbath, Festivals and Ceremonies.* New York: St. Martin's Press, 1982. A brief introduction to the holidays, with recipes.

Greenberg, Irving. *The Jewish Way.* New York: Summit, 1991. Not a how-to book, this is a theology of the holidays, whose theme, says Greenberg, is redemption.

Nathan, Joan. *The Jewish Holiday Kitchen.* New York: Schocken, 1988. An introduction to the world of Jewish cuisine, which includes a lot more than bagels and chicken soup.

Salkin, Jeffrey. *Putting God on the Guest List: How to Reclaim the Spiritual Meaning of Your Child's Bar or Bat Mitzvah.* Woodstock, Vt.: Jewish Lights Publishing, 1992. The title says it all.

Strassfeld, Michael. *The Jewish Holidays: A Guide and Commentary.* New York: Harper and Row, 1985. Comprehensive and chock-full of information.

Waskow, Arthur. *Seasons of Our Joy.* New York: Beacon Press, 1991. Informal, poetic; a New Age approach with broad appeal.

See also: Diamant, *Living a Jewish Life,* and Strassfelds, *The Jewish Catalog, Volumes 1, 2, and 3* Philadelphia, Pa.: Jewish Publication Society.

The Interfaith Family and Conversion

Cowan, Paul and Rachel. *Mixed Blessings: Marriage Between Christians and Jews.* New York: Doubleday, 1987. An intelligent overview of the challenges of interfaith couples based on interviews and workshops and also the experience of the authors.

Kukoff, Lydia. *Choosing Judaism*. New York: Union of American Hebrew Congregations, 1981. A first-person account.

Romanoff, Lena, with Lisa Holstein. *Your People, My People: Finding Acceptance and Fulfillment as a Jew by Choice*. Philadelphia, Pa.: Jewish Publication Society, 1990.

Schneider, Susan Wiedman. *Intermarriage: The Challenge of Living with Differences between Christians and Jews*. New York: Free Press, 1989.

The Bible and Other Basic Jewish Texts

Hertz, J.H. *The Pentateuch and Haftorah*. London: Soncino Press, 1972. The classic Torah commentary.

Holtz, Barry, ed. *Back to the Sources*. Summit Books, 1984. Eight essays by leading experts on the major Jewish texts. Holtz's introductory essay is an elegant and succinct explanation of why people continue to read the classical sources of Judaism.

Holtz, Barry, ed. *Finding Our Way: Jewish Texts and the Lives We Lead Today*. New York: Schocken, 1990. Applying the texts to modern life.

Plaut, Gunther W. *The Torah: A Modern Commentary*. New York: Union of American Hebrew Congregations, 1981. A good volume for study.

Rosenberg, David, ed. *Congregation: Contemporary Writers Read the Jewish Bible*. New York: Harcourt Brace Jovanovich, 1987. A collection of essays about the books of the Bible by poets, novelists, humorists, editors, and literary critics.

Adin Steinsaltz. *Everyman's Talmud*. New York: Bantam Books, 1976. A brief and lucid introduction to Talmud.

Spirituality

Rabbi Lawrence Kushner's books provide an accessible and inspiring introduction to Jewish spirituality.

Kushner, Lawrence. *The Book of Letters: A Mystical Hebrew Alphabet.* Woodstock, Vt.: Jewish Lights Publishing, 1990.

Kushner, Lawrence. *God Was in This Place and I, I Did Not Know: Finding Self, Spirituality, and Ultimate Meaning.* Woodstock, Vt.: Jewish Lights Publishing, 1991.

Kushner, Lawrence. *Honey From The Rock: An Easy Introduction to Jewish Mysticism.* Woodstock, Vt.: Jewish Lights Publishing, 1990.

Kushner, Lawrence. *River of Light: Spirituality, Judaism and Consciousness.* Woodstock, Vt.: Jewish Lights Publishing, 1992.

Kushner, Lawrence. *The Book of Words: Talking Spiritual Life, Living Spiritual Talk.* Woodstock, Vt.: Jewish Lights Publishing, 1993.

Glossary

ALEF-BET — Name of the Hebrew alphabet; also, its first two letters.

ALIYAH — Literally, "to go up." In the synagogue, to be called to the Torah. "Making aliyah" refers to moving to the land of Israel.

APOCHRYPHA — Fourteen "writings," including the Book of Esther, that were not included in the final version of the Bible, but which are, nevertheless, important Jewish texts.

ARAMAIC — Ancient Semitic language closely related to Hebrew. The Talmud was written in Aramaic.

ASHKENAZIC — Jews and Jewish culture of eastern and central Europe.

AUFRUF — Literally, "calling up." Recognition given when people are called up to the Torah on *Shabbat,* typically related to a life-cycle event.

BAAL SHEM TOV — Israel ben Eliezer, the founder of Hasidism, the 18th-century mystical revival movement.

BARUCH ATA ADONAI — Words that begin Hebrew blessings, most commonly rendered in English as "Blessed art Thou, Lord our God, King of the Universe." This book contains a number of alternatives to that translation.

BAT — Daughter, or daughter of, as in *bat mitzvah,* daughter of the commandment. Pronounced *baht.*

B.C.E. — Before the Common Era. Jews avoid the Christian designation B.C., which means Before Christ.

BEIT DIN — A court (literally a house of law) of three rabbis that is convened to witness and give communal sanction to events such as conversions to Judaism.

BRIS — Yiddish for *brit,* the most common way of referring to the covenant of circumcision.

BRIT — Covenant. In this book, the term applies to covenant ceremonies.

BRIT MILAH — The covenant of circumcision.

BUBBE — Yiddish word for grandma.

C.E. — Common Era. Jews avoid A.D., which stands for *anno domini,* or the year of our lord.

CHALLAH — Braided loaf of egg bread, traditional for *Shabbat,* the holidays and festive occasions.

CHAVURAH — Fellowship. Also, small participatory groups that meet for prayer, study, and celebration.

CHAZZAN — Cantor.

CHUPAH — Wedding canopy.

CONSERVATIVE — A religious movement developed in the United States during the 20th century as a more traditional response to modernity than that offered by Reform.

DAVEN — Pray.

DIASPORA — Exile. The dwelling of Jews outside the Holy Land.

D'RASH — Religious insight, often on a text from the Torah.

D'VAR TORAH — Literally, "words of Torah": an explication of a portion of the Torah.

Glossary

DREIDL — A top used for playing a child's game of chance during the festival of *Chanukah*.

EREV — "The evening before" the day. Jewish days begin at sunset, not sunrise.

FLEISHIG — Meat food, which according to *kashrut,* or traditional laws governing what Jews eat, may not be mixed with dairy products

HAIMISH — Yiddish for homelike, giving one a sense of belonging.

HAGGADAH — The book containing the liturgy of the Passover *seder.*

HALACHAH — Traditional Jewish law, contained in the Talmud and its commentaries.

HASIDISM — Eighteenth-century mystical revival, a movement that stressed God's presence in the world and the idea that joy could be seen as a way of communing with God.

HAVDALAH — Separation. The Saturday evening ceremony that separates *Shabbat* from the rest of the week.

KASHRUT — Traditional system of laws that govern what and how Jews eat.

KIDDUSH — Sanctification, also the blessing over wine.

KOHANE — The biblical social class that comprised the priesthood.

KOSHER — Foods deemed fit for consumption according to the laws of *kashrut.*

K'TUBAH — Marriage contract.

KVATTER, KVATTERIN — Godfather, godmother.

MAVEN — An expert.

MAZEL TOV — Literally, "good luck." In common use, it means "congratulations."

MENSCH — Person; an honorable, decent person.

MEZUZAH — First two paragraphs of the *Shema,* a Jewish prayer, written on a parchment scroll and encased in a small container, affixed to the doorposts of a home.

MILAH — Circumcision. *Brit milah* is the covenant of circumcision.

MILCHIG — Diary foods, which, according to *kashrut,* may not be mixed with meat.

MIDRASH — Imaginative exposition of stories based on the Bible.

MIKVAH — Ritual bath.

MINHAG — Custom.

MINYAN — A prayer quorum of ten adult Jews.

MISHNAH — The first part of the Talmud, comprised of six "orders" of laws regarding everything from agriculture to marriage.

MITZVAH — A sacred obligation or commandment, mentioned in the Torah.

MOHEL — One who is trained in the rituals and procedures of *brit milah,* circumcision. Pronounced mo-*hail,* in Hebrew; *moil* in Yiddish.

MOTZI — Blessing over bread recited before meals.

NACHAS — Special joy from the achievements of one's children.

NIGGUN — A wordless, prayer-like melody.

ONEG SHABBAT — Literally, joy of the Sabbath. A gathering, for food and fellowship, after Friday night synagogue services.

ORTHODOX — In general use, the term refers to Jews who follow traditional Jewish law. The modern Orthodox movement developed in the 19th century in response to the Enlightenment and Reform Judaism.

PARASHAH — The weekly Torah portion.

PESACH — Passover.

PIDYON HABEIN — The ceremony of "redeeming" a first-born son from the ancient obligation of Temple service.

RABBI — Teacher. A rabbi is a seminary-ordained member of the clergy. "The rabbis" refers to the men who codified the Talmud.

RECONSTRUCTIONIST — A religious movement begun in the United States in the 20th century by Mordecai Kaplan, who saw Judaism as an evolving religious civilization.

REFORM — A movement begun in 19th-century Germany that sought to reconcile Jewish tradition with modernity. Reform Judaism does not accept the divine authority of *halachah*.

ROSH CHODESH — First day of every lunar month; the New Month, a semi-holiday.

SANDEK — Jewish godfather; the one who holds the baby during a circumcision. *Sandeket* is a new term for Jewish godmother.

SHABBAT — Sabbath. In Yiddish, *Shabbos.*

SHECHINAH — God's feminine attributes.

SHEHECHEYANU — A common prayer of thanksgiving for new blessings.

SHEVA BRACHOT — The seven marriage blessings.

SH'MA — The Jewish prayer that declares God's unity.

SHTETL — A general name for the small towns inhabited by Ashkenazic Jews before the Holocaust.

SHUL — Synagogue.

SIDDUR — Prayerbook.

SIMCHA — Joy and the celebration of joy.

S'UDAT MITZVAH — A commanded meal; the festive celebration of a milestone.

TALLIS, TALLIT — Prayer shawl. *Tallis* is Yiddish, *tallit* Hebrew.

TALMUD — Collection of rabbinic thought and laws; 200 B.C.E. to 500 C.E.

TIKKUN OLAM — Repairing the world. A fundamental Jewish concept of taking responsibility in and improving the temporal world.

TOHORAT HAMISHPACHAH — Laws of family purity prescribing women's sexual availability and the use of *mikvah*.

TORAH — First five books of the Hebrew Bible, divided into 54 portions that are read aloud and studied in an annual cycle.

TZEDAKAH — Charity; righteous giving or action toward the poor.

YIDDISH — Language spoken by Ashkenazic Jews, a combination of early German and Hebrew.

YICHUS — Family status. Pride in family members' achievements.

YOM KIPPUR — Day of Atonement, the holiest of the High Holy Days.

Notes

Notes

 # Directory of Calligraphers and Artists

Works by the following calligraphers and artists appear in *The New Jewish Baby Book:*

Elaine Adler
3 Sunny Knoll Terrace
Lexington, MA 02173

Peggy Davis
389 Adamsville Road
Colrain, MA 01340

Leslie Gattman and Eugene Frank
7410 Poplar Drive
Forestville, CA 95436

Betsy Platkin-Teutsch
629 West Cliveden Street
Philadelphia, PA 19119

 Notes

Conception

1. For a fuller explanation of *mikvah,* see Diamant, Anita. *The New Jewish Wedding.* New York: Summit Books, 1985, p. 150.

2. Zborowski, Mark and Herzog, Elizabeth. *Life is with People.* New York: Schocken Books, 1952, p. 312.

3. Penzner, Barbara Rosman and Zweiback-Levenson, Amy. "Spiritual Cleansing: A Mikveh Ritual for Brides," *Reconstructionist Magazine,* September, 1986, pp. 25–28.

Pregnancy

1. Zborowski and Herzog, pp. 313–317. According to Jewish folklore, Lilith, Adam's first wife, was punished for her behavior with the awful fate of having to give birth to multitudes of demon babies who were then murdered. Lilith took a grisly revenge in killing Jewish newborns.

2. Rosenthal, Rabbi David Simcha. *A Joyful Mother of Children.* Jerusalem: Feldheim Publishers, Ltd., 1982.

3. © Rabbi Judy Shanks, 1983. Recited as part of the *Sh'ma al Ha-mitah.* Reprinted with permission of the author.

4. Adelman, Penina V. *Miriam's Well: Rituals for Jewish Women Around the Year.* Fresh Meadows, N.Y.: Biblio Press, 1986.

5. Zonderman, Shoshana. "Spiritual preparation for parenthood," *Response,* Vol. XIV, No. 4. Spring, 1985, pp. 29–39.

Birth

1. *Kol Haneshama, Shirim Uvrahot—Songs, Blessings and Rituals for the Home,* Wyncote, Pa.: The Reconstructionist Press, 1991, pp. 114–115. According to the authors of this new blessing, Seth Reimer, Betsy Platkin-Teutsch, and David Teutsch, "While it is crafted from biblical verses and rabbinic prayer forms, the synthesis that it embodies is something new. It emerges from a recognition that, because of our distinct gender roles, generally women were excluded from the prayer-house and men from the birthing room. Both were shortchanged. Today we are enriched by the possibility of sharing in both experiences. This affords an opportunity for new words of prayer. These express the joy and wonder of birth."

A Jewish Name

1. Gottlieb, Nathan. *A Jewish Child is Born.* New York: Bloch Publishing Co., 1960, p. 111.

2. Kolatch, Alfred. *The Name Dictionary.* Middle Village, N.Y.: Jonathan David Publishers, 1967, p. xi.

3. Kaganoff, Benzion C. *A Dictionary of Jewish Names and Their History.* New York: Schocken Books, 1977, p. 49.

4. Kaganoff, p. 53.

5. Dobrinski, Rabbi Herbert C. *A Treasury of Sephardic Laws and Customs.* New York and Hoboken, N.J.: Yeshiva University & Ktav, 1986, p. 4.

6. Dobrinski, p. 61. The history of Jewish surnames is another fascinating story. In Europe, it was not until the Middle Ages that Jews commonly added family names, mostly to facilitate dealings with the non-Jewish world. In Northern Europe, Jews did not take family names until the 19th century, and then usually under compulsion by Christian governments.

7. Dobrinski, p. 4.

8. Nesvisky, Matthew. "There's Miki, Riki, Tiki, Suki, Shuli, Tzippi, Tzuri, Uri and Nuri," *Moment Magazine,* Vol. 9, no. 8, September 1984/ Elul 5744, pp. 47–51.

9. In the past, Jews tended to adopt Jewish children. But the ancient ritual statuses of *kohane* and *levite* (groups for whom certain special laws and privileges are in effect) are inherited from one's biological parents only. Thus, the adoptive child of Cohen or Levinson parents would be called the Torah as "son of Abraham and Sarah," the generic convert's name. Because the vast majority of children adopted by Jewish parents today are not born Jews, this is a rare consideration.

10. Nesvisky, p. 50.

Brit Milah

1. Altman, Lawrence K. "Pediatricians Find Medical Benefit to Circumcision," *The New York Times,* Monday, March 6, 1989.

2. Maimonides, Moses. *Guide for the Perplexed,* translated from the Arabic by M. Friedlander. New York: Dover, 1956, p. 378.

3. Romberg, Henry C., M.D. *Bris Milah.* New York and Jerusalem: Feldheim Publishers, Ltd., 1982, p. 94.

4. Kushner, Rabbi Lawrence. "Save this Article," Bulletin of Congregation Beth El of the Sudbury River Valley, Sudbury, Mass. Vol. VIII, no. 6., *Sivan/Tammuz* 5742, p. 3.

5. "Policy Report of the Task Force on Circumcision," *AAP News,* March, 1989, p. 7. "Properly performed newborn circumcision prevents phimosis, paraphimosis and balanoposthitis."

6. Korones, Sheldon B., M.D. *High Risk Newborn Infants.* St. Louis, Mo.: The C.V. Mosby Co., 1976.

7. The traditional practice of circumcision was even more dramatically sexual. The *halachicly* prescribed practice of *m'tzitzah*—the drawing of blood away from the wound—was, for centuries, accomplished by the *mohel* with his lips. The erotic and homoerotic suggestions in that act are clearly disturbing. *Mohels* now either omit *m'tzitzah* or use a pipette to ritually remove the blood.

Notes

8. Exodus 4:24–25.

9. *Jewish Encyclopedia*, p. 570.

10. Gaster, Theodore H. *The Holy and the Profane*, pp. 53–54.

11. Krohn, Rabbi Paysach J. *Bris Milah; Circumcision—The Covenant of Abraham*. Brooklyn, N.Y.: Mesorah Publications, 1969, pp. 62–63.

12. *Midrash Tanchuma* on *T'tzaveh*, 1.

13. Schauss, Hayyim. *The Lifetime of a Jew throughout the Ages of Jewish History*. New York: Union of American Hebrew Congregations, 1950, p. 33.

14. Schauss, p. 25.

15. Weiss, Charles. "A Worldwide Survey of the Current Practice of *Milah*," *Jewish Social Studies*, Number 24, 1962, p. 43. The United Kingdom is one of few places with a system for training and regulation of *milah*, begun in 1745 in London. *Mohels* must pass both a medical examination and a test given by a religious court.

16. Isserles, *Shulchan Aruch, Yoreh Deah* 264:1. "A man should seek around to find the best and most pious *mohel* and *sandek*."

17. Ausubel, Nathan. *The Book of Jewish Knowledge*. New York: Crown Publishers, Inc. 1964, p. 114.

18. Krohn, p. 98.

19. Elijah's chair may be a vestigial link to the very ancient custom of leaving out food, tables, and chairs to appease pagan household gods. Schauss, pp. 36–37.

20. Krohn, pp. 131–132. This passage is often left untranslated, and in some revised ceremonies, is even replaced with other citations from Torah and Talmud. The line, "I saw you wallowing in your blood," invites all kinds of interpretation. The mention of blood, forbidden by Jewish law in so many other contexts, seems to affirm the physical reality of human life, which includes danger, dread, and death as well as spiritual aspirations. According to tradition, this passage connects the covenant of *milah* with the covenant of the Hebrew people forged by the physical suffering during the Egyptian captivity. Similarly, the repeated line, "because of your blood you shall live," is linked to two signs of Jewish peoplehood: the blood of *milah* and the blood of the Paschal offering.

21. Krohn, p. 125.

22. Kushner, p. 3.

23. From a ceremony by Rabbi Edward Treister and Rochelle Treister, June 17, 1986, Houston, Texas.

24. Based on the ceremony by Rabbi Sandy Eisenberg Sasso. The same introductory readings (changed for gender) are used in her *Brit B'not Yisrael* ceremony.

25. Based on a ceremony compiled from many sources, by Rabbi Elaine Zecher and David Eisenberg, for the birth of their son Jacob Zecher Eisenberg.

Brit Bat

I have tried to give credit to everyone whose words appear in this chapter. However, because of the amount of sharing, copying, and rewriting that typify the phenomenon of *brit bat,* I fear that someone, somewhere will find his or her words uncredited or miscredited. For this, I apologize.

I would like to acknowledge the work of the Jewish Women's Resource Center, a project of the National Council of Jewish Women, New York Section, for their library, which is a national resource. Their pamphlet "Birth Ceremonies" was a ground-breaking source, as was "Blessing the Birth of a Daughter: Jewish Naming Ceremonies for Girls," edited by Toby Fishbein Reifman.

Thanks to all the parents and rabbis who shared insights and ceremonies with me. Among them: Fern Amper and Eli Schaap, Aliza Arzt, Rabbi Albert Axelrad, Naomi Bar-Yam, Judith Baskin, Rabbi Gordon Freeman, Randee Rosenberg Freidman, Rabbi Rebecca Jacobs, Carol and Michael Katzman, Stanley H. Hellman, Rabbi Jeffrey A. Perry-Marx, Judith May, Rabbi Barbara Penzner, Rabbi Sandy Eisenberg Sasso, Rabbi Daniel Siegel and Hannah Tiferet Siegel, Rabbi Paul Swerdlow, Rabbi Edward Treister and Rochelle Treister, Rabbi Elaine Zecher.

1. "Raba, son of Rabbi Chana, said to Abaye, 'Go forth and see how the public are accustomed to act.'" *Seder Z'ra-im, Brachot* 45b.

2. Strassfeld, Michael and Sharon. *The Jewish Catalogs I, II, III.* Philadelphia: The Jewish Publication Society of America, 1973, 1976, 1980.

Notes

3. For an interesting discussion of ritual impurity, see Rachel Adler's article "Tumah and Taharah: Ends and Beginnings" in Elizabeth Koltun's book, *The Jewish Woman*. New York: Schocken, 1976, p. 63. One revisionist reading attributes the longer period of ritual impurity for the mothers of daughters to the fact that giving birth to a birth-giver represents a more powerful encounter with the source of life, which requires a longer separation from the mundane.

4. Kushner, Rabbi Lawrence. *The River of Light: Spirituality, Judaism and Consciousness*. Woodstock, Vt.: Jewish Lights Publishing, 1992, p. xii.

5. Jewish Women's Resource Center, "Birth Ceremonies, *Brit Banot; Covenant of Our Daughters*." New York, 1985, p. 2.

6. Greenberg, Blu, *How to Run a Traditional Jewish Household*. New York: Simon and Schuster, 1983, p. 248.

7. Dobrinsky, pp. 3–25.

8. Toby Fishbein Reifman with Ezrat Nashim. *Blessing the Birth of a Daughter; Jewish Naming Ceremonies for Girls*. Englewood, NJ: Ezrat Nashim, 1978. Quoting an unpublished paper by Rabbi Marc Angel of the Spanish and Portuguese Synagogue in New York, p. 27.

9. Reifman, pp. 26–27. From the ceremony that appears in the *Daily and Sabbath Prayer Book* edited by Dr. David de Sola Pool. New York: Union of Sephardic Congregations.

10. Cantor, Debra and Rebecca Jacobs, "Brit Banot,"*Kerem: Creative Explorations in Judaism,* Winter 1992–1993/5753, p. 47. This article includes a *brit bat* ceremony with choices for three different covenant "actions." This work was produced at the behest of the Rabbinical Assembly, the association of Conservative movement rabbis, in preparation for a new rabbis' manual. All citations from this article are protected by the copyright of the Rabbinical Assembly, © 1993. The author would like to thank the Rabbinical Assembly for giving permission to quote from this work.

11. *Shir Hashirim Rabbah* 1, 24.

12. Sasso. This is one of the earliest covenantal blessings, first used in the early 1970s, written by Rabbi Sandy Eisenberg Sasso and Rabbi Dennis Sasso.

13. Proposals for a ritual drawing of blood to parallel *brit milah* have been suggested but have never met with any enthusiasm. Mary Gendler

proposed hymenectomy, piercing a girl's hymen, in an article in *Response Magazine* (Winter 1974–75). The idea was taken up by E. M. Broner in her novel, *A Weave of Women*. New York: Bantam, 1980. Another proposal for ritual ear piercing met with similar negative response. In addition to the general reluctance to cause any pain or draw any blood, pierced ears are a symbol of slavery in the Torah.

14. *Brit r'chitzah* was written by Rabbis Rebecca Alpert, Nancy Fuchs-Kreimer, Linda Holtzman, Sandy Levine, Joy Levitt, Debbie Prinz, Ruth Sohn, Marjorie Yudkin, and Debbie Zecher. The ceremony was first published in *Menorah* magazine, 1983. A long excerpt from the ceremony appears in Susan Weidman Schneider, *Jewish and Female*. New York: Simon and Schuster, 1983, pp. 124–127. *Brit mikvah,* a ceremony by Sharon and Michael Strassfeld, includes the immersion of the baby in a tiny mikvah. It can be found in Reifman, pp. 16–22.

15. Adelman, pp. 63–65.

16. Cantor and Jacobs, pp. 49–50. Reprinted by permission of the Rabbinical Assembly, © 1993.

17. Cantor and Jacobs, pp. 50–52. Reprinted by permission of the Rabbinical Assembly, © 1993.

18. Jewish Women's Resource Center pamphlet.

19. See Marcia Falk's translation. *The Song of Songs*. Harper San Francisco, 1990.

20. Excerpted from a ceremony by Judith Baskin and Warren Ginsberg, written for their daughter and celebrated on October 13, 1985.

21. Excerpted from a ceremony for Rivka Yael by Rabbi Edward S. Treister. Houston, Texas, © 1986/5746. Reprinted with permission.

22. Excerpted from a ceremony by Rabbi Jeffrey Perry-Marx, written for his daughter, Sarah Beth, and celebrated on September 18, 1983. Rabbi Perry-Marx credits the following sources: *brit banot* by Janet Ross Marder; *brit habat* by Sue and Stephen Elwell, *brit r'chitzah,* and *Gates of the Home,* a publication of the Central Conference of American Rabbis. The grandparents' prayer was written by Rabbi Sandy Eisenberg Sasso.

23. For *Shabbat* ceremonies, the Siegels suggest lighting two 24-hour candles on Friday afternoon, holding the baby up to the lights, and saying: "May her eyes be enlightened by Torah."

24. By Ron Laye, at the naming of his daughter, D'vora.

25. Adapted from the Sephardic prayerbook.

26. Excerpted from a ceremony by Hannah Tiferet Siegel and Rabbi Daniel Siegel written for their niece, Adina Sara who was named on December 27, 1987. A complete and annotated version is available from Rabbi Siegel c/o Tucker Foundation, Dartmouth College, Hanover, NH 03755.

27. © The Rabbinical Assembly, 1993. *Brit banot* ceremony reprinted by permission of the Rabbinical Assembly.

Hiddur Mitzvah

1. Krohn, p. 96.

2. Krohn, p. 96.

3. Rabbi Fred V. Davidow, "Blessing of a Newborn-Child," Temple Beth Israel, Plattsburgh, New York. Rabbi Davidow suggests the parents alternate lines and read the last one together.

4. For ideas and patterns, browse through books on Jewish needlepoint. Patterns for other ceremonial objects—tablecloths, *challah* covers, etc.—can be adapted for use on a *wimpel*.

5. Thanks to Cantor Robert Scherr, of Temple Israel in Natick, Massachusetts, for his assistance.

6. See Marcia Falk's translation.

7. For a graceful interpretation of the first psalm see David Rosenberg's *Blues of the Sky*. New York: Harper and Row, 1976.

8. Danny Siegel, © 1985. Reprinted with the permission of the author. Danny Siegel, who wrote this and other poems that appear in this book, is also a *tzedakah*-teacher and the founder and prime mover behind the Ziv Tzedakah Fund, a nonprofit organization that collects and distributes funds to various little-known grassroots projects in Israel and in the United States. Ziv ("radiance") provides money and support for individuals and programs providing direct services to the needy. Ziv has supported an Israeli woman who cares for children with Down syndrome; a Philadelphia teenager who single-handedly began a campaign

to help homeless people; a synagogue shelter in North Carolina. Ziv is also involved in bringing the message of *tzedakah* to communities and schools throughout the United States, Canada, and Israel. For information or to contribute, write: Ziv Tzedakah Fund, c/o Bena Siegel, Treasurer, 11818 Trail Ridge Drive, Potomac, MD 20854.

9. Danny Siegel, © 1983. Reprinted with the permission of the author.

10. Danny Siegel, © 1983. Reprinted with the permission of the author.

11. Danny Siegel, © 1992 Reprinted with the permission of the author.

12. Sandy Eisenberg Sasso, © 1988. Reprinted with the permission of the author.

13. Aviva bat Beilah/slr, © 1985 / 29 Heshvan 5746. Reprinted with the permission of the author.

14. Joel Rosenberg, © 1979. Written for Benjamin Yosef Novak, on the eighth day of his life, August 8, 1979 / 15 Av 5739. Reprinted with the permission of the author.

15. Joel Rosenberg, © 1987. Written in honor of Sara Henna Wolf Pollen's birth. Reprinted with the permission of the author.

16. Hanna Tiferet Siegel, © 1985. Reprinted with the permission of the author.

17. Reprinted with permission of the authors.

18. Translation from *V'taher Libbenu,* the prayerbook of Congregation Beth El of the Sudbury River Valley, Sudbury, MA 01776.

19. The original source of this poem is unknown. It has been widely used in *brit* ceremonies for several years.

20. The original source of this poem is unknown. It has been widely used in *brit* ceremonies for several years.

Simcha

1. Dobrinsky, p. 6.

2. A full version of the special *birkat hamazon* that follows a *bris* is given in Krohn, pp. 141–160. For a short, English version, see *Living a Jewish*

Life, by Anita Diamant and Howard Cooper. New York, HarperCollins, 1991, pp. 53–54.

3. Thanks to Rochelle Treister, proprietor of Elijah's Cup, a Judaica gallery in Houston, Texas, for her suggestions. There is a small but growing number of Judaica shops and mail-order companies that sell hand-crafted gifts made by American and Israeli artists. Most synagogue gift shops and Jewish bookstores carry books, games, and tapes for children.

Announcements

Thanks to Elaine Adler, Peggy Davis, Jonathan Kremer, Betsy Platkin-Teutsch, and all the calligraphers who generously shared their work and ideas with me. Thanks also to the parents whose announcements are quoted, excerpted, and featured, and to Phyllis Nissen, who helped me find adoption announcements.

Celebrations and Customs

1. Krohn, p. 5.

2. Exodus.

3. Thirty days was the biblical measure of a child's viability. Babies younger than a month old often died, and it was considered inappropriate to dedicate to God anything or anyone so vulnerable. If the 31st day falls on *Shabbat* or a holiday, the ceremony is postponed until the following day.

4. *Pidyon haben* is not required for first-born sons whose fathers are either *kohanes* or *levites,* or whose mother is the daughter of a *kohane* or *levite* father.

5. Rabbi Marc S. Golub and Rabbi Norman Cohen, "*Kiddush Petter Rechem:* An Alternative to *Pidyon Haben,*" *CCAR Journal,* Winter, 1973, p. 72. The article contains a ceremony of the same name, written by the authors.

6. Sasso, pp. 23–24.

7. This ceremony is based on Sasso. Also see the ritual by Daniel I. Leifer and Myra Leifer, published in Koltun, pp. 26–29.

8. Krohn, p. 73.

9. Krohn, p. 95.

10. Schauss, p. 46.

11. Trepp, Leo. *The Complete Book of Jewish Observance.* New York: Behrman House Inc./Summit Books, 1980, p. 226.

12. For vivid details about Lilith, see Schauss, pp. 67–74.

13. Rabbi Sandy Eisenberg Sasso, © 1993. Reprinted by permission of the author.

Infertility and Genetic Testing

1. *Y'vamot 63b.*

2. A book that addresses many of the issues raised in this section from a traditional perspective is *And Hannah Wept: Infertility, Adoption and the Jewish Couple* by Rabbi Michael Gold. Philadelphia: Jewish Publication Society of America, 1988.

3. Rabbi Rebecca T. Alpert © 1993. Reprinted by permission of the author.

4. Rabbi Nina Beth Cardin © 1993. Reprinted by permission of the author.

Adoption

Special thanks to Rabbi Daniel Shevitz for his insight, as well as for his thoughtful comments on an early draft of this chapter. Thanks also to members of the Stars of David, Phyllis Lowenstein, executive director of International Adoptions, Inc. in Waltham, Massachusetts, and Alma Orchnick of the Jewish Family and Children's Service in Boston.

1. This poem has been reproduced, without attribution and with some variation, in many places over the past decade.

2. Shevitz, Rabbi Daniel. "A Guide for the Jewish Adoptive Parent," *Response,* No. 48, Spring, 1985, pp. 107–126. This is an excellent source for *halachic* information as well as a sensitively written account by an adoptive parent.

3. For specific information regarding the adoption of Jewish children, see Shevitz. Also, consult your rabbi.

4. Kaplan, Rabbi Aryeh. *Waters of Eden: The Mystery of the Mikvah.* New York: National Conference of Synagogue Youth/Union of Orthodox Jewish Congregations, 1976, p. 35.

5. Gottlieb, p. 74.

6. Because the right of renunciation is based on the child's knowledge of his or her origins, if the adoption has been kept a secret, he or she cannot decide, and thus his or her Jewish status cannot be not settled.

7. Bohrod, Janelle. "Janelle Bohrod's Story," *Startracks,* Spring, 1986, pp. 5–7.

8. Shevitz, p. 114.

9. Since ritual statuses—like that of *kohane* and *levite*—are inherited biologically, the rabbis wanted to be certain there would be no confusion if a Jewish child took the last name of his adoptive Cohen or Levinson parents.

10. Used by permission of the author.

11. This ceremony was adapted from one written by Rabbi Daniel Shevitz and Susan Shevitz for their son.

The Changing Jewish Family

1. Much of the material in this chapter was inspired by and based on portions of *Putting God on the Guest List: How to Reclaim the Spiritual Meaning of Your Child's Bar or Bat Mitzvah* by Rabbi Jeffrey K. Salkin. Woodstock, Vt.: Jewish Lights Publishing, 1992. Thanks also to Rabbi Lawrence Kushner for his teachings about family systems and to Jane Redmont for reading a draft of this chapter.

The First Year

Thanks to The Jewish Women's Resource Center of the National Council of Jewish Women, New York Section; and especially to Naomi Bar-Yam, Fern Amper and Eli Schaap, and Marga Kamm, whose ceremonies, *divrei Torah* and comments inform much of this chapter.

1. A traditional prayer, based on various biblical quotations and associated with the giving of the wimpel, may be found in Strassfeld and Strassfeld, *The Second Jewish Catalog*, p. 42.

2. *Pesikta D'rav Kahana* 12:2.

3. Thanks to Fern Amper and Eli Schaap for permission to quote from the ceremony for their daughter, which was held on December 11, 1983.

Index

Index

About JEWISH LIGHTS Publishing

People of all faiths and backgrounds yearn for books that attract, engage, educate and spiritually inspire.

Our principal goal is to stimulate thought and help all people learn about who the Jewish People are, where they come from, and what the future can be made to hold. While people of our diverse Jewish heritage are the primary audience, our books speak to the Christian world as well and will broaden their understanding of Judaism and the roots of their own faith.

We bring to you authors who are at the forefront of spiritual thought and experience. While each has something different to say, they all say it in a voice that you can hear.

Our books are designed to welcome you and then to engage, stimulate and inspire. We judge our success not only by whether or not our books are beautiful and commercially successful, but by whether or not they make a difference in your life.

We at Jewish Lights take great care to produce beautiful books that present meaningful spiritual content in a form that reflects the art of making high quality books. Therefore, we want to acknowledge those who contributed to the production of this book.

ART DIRECTION AND PRODUCTION
Rachel Kahn

ART
Liisa Ritter, Woodstock, Vermont

TYPE & HEBREW
Set in Sabon and Optima
Miles Cohen, Bayside, New York

PROOFREADING
Sandra Korinchak

CALLIGRAPHY
Pam Wasserman, Woodstock, Vermont

COVER DESIGN
Nancy Malerba, Reading, Vermont

COVER PRINTING
Phoenix Color Corp., Hingham, Massachusetts

PRINTING AND BINDING
Book Press, Brattleboro, Vermont

Spiritual Inspiration for Family Life

THE NEW JEWISH BABY BOOK
Names, Ceremonies, Customs—A Guide for Today's Families
by *Anita Diamant*

A complete guide to the customs and rituals for welcoming a new child to the world and into the Jewish community, and for commemorating this joyous event in family life—whatever your family constellation. Includes new ceremonies for girls, celebrations in interfaith families, and more.

"A book that all Jewish parents—no matter how religious—will find fascinating as well as useful. It is a perfect shower or new baby gift."
— *Pamela Abrams, Exec. Editor,* Parents Magazine

6" x 9", 328 pp. Quality Paperback Original, ISBN 1-879045-28-1 **$16.95**

BEST RELIGION BOOK OF THE YEAR

PUTTING GOD ON THE GUEST LIST •AWARD WINNER•
How to Reclaim the Spiritual Meaning of Your Child's Bar or Bat Mitzvah
by *Rabbi Jeffrey K. Salkin*

Joining explanation, instruction and inspiration, helps parent and child truly *be there* when the moment of Sinai is recreated in their lives. Asks and answers such fundamental questions as how did Bar and Bat Mitzvah originate? What is the lasting significance of the event? How to make the event more spiritually meaningful? New 2nd Edition.

"I hope every family planning a Bar Mitzvah celebration reads Rabbi Salkin's book." — *Rabbi Harold S. Kushner, author of* When Bad Things Happen to Good People

New! 2nd Ed.

6" x 9", 224 pp. Quality Paperback, ISBN 1-879045-59-1 **$16.95** HC, ISBN -58-3 **$24.95**

BAR/BAT MITZVAH BASICS
A Practical Family Guide to Coming of Age Together
Edited by *Cantor Helen Leneman;* Foreword by *Rabbi Jeffrey K. Salkin, author of* Putting God on the Guest List; Intro. by *Rabbi Julie Gordon*

A practical guide that gives parents and teens the "how-to" information they need to navigate the bar/bat mitzvah process and grow as a family through this experience. For the first time in one book, everyone directly involved offers practical insights into how the process can be made easier and more enjoyable for all. Rabbis, cantors and Jewish educators from the Reform, Conservative and Reconstructionist movements, parents, and even teens speak from their own experience.

"Out of her vast experience as Cantor and educator, Leneman has written an important guide that strengthens and solidifies the family through the wisdom and warmth of Judaism."
—*Rabbi Harold Schulweis, Valley Beth Shalom, Encino, California*

6" x 9", 240 pp. Quality Paperback, ISBN 1-879045-54-0 **$16.95** HC, ISBN -51-6 **$24.95**

EMBRACING THE COVENANT
Converts to Judaism Talk About Why & How
Edited & with Introductions by *Rabbi Allan L. Berkowitz* and *Patti Moskovitz*

This book is a practical and inspirational companion to the conversion process for Jews-by-Choice and their families. Written primarily for the person considering the choice of Judaism, it provides highly personal insights from over 50 people who have made this life-changing decision. But it also will speak to their families—the non-Jewish family that provided his or her spiritual beginnings and the Jewish "family" which receives the convert—and help them understand why the decision was made.

"Passionate, thoughtful and deeply-felt personal stories....A wonderful resource, sure to light the way for many who choose to follow the same path."
—*Dru Greenwood, MSW, Director, UAHC-CCAR Commission on Reform Jewish Outreach*

6" x 9", 192 pp. Quality Paperback, ISBN 1-879045-50-8 **$15.95**

Spiritual Inspiration for Family Life

MOURNING & MITZVAH
A Guided Journal for Walking the Mourner's Path Through Grief to Healing

• With over 60 guided exercises •

by *Anne Brener, L.C. S.W.*; Foreword by *Rabbi Jack Riemer*; Introduction by *Rabbi William Cutter*

"Fully engaging in mourning means you will be a different person than before you began." For those who mourn a death, for those who would help them, for those who face a loss of any kind, Brener teaches us the power and strength available to us in the fully experienced mourning process. Guided writing exercises help stimulate the processes of both conscious and unconscious healing.

"A stunning book! It offers an exploration in depth of the place where psychology and religious ritual intersect, and the name of that place is Truth."
—*Rabbi Harold Kushner, author of* When Bad Things Happen to Good People

7 1/2" x 9", 288 pp. Quality Paperback Original, ISBN 1-879045-23-0 **$19.95**

WHEN A GRANDPARENT DIES
A Kid's Own Remembering Workbook for Dealing with Shiva and the Year Beyond
by *Nechama Liss-Levinson, Ph.D.*

Drawing insights from both psychology and Jewish tradition, this workbook helps children participate in the process of mourning, offering guided exercises, rituals, and places to write, draw, list, create and express their feelings.

"Will bring support, guidance, and understanding for countless children, teachers, and health professionals."
—*Rabbi Earl A. Grollman, D.D., author of* Talking about Death

8" x 10", 48 pp. Hardcover, illus., 2-color text, ISBN 1-879045-44-3 **$14.95**

HEALING OF SOUL, HEALING OF BODY
Spiritual Leaders Unfold the Strength and Solace in Psalms
Edited by *Rabbi Simkha Y. Weintraub, CSW, for The Jewish Healing Center*

A source of solace for those who are facing illness, as well as those who care for them. The ten Psalms which form the core of this healing resource were originally selected 200 years ago by Rabbi Nachman of Breslov as a "complete remedy." Today, for anyone coping with illness, they continue to provide a wellspring of strength. Each Psalm is newly translated, making it clear and accessible, and each one is introduced by an eminent rabbi, men and women reflecting different movements and backgrounds. To all who are living with the pain and uncertainty of illness, this spiritual resource offers an anchor of spiritual comfort.

"Will bring comfort to anyone fortunate enough to read it. This gentle book is a luminous gem of wisdom."
—*Larry Dossey, M.D., author of* Healing Words: The Power of Prayer & the Practice of Medicine

6" x 9", 128 pp. Quality Paperback Original, illus., 2-color text, ISBN 1-879045-31-1 **$14.95**

SO THAT YOUR VALUES LIVE ON
Ethical Wills & How To Prepare Them
Edited by *Rabbi Jack Riemer & Professor Nathaniel Stampfer*

A cherished Jewish tradition, ethical wills—parents writing to children or grandparents to grandchildren—sum up what people have learned and express what they want most for, and from, their loved ones. Includes an intensive guide, "**How to Write Your Own Ethical Will**," and a topical index. A marvelous treasury of wills: Herzl, Sholom Aleichem, Israelis, Holocaust victims, contemporary American Jews.

"While the book is written from a Jewish viewpoint, its principles can easily be adapted by people of other faiths."
—*The Los Angeles Times*

6" x 9", 272 pp. Quality Paperback, ISBN 1-879045-34-6 **$17.95**

Spiritual Inspiration for Daily Living...

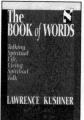

THE BOOK OF WORDS
Talking Spiritual Life, Living Spiritual Talk
by *Lawrence Kushner*

In the incomparable manner of his extraordinary *The Book of Letters: A Mystical Hebrew Alphabet*, Kushner now lifts up and shakes the dust off primary religious words we use to describe the spiritual dimension of life. The *Words* take on renewed spiritual significance, adding power and focus to the lives we live every day.

For each word Kushner offers us a startling, moving and insightful explication, and pointed readings from classical Jewish sources that further illuminate the concept. He concludes with a short exercise that helps unite the spirit of the word with our actions in the world.

"This is a powerful and holy book."
— M. Scott Peck, M.D., *author of* The Road Less Traveled *and other books*

"What a delightful wholeness of intellectual vigor and meditative playfulness, and all in a tone of gentleness that speaks to this gentile."
— *Rt. Rev. Krister Stendahl, formerly Dean, Harvard Divinity School/Bishop of Stockholm*

6" x 9", 152 pp. Hardcover, beautiful two-color text ISBN 1-879045-35-4 **$21.95**

Sample pages from *The Book of Words*

THE BOOK OF LETTERS
A Mystical Hebrew Alphabet
by *Rabbi Lawrence Kushner*

In calligraphy by the author. Folktales about and exploration of the mystical meanings of the Hebrew Alphabet. Open the old prayerbook-like pages of *The Book of Letters* and you will enter a special world of sacred tradition and religious feeling. More than just symbols, all twenty-two letters of the Hebrew alphabet overflow with meanings and personalities of their own.

Rabbi Kushner draws from ancient Judaic sources, weaving Talmudic commentary, Hasidic folktales, and Kabbalistic mysteries around the letters.

•AWARD WINNER•   "A book which is in love with Jewish letters."
— *Isaac Bashevis Singer* (לז)

• **Popular Hardcover Edition**
6" x 9", 80 pp. Hardcover, two colors, inspiring new Foreword.
ISBN 1-879045-00-1 **$24.95**

• **Deluxe Gift Edition**
9" x 12", 80 pp. Hardcover, four-color text, ornamentation, in a beautiful slipcase.
ISBN 1-879045-01-X **$79.95**

• **Collector's Limited Edition**
9" x 12", 80 pp. Hardcover, gold embossed pages, hand assembled slipcase. With silkscreened print.
Limited to 500 signed and numbered copies.
ISBN 1-879045-04-4 **$349.00**
To see a sample page at no obligation, call us

....*The Kushner Series*

GOD WAS IN THIS PLACE & I, i DID NOT KNOW
Finding Self, Spirituality & Ultimate Meaning

Who am I? Who is God? Kushner creates inspiring interpretations of Jacob's dream in Genesis, opening a window into Jewish spirituality for people of all faiths and backgrounds.

In this fascinating blend of scholarship, imagination, psychology and history, seven Jewish spiritual masters ask and answer fundamental questions of human experience.

"Rich and intriguing."
> —*M. Scott Peck, M.D., author of* The Road Less Traveled *and other books*

6" x 9", 192 pp. Quality Paperback, ISBN 1-879045-33-8 **$16.95** HC, ISBN -05-2 **$21.95**

HONEY FROM THE ROCK

"Quite simply the easiest introduction to Jewish mysticism you can read."
An introduction to the ten gates of Jewish mysticism and how it applies to daily life.

"Captures the flavor and spark of Jewish mysticism. . . . Read it and be rewarded."
> —*Elie Wiesel*

"A work of love, lyrical beauty, and prophetic insight. "
> —*Father Malcolm Boyd*, The Christian Century

6" x 9", 168 pp. Quality Paperback, ISBN 1-879045-02-8 **$14.95**

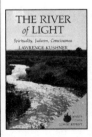

THE RIVER OF LIGHT
Spirituality, Judaism, Consciousness

A "manual" for all spiritual travelers who would attempt a spiritual journey in our times. Taking us step by step, Kushner allows us to discover the meaning of our own quest: "to allow the river of light—the deepest currents of consciousness—to rise to the surface and animate our lives."

"Philosophy and mystical fantasy...exhilarating speculative flights launched from the Bible....Anybody—Jewish, Christian, or otherwise...will find this book an intriguing experience."
> —*The Kirkus Reviews*

6" x 9", 180 pp. Quality Paperback, ISBN 1-879045-03-6 **$14.95**

INVISIBLE LINES OF CONNECTION
Sacred Stories of the Ordinary

Through his everyday encounters with family, friends, colleagues and strangers, Kushner takes us deeply into our lives, finding flashes of spiritual insight in the process. This is a book where literature meets spirituality, where the sacred meets the ordinary, and, above all, where people of all faiths, all backgrounds can meet one another and themselves.

"Does something both more and different than instruct—it inspirits. Wonderful stories, from the best storyteller I know."
> — *David Mamet*

"A wonderful collection of stories charmingly told by a gifted storyteller."
> — Booklist (*American Library Association*)

5.5" x 8.5", 160 pp. Hardcover, ISBN 1-879045-52-4 **$21.95**

Motivation and Inspiration for Recovery

TWELVE JEWISH STEPS TO RECOVERY
A Personal Guide To Turning From Alcoholism & Other Addictions...Drugs, Food, Gambling, Sex

by *Rabbi Kerry M. Olitzky & Stuart A. Copans, M.D.* / Preface by *Abraham J. Twerski, M.D.* / Introduction by *Rabbi Sheldon Zimmerman* / Illustrated by *Maty Grünberg* / "Getting Help" by *JACS Foundation*

A Jewish perspective on the Twelve Steps of addiction recovery programs with consolation, inspiration and motivation for recovery. It draws from traditional sources, and quotes from what recovering Jewish people say about their experiences with addictions of all kinds. Inspiring illustrations of the twelve gates of the Old City of Jerusalem.

6" x 9", 136 pp. Quality Paperback, ISBN 1-879045-09-5 **$13.95**   HC, ISBN -08-7 **$19.95**

RECOVERY FROM CODEPENDENCE
A Jewish Twelve Steps Guide to Healing Your Soul

by *Rabbi Kerry M. Olitzky* / Foreword by *Marc Galanter, M.D., Director, Division of Alcoholism & Drug Abuse, NYU Medical Center* / Afterword by *Harriet Rossetto, Director, Gateways Beit T'shuvah*

For the estimated 90% of America struggling with the addiction of a family member or loved one, or involved in a dysfunctional family or relationship.

"The disease of chemical dependency is also a family illness. Rabbi Olitzky offers spiritual hope and support."

—Jerry Spicer, President, Hazelden

6" x 9", 160 pp. Quality Paperback Original, ISBN 1-879045-32-X **$13.95**
HC, ISBN -27-3 **$21.95**

RENEWED EACH DAY
Daily Twelve Step Recovery Meditations
Based on the Bible

by *Rabbi Kerry M. Olitzky & Aaron Z.*

VOLUME I: Genesis & Exodus
Intro. by *Rabbi Michael A. Signer*; Afterword by *JACS Foundation*

VOLUME II: Leviticus, Numbers & Deuteronomy
Intro. by *Sharon M. Strassfeld*; Afterword by *Rabbi Harold M. Schulweis*

Using a seven day/weekly guide format, a recovering person and a spiritual leader who is reaching out to addicted people reflect on the traditional weekly Bible reading. They bring strong spiritual support for daily living and recovery from addictions of all kinds.

"Meets a vital need; it offers a chance for people turning from alcoholism and addiction to renew their spirits and draw upon the Jewish tradition to guide and enrich their lives."
—Rabbi Irving (Yitz) Greenberg, President, CLAL,
The National Jewish Center for Learning and Leadership

Beautiful Two-Volume Slipcased Set 6" x 9", V. I, 224 pp. / V. II, 280 pp.
Quality Paperback Original, ISBN 1-879045-21-4 **$27.90**

ONE HUNDRED BLESSINGS EVERY DAY

Daily Twelve Step Recovery Affirmations, Exercises for Personal Growth & Renewal Reflecting Seasons of the Jewish Year

by *Dr. Kerry M. Olitzky* / with selected meditations prepared by *Rabbi James Stone Goodman, Danny Siegel,* and *Rabbi Gordon Tucker* / Foreword by *Rabbi Neil Gillman, The Jewish Theological Seminary of America* / Afterword by *Dr. Jay Holder, Director, Exodus Treatment Center*

Recovery is a conscious choice from moment to moment, day in and day out. In this helpful and healing book of daily recovery meditations, Rabbi Olitzky gives us words to live by day after day, throughout the annual cycle of holiday observances and special Sabbaths of the Jewish calendar.

4.5" x 6.5", 432 pp. Quality Paperback Original, ISBN 1-879045-30-3 **$14.95**

Spirituality

BEING GOD'S PARTNER
How to Find the Hidden Link
Between Spirituality and Your Work

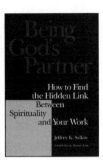

by *Jeffrey K. Salkin* Introduction by *Norman Lear*

A book that will challenge people of every denomination to reconcile the cares of work and soul. A groundbreaking book about spirituality and the work world, from a Jewish perspective. Helps the reader find God in the ethical striving and search for meaning in the professions and in business. Looks at our modern culture of workaholism and careerism, and offers practical suggestions for balancing your professional life and spiritual self.

Being God's Partner will inspire people of all faiths and no faith to find greater meaning in their work, and see themselves doing God's work in the world.

"Will challenge not only Jews caught up in the hustle and the hassle...but everyone of whatever denomination concerned about making sense of our life and responding to the longings of the spirit within the soul."
—*Fr. Andrew M. Greeley, Prof. of Social Science, The University of Chicago*

"This engaging meditation on the spirituality of work is grounded in Judaism but is relevant well beyond the boundaries of that tradition."
—*Booklist*

6 x 9, 192 pp. Hardcover, ISBN 1-879045-37-0 **$19.95**

SELF, STRUGGLE & CHANGE

Family Conflict Stories in Genesis
and Their Healing Insights for Our Lives
by *Norman J. Cohen*

How do I find greater wholeness in my life and in my family's life?

The stress of late-20th-century living only brings new variations to timeless personal struggles. The people described by the biblical writers of Genesis were in situations and relationships very much like our own. We identify with them. Their stories still speak to us because they are about the same problems we deal with every day.

A modern master of biblical interpretation brings us greater understanding of the ancient text and of ourselves in this intriguing re-telling of conflict between husband and wife, father and son, brothers, and sisters.

"Delightfully written ... rare erudition, sensitivity and insight."
— *Elie Wiesel*

6 x 9, 224 pp. Quality Paperback, ISBN 1-879045-66-4 **$16.95** Hardcover, ISBN 19-2 **$21.95**

THE EMPTY CHAIR: FINDING HOPE & JOY
Timeless Wisdom from a Hasidic Master,
Rebbe Nachman of Breslov

Adapted by *Moshe Mykoff* and *the Breslov Research Institute*

A "little treasure" of aphorisms and advice for living joyously and spiritually today, written 200 years ago, but startlingly fresh in meaning and use. Challenges and helps us to move from stress and sadness to hope and joy.

Teacher, guide and spiritual master—Rebbe Nachman provides vital words of inspiration and wisdom for life today for people of any faith, or of no faith. **AWARD WINNER**

"For anyone of any faith, this is a book of healing and wholeness, of being alive!"
— *Bookviews*

4 x 6, 128 pp., 2-color text, Deluxe Paperback, ISBN 1-879045-67-2 **$9.95**

Spirituality

Minding the Temple of the Soul

Balancing Body, Mind & Soul through Traditional Jewish Prayer, Movement & Meditation

MINDING THE TEMPLE OF THE SOUL
Balancing Body, Mind & Soul through Traditional Jewish Prayer, Movement & Meditation
by *Dr. Tamar Frankiel* and *Judy Greenfeld*

This new spiritual approach to physical health introduces readers to a spiritual tradition that affirms the body and enables them to reconceive their bodies in a more positive light. Relying on Kabbalistic teachings and other Jewish traditions, it shows us how to be more responsible for our own psychological and physical health. Focuses on the discipline of prayer, simple Tai Chi-like exercises and body positions, and guides the reader throughout, step by step, with diagrams, sketches and meditations.

7 x 10, 144 pp (est), Quality Paperback Original, illus., ISBN 1-879045-64-8 **$15.95**

BEST REFERENCE BOOK OF THE YEAR

HOW TO BE A PERFECT STRANGER
A Guide to Etiquette in Other People's Religious Ceremonies, Vol. 1
Edited by *Arthur J. Magida*

AWARD WINNER

Explains the rituals and celebrations of America's major religions/denominations, helping an interested guest to feel comfortable, participate to the fullest extent possible, and avoid violating anyone's religious principles. **"A book that belongs in every living room, library and office."**

"The things Miss Manners forgot to tell us about religion."
— *Los Angeles Times*

"Concise, informative, and eminently practical."
— *Rev. Christopher Leighton, Executive Director, Institute for Christian-Jewish Studies*

"Finally, for those inclined to undertake their own spiritual journeys...tells visitors what to expect."
—*The New York Times*

6 x 9, 432 pp. Hardcover, ISBN 1-879045-39-7 **$24.95**

VOL. 2: 17 ADDITIONAL FAITHS
6 x 9, 416 pp, Hardcover, ISBN 1-879045-63-X **$24.95**

SPIRITUALITY...OTHER BOOKS:

Lifecycles, V. 1: Jewish Women on Life Passages & Personal Milestones
Ed. by Rabbi Debra Orenstein. 6 x 9, 480 pp, HC, ISBN 1-879045-14-1 $24.95

Lifecycles, V. 2: Jewish Women on Biblical Themes in Contemporary Life
Ed. by Rabbi Debra Orenstein & Rabbi Jane Rachel Litman. 6 x 9, 464 pp, HC, ISBN 1-879045-15-X $24.95

Finding Joy: A Practical Spiritual Guide to Happiness
by Dannel Schwartz with Mark Hass. 6 x 9, 192 pp, HC, ISBN 1-879045-53-2 $19.95

Tormented Master: The Life and Spiritual Quest of Rabbi Nahman of Bratslav
by Arthur Green. 6 x 9, 408 pp, Quality Pb, ISBN 1-879045-11-7 $17.95

Your Word Is Fire: The Hasidic Masters on Contemplative Prayer
Edited & transl. by Arthur Green & Barry W. Holtz. 6 x 9, 152 pp, Quality Pb, ISBN 1-879045-25-7 $14.95

Spirituality

AWARD WINNER

GODWRESTLING—ROUND 2
Ancient Wisdom, Future Paths
by *Arthur Waskow*

BEST RELIGION BOOK OF THE YEAR

This 20th anniversary sequel to a seminal book of the Jewish renewal movement deals with spirituality in relation to personal growth, marriage, ecology, feminism, politics, and more. Including new chapters on recent issues and concerns, Waskow outlines original ways to merge "religious" life and "personal" life in our society today.

"A delicious read and a soaring meditation."
—*Rabbi Zalman M. Schachter-Shalomi*

"Vivid as a novel, sharp, eccentric, loud....An important book for anyone who wants to bring Judaism alive."
—*Marge Piercy*

6 x 9, 352 pp. Hardcover, ISBN 1-879045-45-1 **$23.95**

GOD & THE BIG BANG
Discovering Harmony Between Science & Spirituality
by *Daniel C. Matt*

Mysticism and science: What do they have in common? How can one enlighten the other? By drawing on modern cosmology and ancient Kabbalah, Matt shows how science and religion can together enrich our spiritual awareness and help us recover a sense of wonder and find our place in the universe.

"This poetic new book...helps us to understand the human meaning of creation."
—*Joel Primack, leading cosmologist, Professor of Physics, University of California, Santa Cruz*

6 x 9, 216 pp. Hardcover, ISBN 1-879045-48-6 **$21.95**

THEOLOGY & PHILOSOPHY

Aspects of Rabbinic Theology
by Solomon Schechter. 6 x 9, 440 pp, Quality Paperback, ISBN 1-879045-24-9 $18.95

The Earth Is the Lord's: The Inner World of the Jew in Eastern Europe
by Abraham Joshua Heschel. 5.5 x 8, 112 pp, Quality Paperback, ISBN 1-879045-42-7 $12.95

The Last Trial: On the Legends and Lore of the Command to Abraham to Offer Isaac as a Sacrifice
by Shalom Spiegel. 6 x 9, 208 pp, Quality Paperback, ISBN 1-879045-29-X $17.95

A Passion for Truth: Despair and Hope in Hasidism
by Abraham Joshua Heschel. 5.5 x 8, 352 pp, Quality Paperback, ISBN 1-879045-41-9 $18.95

Seeking the Path to Life: Theological Meditations on God and the Nature of People, Love, Life and Death
by Rabbi Ira F. Stone 6 x 9, 132 pp, Quality Paperback, ISBN 1-879045-47-8 $14.95;
HC, ISBN -17-6 $19.95

The Spirit of Renewal: Finding Faith After the Holocaust
by Edward Feld 6 x 9, 224 pp, Quality Paperback, ISBN 1-879045-40-0 $16.95
HC, ISBN -06-0 $22.95

Children's

BUT GOD REMEMBERED
Stories of Women from Creation to the Promised Land
by *Sandy Eisenberg Sasso*
Full color illustrations by *Bethanne Andersen*

NONSECTARIAN, NONDENOMINATIONAL.
A fascinating collection of four different stories of women only briefly mentioned in biblical tradition and religious texts, but never before explored. Award-winning author Sasso brings to life the intriguing stories of Lilith, Serach, Bityah, and the Daughters of Z, courageous and strong women from ancient tradition. All teach important values through their faith and actions.

"Exquisite....a book of beauty, strength and spirituality."
—Association of Bible Teachers

For ages 8 and up

9 x 12, 32 pp. Hardcover, Full color illus., ISBN 1-879045-43-5 **$16.95**

AWARD WINNER

IN GOD'S NAME
by *Sandy Eisenberg Sasso*
Full color illustrations by *Phoebe Stone*

For ages 4-8

MULTICULTURAL, NONSECTARIAN, NONDENOMINATIONAL.
Like an ancient myth in its poetic text and vibrant illustrations, this modern fable about the search for God's name celebrates the diversity and, at the same time, the unity of all the people of the world. Each seeker claims he or she alone knows the answer. Finally, they come together and learn what God's name really is, sharing the ultimate harmony of belief in one God by people of all faiths, all backgrounds.

"I got goose bumps when I read *In God's Name,* its language and illustrations are that moving. This is a book children will love and the whole family will cherish for its beauty and power."
—Francine Klagsbrun, author of *Mixed Feelings*

"What a lovely, healing book!"
—Madeleine L'Engle

Selected by Parent Council Ltd.™

9 x 12, 32 pp. Hardcover, Full color illus., ISBN 1-879045-26-5 **$16.95**

For ages 4-8

GOD'S PAINTBRUSH
by *Sandy Eisenberg Sasso*
Full color illustrations by *Annette Compton*

MULTICULTURAL, NONSECTARIAN, NONDENOMINATIONAL.
Invites children of all faiths and backgrounds to encounter God openly in their own lives. Wonderfully interactive, provides questions adult and child can explore together at the end of each episode.

"An excellent way to honor the imaginative breadth and depth of the spiritual life of the young."
—Dr. Robert Coles, Harvard University

AWARD WINNER

11x 8½, 32 pp. Hardcover, Full color illustrations, ISBN 1-879045-22-2 **$16.95**

Children's

A PRAYER FOR THE EARTH
The Story of Naamah, Noah's Wife

For ages 4-8

by *Sandy Eisenberg Sasso*
Full color illustrations by *Bethanne Andersen*

NONSECTARIAN, NONDENOMINATIONAL.

This new story, based on an ancient text, opens readers' religious imaginations to new ideas about the well-known story of the Flood. When God tells Noah to bring the animals of the world onto the ark, God *also* calls on Naamah, Noah's wife, to save each plant on Earth. *A Prayer for the Earth* describes Naamah's wisdom and love for the natural harmony of the earth, and inspires readers to use their own courage, creativity and faith to carry out Naamah's work today.

"A lovely tale....Children of all ages should be drawn to this parable for our times."
—*Tomie dePaola, artist/author of books for children*

9 x 12, 32 pp. Hardcover, Full color illustrations, ISBN 1-879045-60-5 **$16.95**

THE 11TH COMMANDMENT
Wisdom from Our Children
For all ages
by The Children of America

MULTICULTURAL, NONSECTARIAN, NONDENOMINATIONAL.

"If there were an Eleventh Commandment, what would it be?"
Children of many religious denominations across America answer this question—in their own drawings and words—in *The 11th Commandment*. This full-color collection of "Eleventh Commandments" reveals kids' ideas about how people should respond to God.

"Wonderful....This unusual book provides both food for thought and insight into the hopes and fears of today's young."
—*American Library Association's* Booklist

8 x 10, 48 pp. Hardcover, Full color illustrations, ISBN 1-879045-46-X **$16.95**

# of Copies	Order Information	$ Amount
_____	Aspects of Rabbinic Theology (pb), $18.95	_____
_____	Bar/Bat Mitzvah Basics (hc), $24.95; (pb), $16.95	_____
_____	Being God's Partner (hc), $19.95	_____
_____	But God Remembered (hc), $16.95	_____
_____	Earth is the Lord's (pb), $12.95	_____
_____	11th Commandment (hc), $16.95	_____
_____	Embracing the Covenant (pb), $15.95	_____
_____	Empty Chair (pb), $9.95	_____
_____	Finding Joy (hc), $19.95	_____
_____	God & the Big Bang (hc), $21.95	_____
_____	God's Paintbrush (hc), $16.95	_____
_____	Godwrestling—Round 2 (hc), $23.95	_____
_____	Hanukkah (pb), $16.95	_____
_____	Healing of Soul, Healing of Body (pb), $14.95	_____
_____	How to Be a Perfect Stranger Vol. 1 (hc), $24.95	_____
_____	How to Be a Perfect Stranger Vol. 2 (hc), $24.95	_____
_____	In God's Name (hc), $16.95	_____
_____	Israel: An Echo of Eternity (pb), $18.95	_____
_____	Last Trial (pb), $17.95	_____
_____	Lifecycles, Vol. 1 (hc), $24.95	_____
_____	Lifecycles, Vol. 2 (hc), $24.95	_____
_____	Minding the Temple of the Soul (pb), $15.95	_____
_____	Mourning & Mitzvah (pb), $19.95	_____
_____	NEW Jewish Baby Book (pb), $16.95	_____
_____	One Hundred Blessings Every Day (pb), $14.95	_____
_____	Passion for Truth (pb), $18.95	_____
_____	Passover Seder (pb), $16.95	_____
_____	Prayer for the Earth (hc), $26.95	_____
_____	Putting God on the Guest List (hc), $24.95; (pb), $16.95	_____
_____	Prayer for the Earth (hc), $16.95	_____
_____	Recovery from Codependence (hc), $21.95; (pb), $13.95	_____
_____	Renewed Each Day, 2-Volume Set (pb), $27.90	_____
_____	Seeking the Path to Life (hc), $19.95; (pb), $14.95	_____
_____	Self, Struggle & Change (hc), $21.95; (pb), $16.95	_____
_____	Shabbat Seder (pb), $16.95	_____
_____	So That Your Values Live On (hc), $23.95; (pb), $17.95	_____
_____	Spirit of Renewal (hc), $22.95; (pb), $16.95	_____
_____	Time to Mourn, Time to Comfort (pb), $16.95	_____
_____	Tormented Master (pb), $17.95	_____
_____	Twelve Jewish Steps to Recovery (hc), $19.95; (pb), $13.95	_____
_____	When a Grandparent Dies (hc), $14.95	_____
_____	Your Word is Fire (pb), $14.95	_____
_____	Other:_____	

• The Kushner Series •

_____	Book of Letters (hc), $24.95	_____
_____	Book of Words (hc), $21.95	_____
_____	God Was in This Place...(hc), $21.95; (pb), $16.95	_____
_____	Honey From the Rock (pb), $14.95	_____
_____	Invisible Lines of Connection (hc), $21.95	_____
_____	River of Light (pb), $14.95	_____

Check enclosed for $_____ *payable to:* JEWISH LIGHTS Publishing

Charge my credit card: ❏ MasterCard ❏ Visa

Credit Card #_____ Expires _____

Name on card _____

Signature _____ Phone (_____)_____

Name _____

Street _____

City / State / Zip _____

Phone, fax, or mail to: JEWISH LIGHTS Publishing
P. O. Box 237, Sunset Farm Offices, Route 4, Woodstock, Vermont 05091
Tel (802) 457-4000   *Fax* (802) 457-4004   www.jewishlights.com
Credit card orders (800) 962-4544 (9AM–5PM ET Monday–Friday)
Generous discounts on quantity orders. SATISFACTION GUARANTEED. Prices subject to change.

AVAILABLE FROM BETTER BOOKSTORES. TRY YOUR BOOKSTORE FIRST.